# ◆ LORCA ◆

for
Francisco Mena Soto
with gratitude for his friendship
and belief in his poetry

# ◆ **LORCA** ◆
## ◆ THE GAY IMAGINATION ◆

## ◆ PAUL BINDING ◆

First published in October 1985 by GMP Publishers Ltd,
   P O Box 247, London N15 6RW
World copyright © 1985 Paul Binding

**British Library Cataloguing in Publication Data**

Binding, Paul
Lorca: the gay imagination.
1. Garcia Lorca, Federico—Criticism and
interpretation   2. Homosexuality in literature
I. Title
861'.62     PQ6613.A763Z/
ISBN 0-907040-37-3
ISBN 0-907040-36-5 Pbk

Cover art by Christopher S. Brown
Photoset by MC Typeset, Chatham, Kent
Printed and bound by Billing & Sons Ltd, Worcester

# Contents

# Acknowledgements

I owe so much to so many people in both England and Spain that truly it is difficult to convey the measure of my debts. This statement does not, however, cover the opinions expressed in this study, which are my own and for which I take full responsibility.

Pride of place must go to those three doyens of Lorquian studies: J.L. Gili, Rafael Martínez Nadal, Ian Gibson. They have shown themselves to be as generous in spirit and time as admirers of Lorca would hope. I also must thank Sir Stephen Spender for the many interesting conversations about Lorca that we have had, and for his accounts of translating poems in collaboration with J.L. Gili. I must offer thanks to Olga Kenyon of Morley College who invited me to give a lecture which formed part of my book in progress. The response was extremely stimulating.

The book would not be what it is without the help of Juan-Antonio and Mary Blanco; Marion Boyars; Franco Cimarra; Francisco Mena Soto; Roger and Theresa Mortimore; Simon North; Jordi Palacios; Rachel Scott; Natasha Spender; Mark Todd; Luis-Antonio de Villena.

My debt to my editor at GMP, David Fernbach, is one I am very proud to acknowledge, No one could have met with more patience, meticulousness and intellectual precision than I have for this book.

★

The following permissions are kindly acknowledged:

Federico García Lorca, *Five Plays*, translated by James Graham-Lujan and Richard L. O'Connell, with an introduction by Francisco García Lorca. Copyright © 1963 New Directions Publishing Corporation. Reprinted by permission of New Directions Publishing Corporation (USA and Canada) and Martin Secker and Warburg Ltd (UK and Commonwealth).

Federico García Lorca, *Three Tragedies*, translated by James Graham-Lujan and Richard L. O'Connell, with an introduction by Francisco García Lorca. Copyright © 1947, 1955 New Directions Publishing Corporation. Reprinted by permission of New Directions Publishing Corporation (USA and Canada) and Martin Secker and Warburg Ltd (UK and Commonwealth).

Federico García Lorca, *Selected Letters*, edited and translated by David Gershator. Copyright © Herederos de Federico García Lorca 1954, David Gershator 1983. Reprinted by permission of New Directions Publishing Corporation (USA and Canada) and Marion Boyars Publishers Ltd (UK and Commonwealth).

Federico García Lorca, *Deep Song and Other Prose*, edited and translated by Christopher Maurer. Copyright © Herederos de Federico García Lorca 1954, Christopher Maurer 1980. Reprinted by permission of New Directions Publishing Corporation (USA and Canada) and Marion Boyars Publishers Ltd (UK and Commonwealth).

Federico García Lorca, *Obras completas* tomo I, edited by Arturo del Huyo. Copyright © Herederos de Federico García Lorca 1973. Reprinted by permission of the Federico García Lorca estate.

# Introduction

This book is a critical study of the work of Federico García Lorca (1898–1936), a poet and dramatist whose emotional depth, imaginative scope and technical power make him not only one of modern Spain's greatest writers but one of the few supreme creative artists of this century. Almost from his first entry into the Spanish literary world, in his own and the century's early twenties, Lorca was recognised as a phenomenal spirit – and this in a climate remarkably productive of creative talent of a high order (Buñuel, Dalí, Alberti, Aleixandre, etc.). In his expansive personal introduction to the standard edition of Lorca's *Obras completas*, one of these other creative talents, Jorge Guillén wrote:

> Federico García Lorca fue una criatura extraordinaria.
> 'Criatura' significa esta vez más que 'hombre'.
>
> Federico García Lorca was an extraordinary creature.
> 'Creature' means on this occasion more than 'man'.[1]

The attention paid to Lorca's writings from his early manhood onwards might seem enviable today, but in fact Lorca became too often a victim of this kind of attitude towards him (though not, it must be said, at Guillén's hands). Those excitingly ambitious works *El poeta en Nueva York* (*The Poet in New York*), *El público* (*The Public*) and *Así que pasen cinco años* (*When Five Years Have Passed*) were not on the whole well or understandingly received by those to whom he read or showed them, and never in his lifetime reached a wider readership. Though there are external reasons why the *Sonetos del amor oscuro* (*Sonnets of the Dark Love*) have been available to the public only very recently, somehow this long delay seems symbolic of an important aspect of Lorca's history.

The picture of Lorca that he came so to resent – of a sort of 'natural', an inspired *cantaor* of Andalucía – has outlasted his tragically short life. As late as 1981 the great French Lorquian scholar André Belamich felt it necessary to introduce the Pléiade edition of the poems and prose pieces with reminders of how little of Lorca's work corresponds to this image of him; he goes on to emphasise and adumbrate the poet's metaphysical and socio-cultural preoccupations, and to salute the tragic visionary quality of his greatest achievements, a quality that he sees as due to deep though creative divisions in the artist himself.

A significant reason for the persistence of this view of Lorca must be the cultural condition of Franco's Spain. The brutal murder of the poet could be presented as a terrible mistake shrouded in mystery, but Lorca had to be dissociated not only from the reality of his death but from the complex reality of his life. Statements of his that he felt for Spain as an entirety were used to imply his essential non-partisanship in the cruel social and political rift of the Thirties, despite plenty of evidence to the contrary. Other facts about him conveniently receded too: his extensive and creative knowledge of cosmopolitan cultural movements; his almost certain religious heterodoxy (despite deep veneration for Catholic tradition and devotion); and – inextricably related to these two last – his sexual persuasion.

In 1973 Ian Gibson published *The Death of Lorca*, one of the most important literary-historical studies of its decade, since its implications force the mind beyond even the interest of its actual subject. Painstakingly and enthrallingly Gibson showed how, far from being a mysterious blunder – round which a whole host of lurid stories had accrued, and been largely allowed to do so – Lorca's death was authorised by key Nationalists. Lorca had not been some apolitical naif, but had behind him an exemplary anti-fascist record,† while his imaginative daring and his freedom from conventionalism had not endeared him to the Falangist, authoritarian mentality. The truth of his book was endorsed by so many people that Gibson expanded it into *The Assassination of Federico García Lorca*. This came out in 1979, in the hopeful if uncertain years following Franco's death, when in Spain the unmentionable could again be mentioned – and reviewed. Since then Gibson has addressed himself not only to critical editing of Lorca's poetry, but also to the definitive biography of Lorca, a work of the greatest amplitude, the first volume of which has just appeared.

More or less coevally with Gibson's researches, the French scholar André Belamich and Lorca's old friend and literary intimate Rafael Martínez Nadal were making the reading world aware of that darker, intellectually adventurous Lorca that had gone too long unhailed. It became possible to compare versions of poems through the publication of manuscripts, and the complexity, the strivings of the creator's unique mind were ever more clearly shown. Martínez Nadal made possible familiarity with the baffling, sui generis and hitherto unpublished drama, *El público*; Belamich was able to include in his Pléiade edition the almost legendary *Sonetos del amor oscuro*, rescued from family archives. Both these works are distinguished by a remarkable independence of spirit and intricacy of art. Both too have at their centre homosexual life in both its interior and exterior manifestations.

The critical examination of Lorca's work that follows has been

†See Chronology, which makes Lorca's position during these years quite plain.

undertaken in the belief that, for the deepest understanding of it, appreciation of its homosexual content and nature is essential. My book is in no sense a biography, and has nothing to say about Lorca's specific emotional and sexual relationships. I have kept biographical detail to a necessary minimum; accounts of experiences or states of mind – given because they seemed particularly to illuminate a poem or play – have been taken, almost without exception, from Lorca's own published writings and letters. The progress of his apprehension of himself as homosexual and of his wish and need to use his sexual position creatively, as a moral and philosophic vantage-point, is all there in the oeuvre as one reads it through. This last sentence suggests, I realise, what I am convinced is the case: that Lorca's literary journey was one of forward movement, and that the increase in profundity and complexity at a certain point in it is indissolubly connected with his relationship to his homosexual nature. This conviction was central to my desire to write this study, because I felt it could shed light on the relationship of homosexuality to the creative process.

My own reading experience of Lorca can perhaps be paralleled among many of my generation. I first knew what I call in this book the 'classical works', the three great rural tragedies *Bodas de sangre* (*Blood Wedding*), *Yerma* and *La casa de Bernarda Alba* (*The House of Bernarda Alba*), works of great intensity and purity of art which I could relate both to the psychological and compressed dramas of Ibsen and Strindberg and also to the contemporaneous and epical post-expressionist theatrical ventures of Brecht (at the time of my reading perhaps at the very height of his reputation in this country). I then found the *Romancero gitano* (*Gypsy Balladeer*), and many of its poems became part of my own mental landscape. It was not, however, until some years later, when I read *El poeta en Nueva York* – then still apt to be regarded as something of a sport among the poet's work – that the full force and originality of Lorca's mind impressed itself upon me. I started reading the whole corpus of his productions, and soon realised that important features of this poem-cycle had been anticipated in earlier works and were to be absorbed in the largely more restrained achievements of the later years. This realisation intensified as more, and diverse, works of Lorca's became available, as has already been described. The present study therefore begins with *El poeta* and moves backwards and then forwards from it, a method appropriate to my subject since it is the first work in which the homosexual situation of the creator is truly manifested. The homosexual animus of Lorca's output is the more interesting to consider since in important respects – above all in what I regard as his finest performances – the poems of the *Diván del Tamarit* – Lorca is a near-hermetic artist; his creations are elaborately worked, self-contained wholes, free from autobiographical intrusion.

Two beliefs of mine should, I think, be put on record in this introduction. In my view the homosexual artist has his own special contribution to make to the creative illumination of life. This opinion seems to me the reverse of sectarianism; it is part of an acknowledgement of the value and beauty of human diversity. Second, I believe, and after many years of reading him, that Lorca being one of the few truly great artistic geniuses of modern times, his work can be studied with profit from many different angles, and of this I hope I give ample evidence in my book. For he is of the company, I am sure, of Rilke, Yeats, Eliot, Montale – or to turn to the sister-art of music, as seems peculiarly apt for him – of Janáček, Falla, Stravinsky, Bartók.

In the dark times in which we live now, when not only humankind but the very earth and all living things upon it are under unprecedented and evil threat – we have, I feel, more need than ever of the productions of such minds. Perhaps it is no coincidence that it is now – both within and outside the Hispanic world – that Lorca's achievements have come at last fully into their own; studying him is felt to be somehow on the side of life – honouring civilisation.

When I try to consider in what Lorca's greatness resides, I am always reminded of one of Yeats' late masterpieces in which ability to accept and to transcend the tragic nature of existence is so wonderfully praised – 'Lapis Lazuli':

> I have heard that hysterical women say
> They are sick of the palette and fiddle-bow,
> Of poets that are always gay,
> For everybody knows or else should know
> That if nothing drastic is done
> Aeroplane and Zeppelin will come out,
> Pitch like King Billy bomb-balls in
> Until the town lie beaten flat.
>
> All perform their tragic play,
> There struts Hamlet, there is Lear,
> That's Ophelia, that Cordelia;
> Yet they, should the last scene be there,
> The great stage curtain about to drop,
> If worthy their prominent part in the play,
> Do not break up their lines to weep.
> They know that Hamlet and Lear are gay;
> Gaiety transfiguring all that dread.

Lorca was gay in a sense not intended by Yeats, and I hope that this book can show that his finest work is an expression indeed of a gaiety that transfigures all our dread.

Paul Binding
June 1985

# PART ONE

## Chapter One

# Confrontations

I feel depressed and full of regrets. I am hungry for my own country . . . I don't know why I have left; I ask myself this a hundred times a day. I look at myself in the mirror of the narrow cabin and I don't recognise myself. I appear another Federico.[1]

So wrote Federico García Lorca to his friend, the Chilean diplomat Carlos Morla Lynch, on 19 June 1929, while making the Atlantic crossing from Southampton to New York. At thirty-one he was the most acclaimed Spanish poet of his brilliant generation, but awareness of this fact increased rather than alleviated his mental distress. Insecurity of identity persisted long after his ship's arrival in New York on 25 June and determined the nature of his confrontation with the city. This confrontation can now be seen as a real watershed in Lorca's life and art, and a momentous event in the cultural history of our century; out of its anguish and uncertainty came ambitious work of major quality, different in important respects from anything the poet had written before. For many of Lorca's habit-blind contemporaries this was a bad thing; they thought a wrong turning had been taken. Today we evaluate the work otherwise. Adventurous and complex both in ideas and form, it seems to us to possess a remarkable universality of reference. Nor does it seem so unrelated to Lorca's previous productions as was once believed. The New York period can be viewed with hindsight as the crucible through which Lorca's genius had to pass.

Pre-eminently out of New York came a long poem-cycle, *El poeta en Nueva York (The Poet in New York)*. Its publishing history has been complicated. Individual poems were printed in reviews between 1930 and 1933. From 1932 to 1934 Lorca read out in public important sections of the work, both in Spain and in South America, and in 1935 began to prepare the text for publication, which was never to take place in his lifetime. *El poeta en Nueva York* did not, in fact, appear until 1940, four years after Lorca's death, and then outside Spain and incomplete. There were, however, among all those critics who thought Lorca had in these poems gone away from that which he could do best, discerning people who felt that he had truly fulfilled what he had declared was his ambition for the work: to create 'a bitter but living poetry to lash open [the public's] eyes'.[2] The cycle was the poet's agonised response to the double challenge New York forced upon him: to understand and evaluate the city's harsh, tumultuous life; and to understand and evaluate, in this new and disturbing context, his own predicament, personal and ontological.

In a *conferencia* (lecture) that he gave many times on the subject of his New York poems, Lorca wondered whether he should talk about 'New York in a poet' rather than 'a poet in New York'.[3] By extension the same doubts could be entertained about the title of the whole sequence: the poet in New York or New York in the poet? – the poet being so compoundly an outsider: Spanish not American, Latin not Anglo-Saxon, Catholic not Protestant, Gentile not Jewish, homosexual not heterosexual, lover of old cities not denizen of a history-less megalopolis.

Because he chose to accept and not evade these challenges Lorca was able to proceed with work on two highly unconventional plays: *Así que pasen cinco años (As Soon as Five Years Pass)* and *El público (The Public)*. Themes important to the cycle inform both these works. Their history has been similar to that of *El poeta en Nueva York* in that they have not been incorporated into the Lorquian canon until comparatively recently and were for a long time dismissed as inchoate, untypical, eccentric.

Lorca's New World experiences, and the work he did there, not only resulted in a courageous coming to terms with America and with himself, they also brought about in him a new appreciation of Spain and Hispanitude. In the spring of 1930 Lorca accepted the invitation of the Institución Hispano–Cubana de Cultura to lecture in Havana, Cuba, where he felt the intensest pleasure at being back in a Spanish society again; Latin America was for him 'God's America'. In Havana he delivered his most famous lecture, on the *duende*, that Andalusian spirit inextricably associated with acceptance of death, which Lorca saw as embodying not only the quintessence of Spain but what Spain uniquely could give to other societies and cultures.

On his return to Spain Lorca proceeded to write poems and plays which soon won him back the popularity and esteem that had been his after the *Romancero gitano (Gypsy Balladeer)* of 1928. Some of these have become unquestionably the best-known works of Spanish literature of their period, and possibly of the century. More, they have earned the firmest of places for themselves in the international literary repertoire: the elegy 'Llanto por Ignacio Sánchez Mejías' ('Lament for Ignacio Sánchez Mejías'), the plays *Bodas de sangre (Blood Wedding)*, *Yerma (The Barren Woman)* and *La casa de Bernarda Alba (The House of Bernarda Alba)*. All are characterised artistically by a Hispanitude in comparative retreat in those works written in New York (which show the influence of cosmopolitan literary movements). They also have an extraordinary directness of emotional address which explains their popularity far beyond the Spanish-speaking world. These now classical masterpieces could not have been created had Lorca not undergone his crisis in New York and written there his three unorthodox works, above all *El poeta en Nueva York* with which, in the words of the editor of Lorca's letters, David Gershator, 'he reached farthest into the twentieth century'.[4]

The sufferings that Lorca knew had external as well as internal causes. New York in 1929 was in the throes of the Depression, and Lorca very quickly became aware of the widespread misery within the city and of the callousness towards this of too many Americans. Almost from the first he saw this misery as an emanation – indeed, as an inevitable consequence – of the society's dominant philosophy:

> The two elements the traveller first captures in the big city are extra-human architecture and furious rhythm. Geometry and anguish. At first glance, the rhythm can seem to be gaiety, but when you look more closely at the mechanism of social life and the painful slavery of both men and machines you understand it as a typical, empty anguish that makes even crime and banditry forgivable means of evasion.
>
> Willing neither clouds nor glory, the edges of the buildings rise to the sky. While Gothic edges rise from the hearts of the dead and buried, these ones climb coldly skyward with beauty that has no roots and no yearning, stupidly sure of themselves and utterly unable to conquer or transcend, as does spiritual architecture, the always inferior intentions of the architect. There is nothing more poetic and terrible than the skyscrapers' battle with the heavens that cover them. Snow, rain, and mist set off, wet, and hide the vast towers, but these towers, hostile to mystery, blind to any sort of play, shear off the rain's tresses and shine their three thousand swords through the soft swan of the mist.
>
> It only takes a few days before you get the impression that that immense world has no roots. . .[5]

Already, in the comparison between the Gothic cathedrals and the skyscrapers, both apparently attempting heaven, we can see a basis for the quarrel in which Lorca was to engage with the United States. The first cities Lorca had known were Granada, Córdoba, Sevilla; Sevilla's mighty cathedral, and the Islamic tower of the Giralda which stands so impressively beside it, came into being as expressions of belief in the infinite, towards which, in imitation of the soul, they soared. The skyscrapers of Manhattan, on the other hand, were built in a spirit of competition, vying with each other in loftiness just as the firms that created them vied one with another in turnover; the faith to which they testify is doctrinaire free enterprise. They arose, moreover, without the support of the past. The great cathedrals of the Old World frequently stand on the sites of earlier 'holy' buildings, and nearly always on ground fertilised by generations of the believing dead.

Lorca was soon to locate the 'terrible, cold, cruel' heart of New York; this was Wall Street:

> Rivers of gold flow there from all over the earth, and death comes with it. There as nowhere else you feel a total absence of the spirit . . .[6]

Wall Street possessed, it seemed to him, a:

> demoniacal respect for the present. And the terrible thing is that the crowd who fills the street believes that the world will always be the same, and that it is their duty to move the huge machine day and night forever.[7]

This belief was, of course, to receive the most resounding blow only a few months after Lorca's arrival in America. On 28 October 1929 Wall Street crashed. The crash has become part of modern consciousness. Those financiers who in their despair threw themselves out of skyscraper windows enact for us still, repeatedly, their country's plight. America's Promethean ambitions which had found such amazing and beautiful realisation in the skyscrapers of New York – and Lorca, too, found them beautiful – brought about a fall of equally Promethean dimensions and importance. In 1930, during Lorca's sojourn in the city, the Empire State Building was finally ready, emerging to cap the towers not of some New Jerusalem but of the centre of world recession. In the streets down below the armies of the unemployed and unemployable grew to horrifying proportions. The young Spanish poet – none of whose earlier experiences had prepared him for this – looked upon them, empathised with them, and made them the subject of outraged poems: 'Paisaje de la multitud que vomita' ('Landscape of the Vomiting Crowd'); 'Paisaje de la multitud que orina' ('Landscape of the Urinating Crowd').

All this was a long way from the 'populous city', the great and splendid 'Mannahatta' of Walt Whitman, the American poet whose work Lorca knew best, through reading him in the translations of the Spanish 'Whitmanesque' poet, León Felipe. Let us remind ourselves of the sort of literary treatment Whitman had given New York City in 1860:

> Rich, hemm'd thick all around with sailships and steamships, an
>     island sixteen miles long, solid-founded,
> Numberless crowded streets, high growths of iron, slender,
>     strong, light, splendidly uprising toward clear skies,

Tides swift and ample, well-loved by me, toward sundown,
The flowing sea-currents, the little islands, larger adjoining islands,
   the heights, the villas,
The countless masts, the white shore-steamers, the lighters, the
   ferry-boats, the black sea-steamers well model'd,
The downtown streets, the jobbers' houses of business, the houses
   of business of the ship-merchants and money-brokers, the
   river-streets,
Immigrants arriving, fifteen or twenty thousand in a week,
The carts hauling goods, the manly race of drivers of horses, the
   brown-faced sailors,
The summer air, the bright sun shining, and the sailing clouds
   aloft,
The winter snows, the sleigh-bells, the broken ice in the river,
   passing along up or down with the flood-tide or ebb-tide,
The mechanics of the city, the masters, well-form'd, beautiful-
   faced, looking you straight in the eyes,
Trottoirs throng'd, vehicles, Broadway, the women, the shops and
   shows,
A million people – manners free and superb – open voices –
   hospitality – the most courageous and friendly young men,
City of hurried and sparkling waters! city of spires and masts!
City nested in bays! my city![8]

Walt Whitman's lyrical apostrophes do indeed testify to certain important and integral features of New York. But Lorca was to ask himself, as we must, whether the vision of America's most famous and *sui generis* poet – however inspiriting in its rhetorical articulations – did not almost wilfully exclude *full* confrontation of his society, of its uglier and more difficult aspects. What were the merchants and money-brokers really up to? Can the mechanics and masters be satisfactorily saluted as 'well-form'd' and 'beautiful-faced' without any hint of what the relationship, not to say the discrepancy, between them might be? Doubts such as these led Lorca into the most intense appraisal of the transcendentalist-humanist-materialist position which Whitman, father-figure of American poetry, seemed to him to embody. Much as he loved Whitman, he had in the end to come down against his *weltanschauung* – or that aspect of it that the American people had so taken to their bosom. For Lorca the gulf between America's Platonic vision of itself and reality, as in this dark period of 1929–30 he encountered it, was too vast and too troubling.

★

Lorca had made the voyage to New York in the company of his old friend and teacher from Granada, Fernando de los Ríos. Ostensibly he had come to America to learn English: shortly after his arrival, therefore, he matriculated at Columbia University and took a room in one of its halls of residence, John Jay Hall, a room he was to retain until the time of his departure (summer 1930). However he was a member of an English class for one week only! Instead of studying he embarked on an exploration of New York by day and by night. Then in August he went to the countryside – first to Vermont, then to the Catskills, where he stayed with his friend, Angel del Río, to whose accounts of Lorca in America every student of the poet is indebted. Lorca returned to New York for the autumn term – and, as we have seen, for the Wall Street crash and its grim aftermath.[9]

Certainly, from del Río's memoir, it would seem that Lorca had begun work on poems with American themes by the time of his summer holiday in upstate New York, and the earliest poems we have antedate this vacation. Certainly, too, Lorca always intended them as parts of a large-scale whole. (In July and August 1929 Lorca worked also, it would seem, on poems that were not to be part of the cycle.) By 30 September 1929 Lorca was writing to an old friend: 'I've written a book of poetry and almost another.'[10] In November Carlos Morla Lynch received a far more buoyant letter than that penned to him during the Atlantic crossing. Now Lorca is calling New York a 'city of unexpected happiness'. 'I've written a lot,' he says, 'I have almost two books of poems and a theatrical piece. . .That Federico of old. . .has been reborn.'[11]

More revealing still is Lorca's letter to his family of January 1930. He vividly evokes an American Christmas and paints a picture of the effect of Prohibition on American life, then goes on:

> I'm working steadily. I'm writing a book of poems of interpretations of New York which makes an enormous impression on my friends because of its forcefulness. I believe that everything of mine pales alongside these things which in a certain way are *symphonic* like the noise and complexity of New York.[12]

There can be no doubt that on beginning what was to become *El poeta en Nueva York* Lorca felt himself launched on an enterprise of greater imaginative and emotional scope than anything he had hitherto attempted, and so it turned out. He intended the poems to be mimetic of the confusions of the city; hence their frequently pellmell-seeming proffering of images. This confusion can only be overcome by the ultimate shapeliness of the artistic whole in which the individual poems are placed.

I find it interesting that even at such a comparatively early stage of the work as January 1930 Lorca is speaking of it as 'symphonic'. This was not a word he would use lightly. He was intensely musical, a friend of composers and musicians, learned in folk-music, a gifted pianist, and himself a composer of genuine if limited talent. *El poeta en Nueva York* works upon us like a symphony; an image turns out to be the germ of a theme which will receive later development, be subjected to elaborate metamorphosis, and achieve ultimate resolution.

'Everything of mine pales alongside these things,' he wrote. Believing this to be the case (and this without any disparagement of earlier work, of the beautiful *Romancero gitano* in particular) I have chosen to begin this study of Lorca with *El poeta en Nueva York*, that achievement in which (as it will be my business to show) the poet's homosexual position is, for the first time, both properly confronted and used as a vantage-point.

★

The chronology within the cycle – i.e. the chronicle of the poet's expanding apprehension and knowledge of New York (and there is never any doubt that we are intended to take the 'I' as Lorca himself) – is not precisely that of Lorca in 1929–30. *El poeta en Nueva York* is an imaginative artefact not an exercise in the confessional; it contains an ordering of experiences according to an internal logic, and illuminates rather than reproduces the course of Lorca's own sojourn in the United States. The work proceeds as follows:

I. 'Poemas de la soledad en Columbia University' ('Poems of Solitude in Columbia University'). These present us with the disorientation of the young poet at finding himself in a city of whose culture he knows nothing, and with the excursions back to his own earlier life that this disorientation imposes upon him. We also receive an impression of a personal conflict gnawing at him and demanding to be resolved.

II. 'Los negros' ('The Blacks'). In the heterogeneity of New York Lorca found *one* group he admired and found sympathetic, the – often despised – Blacks. These poems are a tribute to them, especially the ode 'El rey de Harlem' ('The King of Harlem'), the first indisputably major poem of the cycle.

III. 'Calles y sueños' ('Streets and Dreams'). Poems of the interaction of outer and inner worlds as the poet increases his familiarity with the city. Here are two brooding poems dealing with Lorca's New York Christmas: 'Navidad en el Hudson' ('Christmas on the Hudson') and 'Nacimiento de Cristo' ('Birth of Christ').

IV, V, VI. Pastoral intermezzi in which the poet takes stock of both himself and his experiences in the New World. He also records his often grateful experiences of New England and upstate New York life: 'Poemas del Lago Edem [sic] Mills' ('Poems from Lake Eden Mills'); 'En la cabaña del Farmer' ('In the Farmer's Cabin') and 'Introducción a la muerte' ('Introduction to Death') – subtitled 'Poemas de la soledad en Vermont' ('Poems of Solitude in Vermont').

These introduce us to two children whom Lorca – a great lover of children – had befriended while in the American countryside, 'El niño Stanton' ('Little Boy Stanton') and a little girl whose tragic fate is lamented in 'Niña ahogada en el pozo' ('Little Girl Drowned in the Well'). 'Introducción a la muerte' is ontological in its principal obsessions. It contains a strange homage to the idea of the void: 'Luna y panorama de los insectos' ('Moon and Panorama of the Insects').

VII. 'Vuelta a la ciudad' ('Return to the City'). Absence from New York has only intensified the revulsion from its life that the poet feels to be the only proper response to it. So now Lorca, very deliberately and with a sad defiance, delivers himself of a *denuncia*, denunciation. The poems 'Cementerio judío' ('Jewish Cemetery') and 'Crucifixión' ('Crucifixion') are likewise charged with bitterness and are profuse with images of alarming psychic force.

VIII. 'Dos odas' ('Two Odes'). These two poems 'Grito hacia Roma (Desde la torre de Crysler [sic] Building)' ('Cry to Rome (From the Chrysler Building Tower)') and 'Oda a Walt Whitman' ('Ode to Walt Whitman') form the climax of the entire work. They are also, in their power and their scope, the profoundest creations of Lorca's to date. The 'Oda a Walt Whitman', by general consent the finer of the two, presents us with a vision of America from a homosexual standpoint, the poet here at last facing up to, and making creative use of, the tensions of a lifetime.

IX. 'Huida de Nueva York (Dos valses hacia la civilización)' ('Flight from New York (Two Waltzes Towards Civilisation)').

X. 'El poeta llega a La Habana' ('The Poet Arrives in Havana'). Lorca expresses his joy at having left for 'God's America, Spanish America'. 'But what's this? Spain again? Universal Andalusia? It is the yellow of Cádiz, but a shade brighter; the rosiness of Sevilla, but more like carmine; the green of Granada but gently phosphorescent like a fish. Havana rises up amid canefields and the noise of maracas, cornets, chinas and marimbas. . .'[13]

It will be seen that the cycle suggests a far longer time between the poet's arrival in New York and his departure for the countryside than was the case. The reader of *El poeta en Nueva York* could imagine that Lorca had spent from summer to gone Christmas continuously in the city, Christmas occurring in section III *before* the pastoral interludes. The landscape of these last, however, would appear to be summery as was indeed the case. But even here invention is present. Angel del Río says that the death by drowning of the little girl in Newburg was total fiction, though we must add that it was a fiction that Lorca kept to in life as well as in art.

In opening this study of Lorca with *El poeta en Nueva York* we are, then, opening it with a master-work tackling the present phase of our civilisation at one of its more painful points and judging matters according to the touchstones of Hispanitude and homosexuality, both indissoluble elements of the poet's personality, actual and literary. What, we must ask ourselves, was his inner climate as he began his extensive confrontation of New York, himself, his art?

We cannot do better by way of finding out than to examine the cycle's first section, 'Poemas de la soledad en Columbia University'. If these are difficult poems, which could be accused with some justification of being wilfully obscure, this should not deter us; more, it makes us realise how very far Lorca was from being the naive folklorist-balladeer he is still too frequently seen as. He had a tormented mind, a complex imagination and a passionate soul, and needed a highly-wrought and difficult art to express them.

★

The first poem, 'Vuelta de paseo' ('Back from a Walk'), can be quoted in full:

> Asesinado por el cielo,
> entre las formas que van hacia la sierpe
> y las formas que buscan el cristal,
> dejaré crecer mis cabellos.
>
> Con el árbol de muñones que no canta
> y el niño con el blanco rostro de huevo.
>
> Con los animalitos de cabeza rota
> y el agua harapienta de los pies secos.
>
> Con todo lo que tiene cansancio sordomudo
> y mariposa ahogada en el tintero.
>
> Tropezando con mi rostro distinto de cada día.
> ¡Asesinado por el cielo!

> Murdered by the sky,
> Between the shapes that move towards the snake
> and the shapes that seek the crystal,
> I will let my hair grow.
>
> With the tree of stumps which doesn't sing
> and the child with the white face of an egg.
>
> With the little broken-headed creatures
> and the tattered water of dry feet.
>
> With all that has deaf-and-dumb weariness
> and the butterfly drowned in the inkwell.

> Shambling with my face different every day.
> Murdered by the sky![14]

The first line (to which the last line is identical except that it is an exclamation and not an adjectival phrase) resembles the opening motif of some Sibelius symphony; throughout the work these few pregnant and mysterious notes will undergo development and transmogrification, to emerge as a challenging *tema* in the 'Grito hacia Roma (Desde la torre de Crysler Building)'. On the most literal level '*asesinado por el cielo*' refers to the not uncommon vertiginous sensation that besets most visitors to New York where the sky, viewed from the great canyons of its streets, seems more distant and consequently more alien than in other cities. The sky is ether, the air, the element we live *in* as well as *beneath*: to feel murdered by it is to feel suffocated, poisoned, by life itself. Lorca's telling us how he shambles along his walks with a different face every day suggests his dislocation from all 'norms' of self, and we remember those words of his to Carlos Morla Lynch: 'I look at myself in the mirror of the narrow cabin and I don't recognise myself.' *Cielo* means 'heaven' as well as 'sky'. Does the young man walking back alone to his rooms feel himself to be singled out for punishment from heaven? Or does he envisage this as the state of every person in New York, where lofty buildings challenge God and serve Mammon? Whichever the case, the feeling – to judge by the exclamation marks – would seem distressingly new to the poet.

Nor is this the only agony in his position. He stands perplexed between two competing forms, '*las formas que van hacia la sierpe*' and '*las formas que buscan el cristal*'. The first are those that make for the world of sexuality epitomised, as traditionally, by the serpent, the second those that strive for purity, spirituality, the chaste world of precious stone and white light. Aren't these forms representatives of, respectively, the id and the super-ego, terms with which Lorca, as we shall see, would have been fully cognisant? What Lorca wants is the serenity of the ego, to be *him*self in a society at one with *it*self. But in the amorphous confusion of contemporary life he is denied this: all that is possible for him is a sort of *non serviam*. For surely the gesture of wearing the hair long approximates to this, as Sixties youth was later to demonstrate. Long hair will render the poet androgynous, even – to the conventional world – effeminate. It will confirm his status of outsider, of whom decision-making is not required. Putting oneself outside decision is, of course, a decision in itself, and one with consequences.

One consequence is a feeling of immediate identification with a variety of living beings all of whom suffer from incompleteness or infertility. Thus the tree lacks branches and therefore buds, the child is the colour of the part of the egg that does not contain the sperm, and the water is threatened by drought. The butterfly, that fragile emissary from the Platonic realm of absolutes – as we will find it to be in Lorca's strange first extant play, *El maleficio de la mariposa (The Butterfly's Evil Spell)* – is drowned in that substance, ink, which exists as a medium for their exegesis (e.g. philosophy and literature).

This world in which nothing is whole or hale is surely akin to the Fisher King's territory in Eliot's *Waste Land* (1922), a work which Lorca had been reading in the Spanish translation of Angel Flores (*Tierra baldía*):

> What are the roots that clutch, what branches grow
> Out of this stony rubbish? Son of man,
> You cannot say, or guess, for you know only
> A heap of broken images, where the sun beats,
> And the dead tree gives no shelter, the cricket no relief,
> And the dry stone no sound of water. . .[15]

Eliot's waste land is under a curse of sterility, awaits a saviour and fructifying waters. Lorca too was to become preoccupied with the idea of redemption of a barren world, and indeed the highest point of the poem-cycle, the 'Oda a Walt Whitman', ends with an earnest of the curse being lifted – and by human (Black) agency – from this *tierra baldía* that was New York.

Lorca himself tells us, in the lecture 'Un poeta en Nueva York', that his early, solitary, horrified walks through the city compelled his mind back to his childhood. The second and fourth poems of the opening section, therefore, have childhood as their principal theme: '1910 (Intermedio)' ('1910 (Interlude)') and 'Tu infancia en Menton' ('Your Childhood in Menton'). During the lecture Lorca would, it seems, read these poems consecutively but in the reverse order to that in which they appear in book form. We cannot be concerned here with biographical probings, with a search for the personal realities behind their admittedly many arcane references. Rather do we want to establish the nature of the obsessions that consumed Lorca at the beginning of his American sojourn, at the beginning of the work of his that 'reached farthest into the twentieth century'.

In 1910 the poet had his twelfth birthday; he was therefore on the threshold of puberty but still looked at the world in a comparatively prelapsarian light. At this period of his life, Lorca tells us, his eyes had never looked upon death or even upon its copious counterfeits and advance-guards. Life for him was made up of facades behind which lurked only half guessed-at forces. His young eyes were quite unable to penetrate these walls:

Aquellos ojos míos de mil novecientos diez
vieron la blanca pared donde orinaban las niñas,
el hocico del toro, la seta venenosa
y una luna incomprensible que iluminaba por los rincones
los pedazos de limón seco bajo el negro duro de las botellas.

Those eyes of mine of Nineteen-Ten
saw the blank wall where the little girls were urinating,
the muzzle of the bull, the poisonous mushroom
and an incomprehensible moon that lit up in the corners
the rinds of dry lemon under the hard blackness of bottles.[16]

Thus a girl's orifices, at this time, were associated only with pissing
beneath a wall; the bull had a muzzle merely, was not the fighting
sacrificial animal in whom the later Lorca was to be so interested; the
mushroom was a poisonous fungus not a phallic-shaped aphrodisiac;
the moon, a recurrent symbol in Lorca (appearing indeed in his *oeuvre*
218 times)[17] and connoting death, is not confronted as a *whole* but
known only through its rays as they played upon empty containers of
food and drink (rinds and bottles), like in some still-life by Zurbarán,
a Spanish master Lorca much admired. The poem's last stanza is
pervaded by a considerable sadness. Lorca tells us that all objects,
whether seeking self-preservation or wholeness, in the end discover
only their own emptiness and disintegration. That is what his older
eyes know, and what – he now thinks – his younger eyes feared as the
truth.

'Tu infancia en Menton' sounds a similarly despairing note. It is
prefaced with a line by a great friend of Lorca's, the even then eminent
poet – scholarly yet lyrical – Jorge Guillén:

> Sí, tu niñez ya fábula de fuentes.

> Yes, your childhood, now a fable of fountains.[18]

Lorca reiterates this line insistently throughout the poem. The
fountain, like the butterfly, stands for Platonic absolutes. In childhood
it was a central object in our landscape, refreshing us constantly with
intimations of – literally, with jet-streams from – immortal life. In
adulthood this fountain becomes only faintly audible. Mature life is
too often, cruelly, a matter of the putting-on, the presentation and the
– consequently necessary – stripping-off of masks. Our real identities
– of beings that should be fed by the eternal waters of pure Love, pure
Idea – have become obscured. And this poem reveals Lorca as
passionately involved with the whole question of identity, not just in
general terms but in particular ones. This is a poem addressed to a
loved one:

Norma de amor te di, hombre de Apolo,
llanto con ruiseñor enajenado,
pero, pasto de ruina, te afilabas
para los breves sueños indecisos. . .
Pero yo he de buscar por los rincones
tu alma tibia sin ti que no te entiende,
con el dolor de Apolo detenido
con que he roto la máscara que llevas.
Allí, león, allí furia del cielo,
te dejaré pacer en mis mejillas . . .

A norm of love I gave you, man of Apollo,
a lament with enraptured nightingale,
but, pasture of ruin, you honed yourself
for short indecisive dreams. . .
But I must search the corners
for your lukewarm soul without you that doesn't understand you,
with the pain of a hesitant Apollo
with which I have broken the mask that you wear.
There, lion, there, fury of the sky,
I will let you graze upon my cheeks . . . [19]

Light is cast upon this passage by a proper knowledge of the significance of Apollo; Lorca was learned in Greek mythology and interested in putting it to new uses. Apollo was the first Greek god to make love to a member of the male sex; in certain classical and post-classical literature his name becomes a shorthand for homosexual relations, as surely it does here. The idea of *norma*, the norm, was much to preoccupy Lorca. Here he tells us that he gave a norm of love to a follower of Apollo (i.e. a lover of his own sex), a norm which was not accepted – maybe because he himself offered it too shyly; he was an *Apolo detenido*. By giving a norm Lorca surely means approaching the object of his desire/love with expectation of reciprocity. This would involve physical demonstration; after all in any meaningful heterosexual relation reciprocity is a *sine qua non*. The man for whom Lorca entertained his Apollonian feelings lived (c.f. the previous poem) behind a mask. The poet would appear to have brought about a shattering of this mask, but, so far as his own happiness was concerned, to no avail. The loved one turned out to have a nervous, lukewarm (*tibia*) soul. All he had wanted were *breves sueños indecisos*, inconclusive interludes in daily life.

On an important level, then, this poem can be read as a heartfelt cry for complete and, so to speak, *public* realisation of self in homosexual love. In subsequent lines the poet begs the spirit of love not to castrate animals who live in heaven – '*clínica y selva de la anatomía*' ('clinic and forest of anatomy') – in other words, not to force those possessed by love, which has its sources in the eternal, to forego the blissful consummation their God-given equipment (i.e. genitalia) demands. Lorca here is seeing consummated homosexual love as a norm, differing in no significant respect from consummated heterosexual love. It is *un*consummated homosexual love that is unnatural, a denial of life. Consummation provides a restoration for the adult of that relation to the absolute which we knew in childhood – when the fountains of eternal water played upon us. And if this protest on behalf of full and acknowledged sexual relations between men, informed by a neo-Platonism reminiscent of Vaughan's 'The Retreat' or Words-worth's 'Immortality Ode', seems a long way away from confronta-tion of New York on the eve of the Wall Street crash, I must remind the reader that the work for which these poems are introductory is to culminate in a great ode which puts homosexuality at its imaginative and moral centre.

'Fábula y rueda de los tres amigos' ('Fable and Round of the Three Friends') is, for us now, the third poem of the opening quartet (Lorca in his *conferencia*, perhaps remembering the writing rather than his later ordering, suggests a different place for it) and is the strangest, most elliptical, of them all.

The three friends are depicted, first as *helados* (frozen), then as *quemados* (burned), and finally as *enterrados* (buried). Surely these three conditions are the results of the harshest aspects of the Four Elements; water, fire, earth. And indeed the varying predicaments of the eponymous three men – presented to us, as the poem's title would suggest, in round-form, with now one, now another, leading – ascribe to each man the characteristics of an element, accord him respectively a humour.

But *one* element is missing: air. Air means the sanguine tempera-ment; Jupiter; the Zodiac signs of Gemini, Libra and Aquarius; the South wind, spring and childhood; azure and yellow; sapphires and topazes and marigolds. *Why* should air be missing? Is it not because air is the element of the 'I' who appears after the first round of the friends has been sung, before their self-destructive transformations have got under way? Air is, therefore, the element of Lorca himself.

Certainly Lorca *was* born under air's sign of Gemini. And we should note that this sign often stands for homosexual inclinations or aspirations, the search for one's twin, a spirit and body matching one's own. Spring, air and childhood had been favourite subjects of the young Lorca's poetry, as he must have recalled when writing these disguisedly autobiographical lines. And the demise of the three friends in this 'Fábula y rueda' is presided over by Jupiter – god of air, and so, by extension, of Lorca.

Not that air's representative himself escapes a cruel fate. His fate is indeed the most appalling of all, redeemed though it partly is by a concluding suggestion of posthumous apotheosis. The three friends have meant Lorca no good. In a line, born of Lorca's horrified walks round New York's poorer districts, the Bowery, the Battery, we read how the trio have associated themselves with:

> . . .mi muerte desierta con un solo paseante equivocado.

> . . .my derelict dying with a single mistaken passer-by.[20]

Death is truly the lord of this extraordinary poem. Its last section has become famous because many (for example that pioneer of Lorquian matters in Britain, J.L. Gili) have seen it as an uncanny prophecy of the poet's own dreadful end:

> Cuando se hundieron las formas puras
> bajo el cricri de las margaritas,
> comprendí que me habían asesinado.
> Recorrieron los cafés y los cementerios y las iglesias,
> abrieron los toneles y los armarios,
> destrozaron tres esqueletos para arrancar sus dientes de oro.
> Ya no me encontraron.
> ¿No me encontraron?
> No. No me encontraron.
> Pero se supo que la sexta luna huyó torrente arriba,
> y que el mar recordó ¡de pronto!
> los nombres de todos sus ahogados.

> When the pure forms collapsed
> under the cri-cri of the daisies,
> I understood that they had murdered me.
> They looked through the cafes and the cemeteries and the churches,
> they opened the barrels and the wardrobes,
> they smashed three skeletons in order to pull out their gold teeth.
> Yet they did not find me.
> No. They did not find me.
> But it was known that the sixth moon fled up the torrent,
> and that the sea suddenly remembered
> the names of all its drowned.[21]

Of the meanings *las formas puras* can have for us, foremost is that of 'traditional verse-forms'; Lorca felt that he had, with these new poems, put behind him all the *baladas* and *sonetos, saetas, siguiriyas* and *romances* in which (albeit often with an exuberant licence) he had excelled.

He now craved new and looser literary forms to express the recent tumultuous emancipation of his mind. The lines are surely a reference to that Daliesque surrealism which many see Lorca as embracing in the New York poems. The French critic, C. Martilly,[22] vindicates such a reading with his ingenious interpretation of the most puzzling line of all: '*Pero se supo que la sexta luna huyó torrente arriba*'. Lorca, he points out, had already, in an interview, assigned *Romancero gitano* (in which the moon is so pervasive a symbol) *fifth* place in his *oeuvre*. The *sixth* moon – which significantly has journeyed up the torrent to the source – thus refers to the more challenging, because deeper-seated, poetry that is to follow the *Romancero gitano*, i.e. the present New York sequence.

In the powerful lines that conclude the 'Fábula' we can see how the man of air, spring and childhood – i.e. Lorca himself – is murdered by a conspiracy of representatives of the baser elements. In the terrible ensuing confusion his body is lost. But the sky and the sea – which share his own colour, azure, the colour of infinity – receive him. He thus passes, as befits him, outside time. So was Lorca to be murdered – by Falangists in the orgy of blood-letting that took place in Granada in August 1936 – and his body lost. But his disembodied spirit, particularly as manifested in art, has haunted both Spain and other countries ever since.

I propose to follow now the course of Lorca's mind as it prepared itself for a new literary task of challenging magnitude and so look back at the poet's earlier years and at the country and culture in which they were spent. We shall then return to New York and try to understand the tragic contrasts, as Lorca perceived them, between *its* life and that which he himself had hitherto known and had drawn on for his creative work. There was, of course, a personal animus behind these perceptions, an animus of sexual origin which we will identify and seek out, for – released and confronted – it is responsible for the 'Oda a Walt Whitman' and indeed for Lorca's masterpieces after his return to Spain.

## Chapter Two

# The Inspirited Land

## 1

Andalucía – in which Federico García Lorca was born on 5 June 1898 – has supplied Spaniards and non-Spaniards alike with some of the most potent and durable images of Spain itself. Over the centuries it has received into its varied and beautiful countryside many different races and cultures: Iberians, Celts, Phoenicians, Greeks, Carthaginians, Romans, Vandals (these last may have given Andalucía its name) and Moors. In one of the ballads of the *Romancero gitano*, 'Reyerta' ('Fight'), a judge, confronted with a brawl between gangs of young country-boys, is told by a mysterious voice:

> aquí pasó lo de siempre.
> Han muerto cuatro romanos
> y cinco cartagineses.

> it's happened here as always.
> Four Romans have died
> and five Carthaginians.[1]

So the Romans and Carthaginians continue to this day in the Andalusian countryside!

Andalucía contains huge estates belonging to extremely rich landowners and, toiling for these, many very poor labourers. There are vast rural areas but the province also possesses some of Spain's busiest and most celebrated cities: the great trinity Lorca honoured in numerous poems of Granada, Córdoba and Sevilla, as well as Cádiz, Málaga, Jerez de la Frontera, Jaén. It is a land, on the one hand, of a stubborn, sometimes indolent traditionalism, and, on the other, of an often violent political (leftist) activism. Andalucía has nurtured the anarchosyndicalists and some of Spain's staunchest Communists; it saw some of the Civil War's cruellest, bloodiest passages – while, years later, in the regional elections of 1982 it provided the country, and the watching world, with an earnest of the sweeping Socialist victory of Felipe González in the general election of the autumn of that year.

These paradoxes and coexistences must surely account for Andalucía's quite extraordinary pre-eminence in literature, which, in terms of the modern period, means poetry. The two most dazzling luminaries of the Spanish literary scene at the time of Lorca's growing-up were both Andalusians: Antonio Machado and Juan Ramón Jiménez. And of the circle of young poets that García Lorca was to join in Madrid, no fewer than *five* others were fellow-Andalusians: Vicente Aleixandre, Emilio Prados, Luis Cernuda, Rafael Alberti and Manuel Altolaguirre.

If the place of Lorca's birth is of inestimable importance in any analysis of him, so too is the time, the year, indeed the *point* in the year. Lorca was born in the very middle of the Spanish–American War. Disastrous though it was for Spain, the Lorca family benefited financially by it to a considerable degree. Lorca was to be comfortable, as far as money was concerned, all his life. The war ended on 26 July 1898 with Spain asking the United States for terms, and thus losing her last important colonies: Cuba, Puerto Rico, the Philippines. (This may in part account for the animus against the United States felt by Lorca and other Spaniards of his age.) Her defeat heightened Spain's already severe problem of national identity. Was her greatness solely a matter of the past, of the conquistadores and the golden century? This question, and concomitant ones concerning the country's moral health and relationship to the other European powers, intensely preoccupied the major Spanish intellectuals of the day: Miguel de Unamuno, Pío Baroja, 'Azorín', Antonio Machado, and – later – José Ortega y Gasset; it contributed to the unhappiness and suicide of Angel Gánivet. This group, the *Generación del '98* (Generation of 1898), made the relationship of the individual to the regeneration of Spain a primary subject. When Lorca and his literary friends – the principal among whom have already been named – formed themselves into an informally structured group, the *Generación del '27* (Generation of 1927), they called themselves the *nietos del '98* (grandsons of 1898) so conscious had they been in formative years of the concerns, and the literary expressions of these concerns, of the older men.

★

Lorca's father was a prosperous farmer and landholder, Don Federico García Rodriguez; his mother, Don Federico's second wife, was a sensitive schoolteacher, Doña Vicenta Lorca. (Lorca did not follow the conventional Spanish practice of being known by his middle name or patronymic. 'Lorca', his mother's surname, was preferred to García because far less common.) Three surviving children succeeded Federico: his brother Francisco (Paco, Paquito), to whom he was very close and who was intimately to share his literary interests, and his two sisters, Conchita and Isabel. When he was two months old, Federico suffered a grave illness; apparently he was unable to walk until he was four years old, and retained a limp in after-years. There is a story that before he could walk or talk, he could thump out with his tiny fists accompanying rhythms to the servants' songs.

Prosperous and socially elevated though the García family was, with a highly literate mother and doting servants, Lorca was familiar from the very earliest with both the ancient traditions of the Spanish peasantry and the often harsh life which fostered them. This is brought home to us by one of Lorca's most brilliant lectures, 'Las nanas infantiles' ('Lullabies', 1928). The village women who acted as wet-nurses and nannies for the children of the landholding classes brought with them rich preservations and expressions of the primitive mind in the shape of cradle- and other songs, proverbs and tales. Exploring the subject – after almost a decade of serious interest in folk music and folklore – Lorca came to realise that the lullabies he had known in his own infancy were by no means peculiar to his own part of Andalucía, or even to Andalucía itself, but were the same as, or closely related to, lullabies from all regions of Spain, thus suggesting a deep-rooted kinship between all Spaniards. About these lullabies he found something most curious:

> I found that Spain uses its very saddest melodies and most melancholy texts to darken the first sleep of her children. By no means does this happen in just one model, one song, isolated in this or that region. Every region accentuates its own poetic character, its depth of sadness. . .
>
> The European cradle song tries only to put the child to sleep, not, as the Spanish one, to wound his sensibility at the same time. . .
>
> The Russian cradle songs that I know, though they have the oblique, sad Slavic sound – cheekbone and distance – of all Russian music, do not have the cloudless clarity, the steep obliquity, and emotional simplicity that characterise the Spanish ones. The child is able to bear the sadness of the Russian lullaby as one bears a day of mist beyond the window-panes. Not in Spain. Spain is the country of profiles. There are no smudgy limits one can cross to flee to the other world. Everything is delineated and bounded very exactly. A dead man is deader in Spain than in any other part of the world. Whoever wants to jump into dream wounds his feet on the blade of a barber's razor.[2]

So an atavistic image of life profiled against death was imparted to Spanish children through their folk heritage long before the Church or the rationalism of education could exert themselves. Lorca's own favourite among these dark lullabies seems to have been:

A la nana, nana, nana,
a la nanita de aquel
que llevó el caballo al agua
y lo dejó sin beber.

Lullaby, lullaby, lullaby,
little lullaby of that man
who led the horse to the water
and left him without drink.[3]

The starkness of the words and the plaintive melody contrived to
make for Federico '*that* man and his horse intensely dramatic'. And in
his lecture he went on to remark how 'the strangeness of the man not
watering his horse causes a rare and mysterious anguish'. One can
appreciate this anguish the better if one places the scene in the context
of a sweltering Andalusian summer, when water is scarce and thirst
torments men and beasts alike.

Many of the songs they heard from village-women presented
children with stories – or fragments of stories – of emotional and
familial difficulties among the rural poor: seduction, adultery,
unwanted pregnancies and births, marital quarrels. Because of his
unusual gifts and memory, perhaps also because his infirmity had
rendered him housebound longer than most small boys, Federico not
only retained his knowledge of these songs and of the life with which
they dealt but was later able to see the world of the villagers and other
country people as informed by the sexuality the middle classes
banished. He was also able to appreciate the hardness of their lot. He
was moved in later years by an Asturian lullaby (in the dialect of that
province) which reminded him of Andalusian ones of his childhood,
and, too, of Andalusian lives he'd apprehended:

Todos los trabayos son
para los pobres muyeres,
aguardando por las noches
que los maridos vinieren.

Unos veníen borrachos,
otros veníen alegres;
otros decíen: 'Muchachos,
vamos a matar las muyeres.'

Ellos piden de cenar,
ellas que darles no tienen.
'¿Qué ficiste los dos riales?
Muyer  qué gobierno tienes!'

All the chores are
for the poor women,
waiting at night
for their husbands to come.

Some come drunk,
some come 'merry';
some say: 'Lads,
let's kill our wives!'

They ask for dinner,
from the women who've nothing to give them.
'What did you do with the two *riales*?
Woman, what a household you run!'[4]

For Lorca the less well-off were never to be outside some invisible
pale, and as neither boy nor man did he fail to realise the cruel
exploitation of women – and their helplessness in the face of this.

Nursery songs and tales familiarised Lorca too with the creatures of
Andalusian folklore, felt as living presences, whose credited existence
seems to me somewhat to mitigate Lorca's picture of Spain as a land of
rigid distinctions, of sharp profiles. He came to know about the *bute*,
the *marimante*, the shadowy *coco* who 'wanders round the room but
never shows himself', the *duende* whom later, as we have noted, Lorca
was to apostrophise as the very essence of Spain itself, the *hada* –
whom the young Lorca may or may not have seen clinging to a
curtain! – and the *amargo* or 'bitter one'. The imaginative, impression-
able Federico was vouchsafed a vision of this last creature, an
exceedingly significant experience for his development according to
his account of it in his lecture on the *Romancero gitano*:

> When I was eight years old and was playing in my house at
> Fuente Vaqueros a boy looked in at the window. He seemed a
> giant, and he looked at me with scorn and hatred I shall never
> forget. As he withdrew, he spat at me, and from far away I
> heard a voice calling : '¡Amargo, ven!' 'Amargo, come!'
>
> After that the Amargo grew inside me until I could decipher
> why he looked at me in that way, an angel of death and of the
> despair that keeps the doors of Andalucía. The figure is an
> obsession in my poetic work.[5]

What are we to make of this strange apparition? Lorca himself, it
must be added, went on to say: 'By now I do not know if I saw him,
or if he appeared to me or if I imagined him, or if he has been waiting
all these years to drown me with his bare hands.'

The picture Lorca paints for us in the above passage is not only vivid, it is fertile in symbolic properties. A gentle, slightly lame boy of the moneyed class looks out through the window of his prosperous house to see another boy looking in. Clearly this boy spitting with hatred represents – on one level – the peasantry, the Gypsies, all those who are not part of the big farm at Fuente Vaqueros, and whom a deep-seated – one might say, instinctual – guilt has forced the more privileged child to confront. On another level, the burgeoningly sexual, Lorca must have seen the Amargo hostilely staring because he both feared and wanted to be possessed by him. And the voice calling '¡Amargo, ven!'? Is it some 'genius' of the Andalusian countryside calling the giant-like boy back to his rightful element? Is it the voice of Lorca's waiting sexual self? Or is it – as the poems that commemorate the Amargo suggest – an emanation of that other force with which peasants are frankly familiar but which the bourgeoisie evades: Death?

It was not until Lorca had immersed himself in the ancient Gypsy music of Andalucía, the *cante jondo*, that he was able to release the Amargo from his memories: in 'Diálogo del Amargo' ('Dialogue of the Amargo') and 'Canción de la madre del Amargo' ('Song of the Mother of the Amargo') (both in *El poema del cante jondo*, 1922; pub. in book form 1931) and in the masterly 'Romance del emplazado' ('Ballad of One Doomed to Die') in the *Romancero gitano*. The last of these depicts the death-bed of the strange, churlish young man, endowing it with an unforgettable nobility. It shows how almost twenty years after the apparition Lorca was able to forgive the boy his aggression, to feel for him, to take him tenderly towards death, and indeed, in some of the most hallucinatory lines Lorca ever wrote, beyond it.

In the same year as his vision of the Amargo, Lorca had another experience which was to have a determining effect upon him, for which his already strong 'love of the earth was responsible':

> It was something like 1906. My homeland, a land of farmers, had always been tilled by those wooden ploughs that could scarcely scratch its surface. That year some of the ploughmen had got brand-new Brabante ploughs (the name sticks in my memory) which had won a prize in the Paris Exhibition of 1900. I was a curious little boy, and I followed that vigorous plough of ours all over the fields. I liked seeing how the huge steel prong could open incisions in the earth and draw forth roots instead of blood. On one occasion the plough hit something solid and stopped. The shiny steel blade was pulling up a Roman mosaic on which was inscribed. . .I can't remember, but for some reason I think of the shepherds Daphnis and Chloe. So that the first artistic wonder I ever felt was connected with the earth.[6]

The blade strikes a fragment of Roman pottery, and its antiquity fascinates the small boy who was always later to be stimulated by the relics of the past peoples of his province: in that surrealist drama he wrote in New York, *El público*, Roman remains provide important and determining settings. It is interesting, too, to note that even aged eight Lorca appears to have been familiar with the story of Daphnis and Chloe. Throughout his life, particularly in the Twenties, Lorca was moved by classical myths and literature; we have noticed his rich usage of Apollo in the opening section of *El poeta en Nueva York*. The tale of Daphnis and Chloe may unconsciously have appealed to Lorca because its pastoralism connected with his childish awareness of the peasants' easy, strong sexuality, that awareness implanted by the *nanas*.

## 2

The countryside was a constant source of delight to Lorca throughout his boyhood and youth: the intimate life it harboured, its animals, birds, plants, trees. He used to imagine the poplars were sighing out his own name: 'Fe-de-ri-co.' Certainly the poplars – the *álamo* or common poplar, the *chopo* or black poplar – feature recurrently in Lorca's first book of poems, *Libro de poemas* (1921), many of which were written when he was only twenty and still as close to country things as when a boy. In 'El diamante' ('The Diamond') we read:

> Los chopos niños recitan
> su cartilla; es el maestro
> un chopo antiguo que mueve
> tranquilo sus brazos muertos.

> The boy poplars recite
> their primer; the master is
> an old poplar that moves
> in tranquility its dead arms.[7]

The old poplar stands here like Socrates with his student-disciples. And in 'El concierto interrumpido' ('The Interrupted Concert') night has fallen, the frogs, '*muecines de la sombra*' ('muezzins of the shadow') have fallen asleep, and the *chopo* is revealed as '*el Pitágoras/de la casta llanura*' ('the Pythagoras/of the chaste plain').[8]

The multifarious lives lived, often unnoticed, beneath our feet or hidden in bushes, river-banks, the branches of trees, held – at his own later admission – particular fascination for him. Throughout his early poems – those in *Libro de poemas, El poema del cante jondo* and *Canciones 1921–1924* – bees buzz, butterflies flutter, lizards bask in the sun or flick their way into crevices, cicadas and crickets sing. '¡Cigarra!' he exclaims, '¡Dichosa tú!' ('Cicada, how blessed you are!'). This insect dies '*borracha de luz*' ('drunk with light') and at total harmony with all living beings around it. No wonder, then, that Lorca exclaims:

> Sea mi corazón cigarra
> Sobre los campos divinos.
> Que muera cantando lento
> Por el cielo azul herido . . .

> May my heart be a cicada
> In the divine fields.
> Who dies slowly singing
> In the blue wounded sky . . . [9]

One of his earliest long poems, now lost to us, told the story of a wounded butterfly who fell into the nest of some cockroaches, one of whom became infatuated with her. After her recovery she went away, leaving the boy-cockroach desolate. Another long poem – written in December 1918 and happily not lost but included in the *Libro de poemas* – is called 'Los encuentros de un caracol aventurero' ('The Encounters of an Adventurous Snail'). The snail, '*burgués de la vereda*' ('bourgeois of the pathway') meets, first, two frogs who tell him about eternal life (it is, they say, like living perpetually in unruffled water with a flowery meadow nearby), and next a party of ants carrying one of their kind who has been wounded because '"*Yo he visto a las estrellas*"' '"I have seen the stars"').[10]

Lorca's first surviving play, *El maleficio de la mariposa (The Butterfly's Evil Spell*, put on at the Teatro Eslava in Madrid for one night in March 1920) also treats of insect life: the setting is a lush meadow, and we meet many insects, though our particular concern is with the beetles. The protagonist is a Boybeetle who considers himself a poet and who is enamoured, not of the charming Girlbeetle thought to be a fit bride for him, but of a Butterfly who, as in that lost poem, falls down from the sky wounded. It is a hopeless love. Two features of this play – spectacularly unsuccessful at the time, but, for all its unevenness, palpably Lorquian – should be noted here now (for we will be returning to it later); from these we can learn a great deal about the young Lorca's relationship to the nature that meant so much to him in these earliest days – as well as about the emotional and ontological importance of this relationship.

First, behind the dramatis personae of *El maleficio* there is an eminence, the Gran (sometimes San) Cucaracho (Great or Holy Beetle); his dicta form a sort of bucolic Sermon on the Mount:

'Until you learn to love deeply the stones and the caterpillars, you will not enter the Kingdom of Heaven. . .'

'The kingdom of plants and animals is near at hand; though

Man forgets his Maker, plants and animals are very near the light. . . the rhythm of a leaf swaying in the wind is the same as that of a distant star, and. . .the very words spoken by the fountain in the shade are repeated by the sea, and in the same tone . . .'[11]

'Criticise thou nobody,' – so said the Great Beetle.
'Consider thou thy lives as thou considerest the newborn grass.
Suffer thou amongst thyselves the faults of others,
for in My Kingdom those who sing and play are worthier
than those who spend their lives at works. . .
For thou must be earth and thou must be water,
petals to the rose, bark to the tree.'[12]

The second feature is the character of Boybeetle himself, with whose death the play apparently ended (one says 'apparently', for the last pages have not, alas, survived). This lover, whose passion leads him away from a conventional female of his own kind, is described in the stage directions as:

a trim and refined little boy whose distinction derives from painting the tips of his antennae and his right leg with lily pollen.[13]

Later on – at the height of his infatuation with the butterfly – he appears 'charmingly painted in yellow'. Lorca, also a boy-poet, must have been thinking, part self-defensively, part self-mockingly, about his own behaviour and impact on others when even younger than at the time of writing this play.

When, as a result of the success of the *Romancero gitano* (1928), Lorca was asked by a reporter about his childhood games and amusements, he replied that they had been those 'played by children who are going to turn out to be complete idiots, i.e. poets: saying Mass, making altars, building little stages. . .' The poet's brother Francisco has left us a lively account of what is being referred to here:

For me, Federico's theatre begins with my first childhood memories. The first toy that Federico bought with his own money, by breaking open his savings bank, was a miniature theatre. He bought it in Granada, in a toy store called 'The North Star', which was on the Street of the Catholic Kings. No plays came with this little theatre, so they had to be made up.[14]

And there were puppets in the household for whom parts had to be invented:

I remember that in our childhood we frequently played one of his favourite games. Before an altar made with an image of the Holy Virgin, loaded down with roses and celandines from the garden, he would play priest, costumed in the best he could find. My sisters, I, a few other children and the servants would attend. The almost express and almost tacitly accepted condition was that we had to weep at the time of the sermon. Half in jest, we would weep.[15]

One servant wept in no spirit of jest at all.

Delight in puppets, masques and masquerade was to persist in Lorca long after childhood. These constituted another way in which he entered the folk-life of Andalucía. His first successful play, *Los títeres de cachiporra (The Billy-Club Puppets*, 1922–25) was written with puppets in mind, and was itself the successor of another puppet-play which has unfortunately been lost, *La niña que riega la albahaca y el príncipe preguntón (The Girl who Waters the Basil-Plant and the Inquisitive Prince)*. Lorca's pursuits remind us of those of Henrik Ibsen, Hans Andersen and Robert Louis Stevenson (see the last's delightful essay, 'Penny Plain, Tuppence Coloured'). It can be no accident that all are writers distinguished by a quite unusual ability to combine a highly individual imagination (the forward child imposing his will on a prescribed world of archetypal figures) with an ability to draw on folk or popular culture. Ibsen in *Peer Gynt* (a play of which Lorca was very fond), Hans Andersen in *The Snow Queen*, Stevenson in *The Master of Ballantrae*, Lorca in his comedies and tragicomedies and in *Bodas de sangre (Blood Wedding)*, all not only utilise folkloric properties but actually work in scenes and situations with plain ancestry in traditional devices of puppet or cardboard theatre.

It cannot be unimportant that wherever he went, Lorca took with him his toy theatre – whether he was in Madrid or in the United States.[16] Surely it was for him not only a link with his treasured childhood but a tangible metaphor for Art. Lorca rejoiced in the given, circumscribed form and its challenges. Within the small scale of the puppet-play he could suggest and work emotional plight of universal relevance – as in the fairy-tale (Andersen) or the fable (Stevenson).

*Los títeres de cachiporra*, for instance, is a slight-seeming knockabout farce, in which an ugly and over-bearing older man, Don Cristóbal, tries to marry a young girl already in love with a youth her own age, Cocoliche. This is conventional enough matter for a Punch-and-Judy sort of play, and very deftly Lorca satisfies our conventional demands. But within their confinement he does other things as well. He introduces a second young man, who has also loved and been loved by Rosita, Currito from the Harbour, and with him a strange, and by no means unmoving, melancholy enters, a wistful statement is subtly made that unrequited feelings are an inextricable part of the human lot. Then Lorca stands the whole business of puppetry on its head by making Don Cristóbal turn out actually to *be* a marionette, to the others' flesh-and-blood – and this *in the context of a puppet-play*. This revelation, amusing enough for its toy theatre audience, also has a more serious meaning: the swaggering chauvinism of Don Cristóbal, who thinks every woman should do his bidding, is shown to be a (puppet-like) denial of humanity. Thus a small scale is used to range over a considerable territory of human experience – just as in the Danish master's apparently so delicate fairy-tales.

In the dressing-up games which Lorca so enormously delighted in there surely was (c.f. the Boybeetle and his painting of himself) a strong vein of 'camp': the mixing up, fusing, interchanging and swapping of gender roles and aspects, a sort of gleeful androgyny which was to serve Lorca well in his adult works for the theatre and which is not altogether absent from the poems, as we have already seen ('Vuelta de paseo').

## 3

In 1909 his family had moved to Granada so that Lorca could attend the Colegio del Sagrado Corazón, the director of which was his uncle. The countryside thus became a place for the holidays. Granada where he was educated, where he began as an artist and a writer, and where he was to be murdered in the opening days of the Civil War, pervades Lorca's work. Only a few months before his death Lorca read over the radio an evocation of his city, 'Semana Santa en Granada' ('Holy Week in Granada'), made partly in protest at what he felt to be the creeping commercialisation of the place. (What would he think of the entire south of Spain, so exploited, *now*?) Lorca's love for the city informs the whole piece, but so does a certain feeling of claustrophobia, also present in letters to friends from his late teens on, of a conservatism which made him pleased to have later exchanged it for Madrid. (Even so, in his long Madrid years he made regular and protracted visits to Granada and Valderubio, and spoke, as we shall see, of this area, the *vega*, as his home.)

[the] contemplative man goes to Granada, to be all alone in the breeze of sweet basil, dark moss, and trilling nightingales exhaled by the old hills near that bonfire of saffron, deep gray, and blotting-paper pink, the walls of the Alhambra. To be alone, to ponder an atmosphere full of difficult voices, in an air so beautiful it is almost thought, at a nerve centre of Spain where the *meseta* poetry of St John of the Cross fills with cedars, cinnamons and fountains, and Spanish mysticism can receive

that Oriental air . . . whoever would like to sit down at a cafe
table among phantasms and perhaps find a wonderful old ring
somewhere along the corridors of his heart should go to the
inner, hidden Granada.[17]

Granada with its spectacular setting and architecture is a city with a
complex and extraordinary history, and undoubtedly it shaped
Lorca's ability to view the past in the present, to see a moment as
containing, laterally, many previous moments, days, years. The idea
of the palimpsest – art of one period imposed upon another, itself
often an imposition – was very dear to him artistically (see the
'Palimpsestos' in *Primeras canciones, 1922*).

The Moors – who invaded Spain in 711, establishing themselves as
masters of the whole peninsula within a decade – made Granada a city
of great importance. Under the Nasrids – whose rule began in 1232 –
it knew prosperity, cultural activity, power. It was the last city,
indeed, that the Moors retained; its fall in 1492, that year of such
importance in Spanish and all western history, had even at the time the
strongest symbolic as well as actual significance. But after 781 years of
domination Moorish culture could never wholly die, and certainly
today's Spain *still* feels a special relationship to Arab art and thought.
A young Spanish poet, like the recent prize-winner Luis Antonio de
Villena (born 1951) – an enthusiastic Lorquian – shows a keen interest
in Arab poetry, in which the erotic element resembles some
ingeniously constructed, refreshing garden such as those for which the
Hispano-Moorish cities have become so famous. Lorca was fascinated
by, and proud of, Granada's Moorish past. He found in the air of the
city 'gestures and lines of remote Arabia', knew parts of the *Thousand
and One Nights* by heart, and admired Arab and Persian poets – Ibn
Sa'id, Hafiz – for their fusion of sensuality and sense of death. His
gipsified version of the Biblical story of Amnon's rape of his sister
Thamar ('Thamar y Amnón' in the *Romancero gitano*) has always
seemed to me to infuse a strikingly Arab eroticism into the
Judaeo-gipsy drama. Towards the end of his life Lorca wrote the
poems of the *Diván del Tamarit* – the very title signifies a collection of
Arab-style verses – which contains in its *gacelas* and *casidas* Lorca's
most highly-wrought homage to the culture that also produced the
Alhambra. A number of these treat, if obliquely, the past-in-present
of Granada, its pain as well as its beauty:

> Quiero bajar al pozo,
> quiero subir los muros de Granada,
> para mirar el corazón pasado
> por el punzón oscuro de las aguas.

I want to descend the well,
I want to ascend the walls of Granada,
to look at the heart pierced
by the dark awl of the waters.[18]

In a short lyric, 'Granada y 1850' in the *Canciones 1921–1924*, we receive a strong impression of what the city – seen in the past, before the pressures of the vulgar, exploitative present – meant to the young poet:

Desde mi cuarto
oigo el surtidor.

Un dedo de la parra
y un rayo de sol
señalan hacia el sitio
de mi corazón.

Por el aire de agosto
se van las nubes. Yo,
sueño que no sueño
dentro del surtidor.

From my room
I hear the fountain.

A finger of the vine
and a ray of sun
point towards the place
of my heart.

In the August breeze
the clouds pass away. I,
I dream that I am dreamless
within the fountain.[19]

Thus the city suggests the peace that is possible by entering into its past via sleep and death. In a sense Granada and its environs was always to be '*el sitio de mi corazón*' for Lorca.

Here are some letters written to friends after he had taken up quarters in the Residencia de Estudiantes in Madrid, which show the feelings he entertained for the scenery and atmosphere of Granada and the *vega* and how necessary these were to his creative genius:

*Summer of 1921 to Melchor Fernández Almagro:*
When I arrived you can't imagine the great happiness I felt on seeing the tremulous plain [the *vega*] in a delirium of blue mist. . .I believe I belong among these melodic poplars and lyrical rivers, with their continuous still waters, because my heart is truly at ease . . .[20]

*Tuesday, 2 August 1921 to Adolfo Salazar:*
Everyday I'm convinced more and more of how marvellous this country is. . .A few days ago a purple-green moon came out over the bluish mist of the Sierra Nevada and in front of my door a woman sang a *berceuse* that was like a golden streamer entangling the whole countryside. Especially at twilight one lives in the fullest fantasy, a half erased dream . . .There are times when everything evaporates and we're left in a desert of pearl grey, of rose and dead silver. I can't describe to you the vastness of this plain and this little white village in the midst of dark poplar groves.
At night our very flesh hurts from so many bright stars. . .[21]

*Granada, Autumn 1921 to Melchor Fernández Almagro:*
Autumn changes the plain into a submerged bay. In the tower of the Alhambra, haven't you felt the urge to sail off? Haven't you seen the ideal ships sleepily bobbing at the foot of the towers? Today I realise, in the midst of this pearly grey sunset, that I live in a marvellous Atlantis.[22]†

*Granada, Spring 1922 to Melchor Fernández Almagro:*
I'm going to the country . . . I'm thinking now of doing a lot of work beneath my eternal poplars and 'beneath the pianissimo of gold'. I'd like to produce a calm and serene work this summer; I'm thinking of constructing various ballads with lagoons, ballads with mountains, ballads with stars. . .[23]

In 1914 Lorca matriculated in the faculties of Law and of Philosophy and Letters at the University of Granada. His great interest at this time was in music, but his family discouraged him from pursuit of a musical career. Academically Lorca was an indifferent student but in non-curricular fields a remarkably productive and vigorous one. He read widely – the Greek and Latin masters, the great Spanish classics, the admired Russian and French authors of the day – he studied the

---

†This feeling was to generate one of Lorca's finest and most famous pre-New York poems, the 'Romance sonámbulo' ('Somnambulist Romance') in *Romancero gitano*. Among other things this conveys inland Granada's longing for the distant but nigh-palpable sea.

piano and the guitar, he painted (and was to continue doing so long after his student days were over). He became friendly with a group of young men a number of whom were to remain life-long intimates, all concerned with the arts and the intellectual life. They formed a *tertulia* – that informal Spanish institution as strong in contemporary Spain as ever in the past – a gathering, often taking place in cafes, at which papers or poems are read out and discussion ensues. The *tertulia* of Lorca and his friends was called El Rinconcillo, the little corner, and mostly took place in the Café Alameda.

Lorca attracted the attention of older men too. The socialist professor of law, Fernando de los Ríos – with whom, as we have seen, Lorca was to go to the United States, but who was at this time president of the Centro artístico de Granada – heard the youth play the piano and was deeply impressed. (V.S. Pritchett in *The Spanish Temper* has left us a nice picture of this admirable and percipient man in later years: 'a fine black beard and a soft, educated, and persuasive voice, and a gentle enunciation. . .[he] thought of revolution poetically'.)[24] It was some sonatas by Beethoven that de los Ríos heard Lorca rendering, and I have often thought that the strange blend of tragic awareness and joy, of individual and intricate form and emotional outpouring that we find, say, in Beethoven's Op. 110 and 111, can be counterparted in Lorca's own later writings; that masterpiece 'Llanto por Ignacio Sánchez Mejías' can surely be legitimately regarded as a sonata.

Indeed it would be impossible to underestimate the part of music in Lorca's life and art, and we shall shortly be concerning ourselves with a musical venture of his which had the greatest effect upon his poetry. Lorca was a dedicated student of the piano for nine years; the Lorquian expert Rafael Martínez Nadal has told me that, like many others, he has never been able to forget the beauty of Lorca's playing for him. Lorca's enthusiasm for music led to his meeting the great Spanish pianist, Ricardo Viñes, intimate and associate of Maurice Ravel. Another frequenter of the Café Alameda, and also a friend of Viñes in Spain and Paris, was Manuel de Falla (1876–1946), almost certainly the greatest composer Spain has so far produced, and one of the greatest of his day. Lorca met Falla first in 1917,† that is before he was twenty, but the two, young man and older man, became close friends very quickly. Lorca's art, in my view, is almost unimaginable without this friendship and what it evoked in the precocious, receptive youth. It must have stimulated exceedingly his interest in music, but did not have the effect of making him want to devote himself to his friend's art – not directly, that is. It was after he had met Falla, in the winter of 1917–18, that he began work on poems, poems we know now, since some of them, polished, found their way into the *Libro de poemas*.

†Some chroniclers of the poet's life have put the meeting in 1915.

By 1917 Manuel de Falla had written four of his major works: *La vida breve* (*Life is Short*, 1913), an opera, *Noches en los jardines de España* (*Nights in the Gardens of Spain*, 1917); *Symphonic Impressions* for piano and orchestra; a ballet with songs in one act, *El amor brujo* (*Love the Magician*, 1915); and a full-length ballet in two acts, *El sombrero de tres picos* (*The Three-Cornered Hat*, 1917). Falla – himself an Andalusian, born in Cádiz – was a strong, original, and contradictory personality. He stood aloof from life, and increasingly so as he got older; there was an austerity in his nature which made him reject the messiness of emotional entanglements. He reserved the passion within him for his music and for his religion. Whereas his young friend would seem from an early age to have dissociated himself from orthodox Catholic doctrine and practice, Falla was devout to a degree rarely encountered this century; contemporaries compared him to St John of the Cross. 'Falla was a saint and a doctor of music just as Fray Juan was a saint and doctor of the Church,'[25] said one, but this was not to imply that Falla eschewed prayer and other devotions. At the same time his music is charged with an almost atavistic eroticism, and – particularly in his Paris years from 1907 to 1914 – he knew and was indeed intimately associated with vanguard artists of the day: Debussy, Ravel, Rubenstein, Diaghilev, Stravinsky, Picasso, Ansermet and (in Madrid) Gregorio Martínez Sierra, who was to put on Lorca's first play, *El maleficio de la mariposa*. Like many others of these creative intellects with whom he associated Falla combined in his art – and in his attitude towards other people's – a desire for freedom from the tyrannies of old forms, of outworn conventions, with a deep reverence for ancient musical traditions, particularly church and folk music. (His friend Stravinsky, of whose first works he was an enthusiastic champion, displays a similar union of concerns in *Petrushka, Le sacre du printemps, Les noces*.) Being Spanish he had a particular interest, obviously, in the old musical forms and modes of his own country, and these form the corner-stones of his compositions.

Of the famous works recently completed when he and Lorca became friendly, *Noches en los jardines de España* is the most impressionistic; its first movement attempts to paint in notes the Generalife of Granada, the second is a 'Danza lejana' ('Dance in the Distance'), the third a tribute to the gardens of another great Andalusian city (and at one point in history a rival of Granada), Córdoba. Readers of Lorca's earlier poetry will be able to find pieces that match the moods of these movements. *El amor brujo* and *El sombrero de tres picos* are greater achievements than *Noches*, and Lorca surely learned more deeply from them: their dramatic conveyance of Spanish rural life; their thematic presentation of characters and situations that never isolates them from a carefully shaped larger artistic context; their passionate and obsessive rhythms. There will be more to say vis-à-vis Lorca's debt to Falla when I consider the poet in terms of the artistic movements of his age. What I shall be concerned with more imminently is Falla's burning zeal for the preservation of the old musical form of Andalucía, *cante jondo* (deep song), a zeal by which Lorca was soon and ardently affected.

Lorca was anyway taking the keenest interest in his own province, and for that matter, in his country. One of the results of the agitations of the *Generación del '98* was to make young intellectuals desirous of knowing more about the various regions of Spain, each of which has so distinct a character. In 1916 Lorca went on a university expedition to Castilla and the north-west, taking in El Escorial, Avila, Salamanca, Santiago de Compostella, León, Burgos, Segovia; then, from June to September of the year in which he met Falla he was travelling again, in Castilla la Vieja, León and Galicia, and in 1918 the fruits of his eager travels appeared: a still readable and lively account of what he'd seen, *Impresiones y paisajes* (*Impressions and Landscapes*), published in Granada.[26]

In 1918, during a visit to Baeza, Lorca met that pre-eminent poet of his generation, Antonio Machado, at that time a teacher there. It is poignant to reflect that Machado was not only to outlive the brilliant youth he talked to but to write the greatest of the elegies that his vile and premature death inspired: 'El crimen fué en Granada' ('The Crime was in Granada'). One cannot but wonder if, when confronting the precocious younger poet, Machado appreciated in him those qualities he so hauntingly salutes in his ode. He imagines Federico talking to Death and saying:

> . . .diste el hielo a mi cantar, y el filo
> a mi tragedía de tu hoz de plata. . .
> Hoy como ayer, gitana, muerte mía,
> que bien contigo a sola,
> por estos aires de Granada, mi Granada.

> . . .you gave ice to my song, and the blade
> to my tragedy of your silver sickle. . .
> Today as yesterday, Gypsy-woman, death of mine,
> how good it is with you alone,
> in these breezes of Granada, my Granada.[27]

Andalusian though he was, Machado had spent much of his mature life in Castilla, and it was the Castillian landscape that he had made particularly symbolic of what, to him, was strongest and most individual in the Spanish temperament; certainly the stark, stubborn country round Soria becomes to the reader of Machado a metaphor both for Spain and for Life itself. The rocky uplands beyond the Guadarrama, the solemn old walled cities that stand as islands in a sea of bare land, the treeless sweeps and sudden canyons of the *meseta*, these do somehow suggest a patience in the face of the onslaughts of time and weather, in other words, that *'sentimiento tragico de la vida'* ('tragic sense of life') that Machado's older contemporary and associate Unamuno made so famous and so quintessentially Spanish.

Meeting Machado – mystic celebrant of the Spanish land, philosophic investigator of the human condition, tragic recorder of the movements of the human heart, particularly in sexual love – must greatly have strengthened Lorca's resolve to write poetry. The list of the poems he wrote during 1918 and which find their way into the *Libro de poemas* is most impressive, and not just because of the age of their author: in April he wrote 'Balada triste' ('Sad Ballad') and in May the somewhat Machado-like 'Preguntas' ('Questions'); in June 'Corazón nuevo' ('New Heart'); in July 'Santiago'; in August 'Cigarra' ('Cicada') and 'Mañana' ('Morning'). While November saw the writing of 'Canción otoñal' ('Autumn Song') and 'El canto de la miel' ('The Song of the Honey'), and December the 'Canción menor' ('Minor Song'), 'Elegía a doña Juana la Loca' ('Elegy to Lady Juana the Mad'), 'Elegía', and 'Los encuentros de un caracol aventurero' ('The Encounters of an Adventurous Snail'). With some of these we will be dealing later in Chapter Four, when we try to understand Lorca's emotional predicament. In this chapter, as has already been stated, I am more concerned with his relationship to Spain and to his own Spanishness.

It should already be obvious that for Lorca there exists a transmutability of emotions between the personal and the non-personal worlds. If one says that there is right from the start a pathetic fallacy in Lorca's poetry, this is not to say that insects, trees, mountains, etc. symbolise or represent feelings inside the poet so much as that they *contain* feelings comparable to his own, matching or contrasting with, as the case may be, those dominant in him at the time of writing. Even in *El maleficio de la mariposa* – part of the point of which is to present an emotional predicament – the intensity of the work derives to a very considerable extent from Lorca's more unconscious apprehensions of the insects and the meadow in which they live, from his vision of the entire natural world as inspirited.

## 4

In the spring of 1919 Lorca went to live at the Residencia de Estudiantes in Madrid, an institution run on collegiate lines, where artists and intellectuals could live, study and pursue their own work. Internationally famous men – H.G. Wells, Bergson, Claudel, Mauriac, Keynes, Aragon, Valéry – came to lecture, and brilliant young men were attracted to and benefited from the institution: of his fellow-poets, Rafael Alberti, Jorge Guillén and Pedro Salinas, and among practitioners of the other arts, the future film-director Luís Buñuel and Salvador Dalí. Lorca was to live at the Residencia until 1928, spending his holidays in or near Granada, and we shall be looking later at his relationship to the cultural activity around him in these years. In 1920, as we have already seen, *El maleficio de la mariposa* was produced – by the celebrated dramatist and director Gregorio Martínez Sierra, through, one conjectures, the offices of Falla. The play was a 'stentorian failure', to use the poet's brother's words;[28] the hostility of the audience at the piece's unconventional setting and dramatis personae ensured that its first night was also its last, and the actors had the greatest difficulty in proceeding to the end. (We might also add that this lack of success did not – it would appear – earn the sympathies of Lorca's parents who were insisting that he complete his law studies; he did. Throughout the greater part of the Twenties Lorca's father and mother were worried about unfavourable reception of their son's work and, for all that he pays tribute in letters to their kindness, would seem to have made him feel quite unnecessarily guilty.)

In 1921 however, Falla became responsible for a new stage in Lorca's development towards being a great writer, one far happier and, I think, far longer lasting than the performance of *El maleficio*: Falla's already mentioned zeal brought about Lorca's absorption in the old artistic traditions of Andalucía, above all in *cante jondo*. In the spring of that year Lorca assisted Falla in the Holy Week celebrations of Sevilla; this inspired the 'Poema de la saeta' ('Poem of the Saeta') sequence in *El poema del cante jondo*. By November 1921 his interest in the subject of Andalusian music had resulted in the first clean manuscript volume to be called *El poema del cante jondo*; by New Year 1922 he was writing to a friend, Adolfo Salazar, about a *cante jondo* festival that Falla, himself and some others wanted to organise. This came about in the June of 1922, money being put up by the city of Granada. Its declared object was to safeguard Andalucía's most ancient tradition, which, though living, was under threat; and a competition was held in the Centro artístico. On this occasion Lorca delivered his lecture – one of his finest, 'El cante jondo – primitivo canto andaluz' ('Deep Song – Ancient Andalusian Song'). Some of what Lorca says overlaps with the text of a pamphlet to which Falla put his name, some shows a youthful tendency to generalisation and hyperbole, but the greater part of it is at once passionate and informative; it contains sentences rich in pregnant images that are wholly worthy of the later poet and dramatist at his best, and the entire *conferencia* helps us to understand the direction in which Lorca's art was moving, and why.

But first we should be clear about what is meant by *cante jondo*. It predates by about two centuries the better known *flamenco* which is a derivative or consequence of it, and thus in forms that we know today is at least four centuries old: the forms of *saeta* (arrow), *siguiriya, solea* (or *solear*). Perhaps the most important feature of the art is that in it word and music cannot, and must not, be separated. The emotion of the first dictates the line of the second. This has led many – Falla and Lorca among them – to regard the *cante jondo* as a continuing link with a possible primitive condition, when people sang as birds rather than spoke as their descendants. As Lorca said in beautiful sentences:

> Deep song is akin to the trilling of birds; the song of the rooster, and the natural music of forest and fountain. . .even before I knew of the Maestro's opinion [Falla's views on the primitive and oriental origin of *cante jondo*], the Gypsy *siguiriya* had always evoked. . .an endless road, a road without crossroads, ending at the pulsing fountain of the child Poetry, the road where the first bird died, and the first arrow grew rusty.[29]

And, speaking of the great practitioners of the art – such as Silverio Franconetti and Juan Breva to whom he was to address apostrophising poems – he said:

> When the *cantaor* [Gypsy singer] sings he is celebrating a solemn rite, as he rouses ancient essences from their sleep, wraps them in his voice, and flings them into the wind . . .[30]

Culturally Falla and Lorca accounted for the strange individuality of this Andalusian heritage in three ways: the use of the Byzantine liturgy by the Spanish church up to the eleventh century, the long Moorish presence in Spain, and – most important of all – the arrival in the fifteenth century of the Gypsies. The Gypsies settled in most significant numbers in the environs of Granada, and the music they brought with them has been related by experts to that of Indian antiquity. Musically Falla identifies certain peculiar characteristics of their art: the use (as in Indian songs) of vocal *portamento*, 'the way of leading the voice so as to produce the infinite nuances existing between two joined or distant notes'; 'the repeated, even obsessive, use of one note, as in certain primitive enchantment formulae'; the employment of ornamental features (again as in ancient Oriental songs) only at certain moments 'to express states of relaxation or rapture'; 'the shouts [e.g. *¡Ay!*] with which our people encourage or incite the *cantaores* or *tocaores*, originating in a habit still to be observed in similar cases among the Oriental races'.[31]

Straightway we can see stylistic legacies of *cante jondo* upon Lorca's work: here, too, are reiterations that do indeed, in certain lines, approximate to an enchantment formula, a starkness of diction which nevertheless permits bold images and verbal elaborations at emotionally suitable moments, and cries like '¡*Ay!*' which goad on and rhythmically punctuate the poems. All these features, it should be noted, can be found in *El poeta en Nueva York* as much as in the earlier productions; '¡*Ay Harlem!*' he cries, or '¡*Ay Wall Street!*', bringing a Spanish-Gypsy cry of lament to bear upon the cruelties of twentieth-century American civilisation.

But more important, of course, is the *spiritual* quality of *cante jondo*. After his work in the field of this old art-form, the romantic melancholy which pervades so many poems of the *Libro de poemas* – and, indeed, *El maleficio* itself – gives way to something altogether stronger, purer, deeper:

> The Gypsy *siguiriya* begins with a terrible scream that divides the landscape into two ideal hemispheres. It is the scream of dead generations, a poignant elegy for lost centuries, the pathetic evocation of love under other moons and other winds. . .[32]
>
> There is nothing, absolutely nothing in Spain, to equal the *siguiriya*'s style, atmosphere, and emotional rightness. . .It is wondrous and strange how in just three or four lines the anonymous poet can condense all the highest emotional moments in human life. There are songs where the lyric tremor reaches a point inaccessible to any but a few poets:

> > Cerco tiene la luna,
> > mi amor ha muerto.
> >
> > The moon has a halo,
> > my love has died.

> . . .It is the living, eternal enigma of death. . .Whether they come from the heart of the Sierra, the orange groves of Sevilla, or from harmonious Mediterranean shores, the songs have common roots: love and death. But love and death as seen by the Sibyl, that Oriental personage, the true sphinx of Andalucía.
>
> At the bottom of all these poems lurks a terrible question that has no answer. . .[33]

Let us now try to enumerate those attributes of the *cante jondo* which Lorca himself hailed in his lecture and which belong, equally, to his own art:

1) Emphasis on pain and death. They condition our existence, constitute elements in which we have to live. 'The finest degrees of Sorrow and Pain, in the service of the purest, most exact expression, pulse through the tercets and quatrains of the *siguiriya* and its derivatives.'[34]

2) Emotiveness. 'Seldom do we Andalusians notice the "middle tone". An Andalusian either shouts at the stars or kisses the red dust of the road.'[35] Lorca's emotional range is more considerable than is often realised: a single poem like the 'Romance sonámbulo' can impart longing, love, grief, despair, and tender resignation. As for 'shouting at the stars', the New York poems can be seen as both the most violent and the most sublime expressions of Lorca's anger at the injustice of life.

3) A non-dogmatic pantheism not irreconcilable with Christianity and, indeed, assimilated into it by easier or more primitive societies; related too to the neo-Platonism Lorca must have found in Machado and which was, anyway, almost instinctive with him. 'Deep song. . .consult[s] the wind, the earth, the sea, the moon, and things as simple as a violet, a rosemary, a bird.'[36]

4) A sense of the *cantaor* having Nature herself as sympathetic audience: 'With deep spiritual feeling, the Andalusian entrusts Nature with his whole intimate treasure, completely confident of being heard.'[37]

5) 'The wind is a character who emerges in the ultimate, most emotional moments. He comes into sight like a giant absorbed in pulling down stars and scattering nebulae; and in no popular poetry but ours have I heard him speak and console. . .'[38] In two of the most successful *romances* of the *Romancero gitano* the wind plays a most memorable role. In 'Preciosa y el aire' ('Preciosa and the Wind') the wind is a lusty satyr pursuing the Gypsy girl until she is in a state of fear, a condition which arouses no response in the English consul and his allies, the members of the Guardia Civil, thus showing the imperviousness to realities of Nature of these men.[39] In 'Romance sonámbulo' the wind is laden with passion, '*verde viento*' ('green wind'): it blows at the beginning and at the close of the poem, where it does indeed speak to and console the characters in their distress.[40]

6) The absence in the rendering of a particular scene of the picturesque; the refusal to indulge in decoration either pictorial or audial. Of *cante jondo* itself Lorca says: 'Deep song sings like a nightingale without eyes. It sings blind, for both its words and its ancient tunes are best set in the night. . .'[41] It knows neither morning nor evening, mountains nor plains. It has nothing but the night, a wide night steeped in stars. Nothing else matters. . .It is song without landscape, withdrawn into itself and terrible in the dark. Deep song shoots its arrows of gold right into our heart. In the dark it is a terrifying blue archer whose quiver is never empty.'[42]

Of course in one sense no poems could be less 'without landscape' than Lorca's; we have already seen how an inspirited countryside comes into his work. But on examination it will be seen that Lorca's landscape is for the most part made up of non-particularised and representative features in which an emotion is immanent or at play against others. So that Lorca's image of the *cantaores* making their song in the night is by no means irrelevant to his poems. (It should be noted that of the eighteen *romances* of the *Romancero gitano* the greater number are nocturnal, or partially nocturnal, in setting.)

7) The dominance of the erotic. When the erotic is in the ascendant the poems become 'the expressive sisters of the magnificent verses of Arabian and Persian poets'.[43] Again the artists of the *cante jondo* prefer to work in significant generalities rather than individual details, and so does Lorca. We should say here, though, that Lorca's most memorable erotic passages always have men at their centre, sometimes (for example, the archangels of *Romancero gitano*) as desirable beings whose beauties and charms are extolled, sometimes as in 'La casada infiel' ('The Unfaithful Wife') as *desire-possessed* beings whose performances we're made privy to:

> Aquella noche corrí
> el mejor de los caminos,
> montado en potra de nácar
> sin bridas y sin estribos.

> That night I rode
> the best of roads
> mounted on a nag of mother-of-pearl
> without bridle and without stirrups.[44]

However it should also be said that Lorca's realisation of the power of desire – made through poetry and music as much as through his own experience – enables him peculiarly to defy a society's, even a primitive society's, conventions. 'La casada infiel' takes us into the *machismo* of the Gypsy's mind, yet the poem does not take his side; the woman's right to sexual appetite is tacitly, and very movingly, upheld. And what is perhaps Lorca's greatest achievement in the erotic domain before 1929–30, 'Thamar y Amnón', has incestuous love as its theme.

★

In considering the fruits of Lorca's immersion in *cante jondo* two terms, unfamiliar to those not read in Hispanic matters, should be introduced: *andalucianismo universalizado* ('universalised andalusianism'; the phrase is, for obvious reasons, virtually untranslatable) and *agitaniza-ción*, 'Gypsy-fication'. The two are related. The first was coined by Falla and his friends, the composers Albéniz and Turina, in Paris, when they were engaged on serious works which, they hoped, would express their native country and make use of its musical offering. They did not want to end up practising some regionalist, local-colourist work, however delightful and full of authentic detail. Rather they wanted to create works profoundly rooted in their own cultures but of wide intellectual and emotional reference. The same ambition clearly was Lorca's too: when he thought that the *Romancero gitano* was popular in some quarters because of its picturesque qualities he was deeply upset, and had periods when, fearing the existence of these, he turned against the book. *Agitanización* means rendering the animate and inanimate worlds – more, the very cosmos itself – according to the pantheist, passionate, non-rationalist and mythopoeic vision of the Gypsy. And for Lorca – increasingly, as we shall see in Chapter Four, hostile to the narrowness of the bourgeois, bien-pensant sections of societies like Granada – the Gypsy was, quite simply:

> the loftiest, most profound and aristocratic element of my country, the most deeply representative of its mode, the very keeper of the glowing embers, blood, and alphabet of Andalusian and universal truth.[45]

This paragraph will have demonstrated that when *agitanización* is carried out – on archangels, on the sun and the moon, on death itself – then an *andalucianismo universalizado* has invariably been achieved.

Here is Christ himself, Gypsified so that, in his Andalusian beauty, he illuminates Spain and touches the sensibilities of anyone in the world who feels both the frailty and the strength of male flesh and bone, and the spirit temporarily housed within them:

> Cristo moreno
> pasa
> de lirio de Judea
> a clavel de España.
>
> *¡Miradlo por dónde viene!*
>
> De España.
> Cielo limpio y oscuro,
> tierra tostada,
> y cauces donde corre
> muy lenta el agua.
> Cristo moreno,
> con las guedejas quemadas,
> los pómulos salientes
> y las pupilas blancas.
>
> *¡Miradlo por dónde va!*
>
> Swarthy Christ
> passes
> from the lily of Judea
> to the carnation of Spain.

*Look where he comes!*

Of Spain.
Clear and dark sky,
sun-burnt land,
and ditches where runs
very slowly water.
Swarthy Christ
with burned tresses,
protruding cheek-bones
and white pupils.

*Look where he goes!*[46]

The first major English poet to admire Lorca, Stephen Spender, has said that what first impressed him was the Spanish poet's 'grammar of images'.[47] Of that grammar *El poema del cante jondo* is the first primer. Here we encounter that aggregate of figures and features which at once evoke Lorca's own land and are of wide psychic address: olive trees; orange and lemon groves; mountains with hemlocks and nettles growing on their slopes; oleanders; poplars; prospects of old cities, and of three cities in particular, Sevilla, Granada, Córdoba; rivers and their sluggish backwaters; the phallic-shaped rushes that grow by their banks; the wind; the tantalisingly apprehendable sea; the moon – especially when shining over uninhabited countryside; riders and their horses; white villages; forges; children in the squares of little towns; the *cantaores* and the ordinary Gypsies, old women, young boys, gentle girls.

And Lorca himself described the *Romancero gitano* as a *retablo* (altar-piece; frieze; though the word can also signify 'puppet-show'):

Thus the book is a *retablo* of Andalucía with its Gypsies, horses, archangels, planets, its Jewish and Roman breezes, rivers, crimes, the vulgar note of the contrabandistas, and the celestial note of the naked children of Córdoba who make fun of San Rafael. . .the book is anti-folklore, anti- 'local colour', and anti-flamenco [this being in Lorca's eyes essentially a bastardisation of *cante jondo*] . . . [It] has figures of millenial depths and just one character, *pena*, dark and big as the summer sky, who percolates through the bone marrow and the sap of trees and has nothing to do with melancholy, nostalgia, or any other affliction or disease of the soul, being an emotion more heavenly than earthly. Andalusian *pena*, which is the struggle of the loving intelligence with the incomprehensible mystery that surrounds it.[48]

*Pena* has variously been translated by 'pain', 'sorrow', 'grief'; I myself incline to the last. What is being grieved for – in such an instinctive, inherited way – is nothing less than the fallen, suffering state of the world. We have just seen how to Lorca the art of the *cantaores* laments this state, constitutes indeed a moving proof of it; do they not give vent to screams 'of dead generations', to 'poignant elegies for lost centuries'? The *Romancero gitano* then belongs to the same spiritual world as *cante jondo*, as *El poema del cante jondo* and those *Canciones* which are exercises in this ancient art.

Involvement in *cante jondo* made Lorca – as he is proud to infer in his often delivered lecture on the *Romancero gitano* – able to come to terms with that figure of the Amargo, 'centaur of death and hatred', 'angel of death and of the despair that keeps the doors of Andalucía', incarnation and begetter of *pena*. The first poem that Lorca wrote about the Amargo was 'Diálogo del Amargo' – which, strictly speaking, is not a poem at all but a dialogue in prose which, however, works upon us *as* a poem. In July 1925 he wrote the 'Canción de la madre del Amargo', finally included in the 1931 edition of *El poema del cante jondo*. A little after he had written this last poem, he wrote the third and finest of the Amargo pieces, 'Romance del emplazado' ('Ballad of One Doomed to Die'), included in the *Romancero gitano* of 1928 and one of its glories. If we look at these three works, informed by powerful emotions springing from Lorca's early childhood and yet inextricable from his later appreciation of Andalusia's rich and centuries-old culture, we shall arrive in the very thick of the *Romancero gitano*, that book whose success he was carrying with him to New York, a success both assuring and disconcerting, painful.

5

The setting of the 'Diálogo' is the countryside at night. ('Deep song', we remember, is 'best set in the night'.) Three youths with wide-brimmed hats are waiting for the Amargo to join them for a journey, but when he appears, they realise that they don't really care for travelling in the dark, coming on now ever faster with frogs and crickets singing it in. Night, says one of them, was made for sleeping. But not for the Amargo. Swaggering with hands on hips, he has a strange snatch of *cante jondo* to sing:

> Ay yayayay.
> Yo le pregunté a la muerte.
> Ay yayayay.
>
> Ay yayayay.
> I questioned death.
> Ay yayayay.[49]

This song of his has a strong effect on the youths – 'The scream of his song puts a circumflex accent on the hearts of those who have heard him' – and they leave him alone in a landscape now revealed as wild and mountainous. A horseman appears and offers the Amargo a ride on his mount. He tells the Amargo that he himself, though bound for Granada, has come from Málaga where his three brothers live by selling knives, silver knives and gold knives. 'Knives of gold go by themselves straight to the heart. Silver knives cut the throat like a blade of grass.'[50] The Amargo would seem very unimpressed by the Rider; he is reluctant to accept a seat on his horse, and actually declines the offer of the knife that the man makes him. But the Rider is most insistent. With increasing urgency he praises the knives and stresses the desirability of a ride on this desolate night. The gold knife he takes out has a point which 'shines [in the darkness] like the flame of a candle', and the Amargo has to admit: 'How beautiful it is!'[51]

And now, in stage directions that themselves form a haunting poem, Lorca tells us:

> The night thickens like a hundred-year-old wine. The fat serpent of the South opens his eyes in the dawn, and sleepers feel the infinite desire to jump off the balcony into the perverse magic of the perfume and the distance.[52]

The Amargo suspects that they have lost their way; the Rider agrees but thinks that the lights now appearing in the distance must be those of Granada itself. The Amargo admits to a sadness at the size and loneliness of the world. The admission is followed by the most crucial part of their interchange:

> RIDER. What do you do?
> AMARGO. What do I do?
> RIDER. And if you are in your place, why do you want to be?
> AMARGO. Why?
> RIDER. I ride this horse, and I sell knives, but if I did not do so, what would happen?
> AMARGO. What would happen?[53]

He can only echo the question, not answer it, and we are moved to remember Lorca's own words about the poems of *cante jondo*: 'At the bottom of those poems lurks a terrible question that has no answer.' The Amargo accepts the seat on the horse now, accepts too – with a cry of '¡Ay!', etc. – the knife. Forward the two men and the horse go, and meanwhile the mountains bristle with hemlocks and nettles, those death-connoting plants.

Of the two men taking part in the dialogue, the Rider would appear to be the aggressive, initiatory one. It is he who makes the offers and, through persistence, has them accepted, it is he also who is more intimately associated with the two symbols/instruments of male power and of death, the horse and the knife (for the horse is powerful enough to kill, in addition to its appearance in many mythologies as a taker of men away from life). The Amargo, on the other hand, is a sullen, stubborn creature who boasts of his courage in questioning Death and delivering to him the traditional Gypsy cry of ¡Ay! while in fact only shortly afterwards capitulating to one of his representatives (the Rider). The Amargo, indeed, ends up in collusion with death, yet in doing so attains a curious and moving self-apotheosis which the following two poems about him commemorate.

Oleanders herald in the Amargo at the beginning of the 'Diálogo', and these and the gold knife the Rider gives to him are to be found in the captivating 'Canción de la madre del Amargo', which may as well be quoted in full, as illustrative of the gentleness, the tenderness of Lorca's art, even at this comparatively early stage:

> Lo llevan puesto en mi sábana
> mis adelfas y mi palma.
>
> Día veintisiete de agosto
> con un cuchillito de oro.
>
> La cruz. ¡Y vamos andando!
> Era moreno y amargo.
>
> Vecinas, dadme una jarra
> de azófar con limonada.
>
> La cruz. No llorad ninguna.
> El Amargo está en la luna.
>
> They carry him on my sheet
> my oleanders and my palm.
>
> The twenty-seventh day of August
> with a little knife of gold.
>
> The cross! And there it is!
> He was swarthy and bitter.
>
> Neighbours, give me a pitcher
> of brass full of lemonade.
>
> The cross! Don't cry, anybody.
> The Amargo is on the moon.[54]

So the Amargo has been undone by the Rider's gold knife (and this little knife, *cuchillito*, will reappear, as Lorca himself pointed out, in *Bodas de sangre*, as will also the Greek-style chorus of keening women).[55] It is a tribute to the consistency of Lorca's thought that the chronology inside the Amargo poems is entirely satisfactory; in the above poem we learn that he is buried on 27 August; in the next and last poem we hear that he actually died on 25 August, and was told of his impending death two months before that (25 June).

The 'Romance del emplazado' opens with an arresting exclamation in the first person singular: '*¡Mi soledad sin descanso!*' ('My loneliness without rest!')[56] though the identity of this 'I' is not clear. He stands in a nether world remarkably like the Stygian regions of Greek mythology (Lorca's study of this subject was coeval with his studies of Gypsy culture). The 'I's' sleepless eyes, and his horse's, confront '*un sueño de trece barcos*' ('a dream of thirteen boats'), thirteen a baleful number, boats a traditional symbol for death. Is this 'I' that Rider of the 'Diálogo' entering his own realm? Or is he Lorca, the *romancero* himself?

The second section of the poem connects this land-of-death with the inspirited land-of-life of the Gypsies, in which, however, one Gypsy, *emplazado*, is to die. The connection is made via that grammar of images of which Stephen Spender spoke: in the real world boys are being chased, we learn, by '*densos bueyes del agua*' ('heavy water-oxen'), a country phrase for strong currents of water. Thus the river Styx turns into an Andalusian river with Gypsy boys bathing in it, and also into a forge, where they sing:

> el insomnio del jinete
> y el insomnio del caballo.

> the insomnia of the horseman
> and the insomnia of the horse.[57]

On 25 June the Amargo is told to prepare for death, to paint a cross on his door and to ask for lights and bells (Platonic-Christian emblems of peace which Lorca had used before in his 'Balada de la placeta'):

> Porque dentro de dos meses
> yacerás amortajado.

> Because in two months
> you'll lie down shrouded.[58]

Already we can feel a certain sympathy for this lonely doomed figure, surely representative of the id of the poet, the id within us all, for whom the paraphernalia of orthodox Christianity would seem quite irrelevant. But this sympathy increases in the last part of the poem in which lines of a solemn and gnomic rhythmic intensity convey the passing of these two months. And El Amargo is not alone, of course, in being *emplazado*; he constitutes a *momento mori* for us all:

> Espadón de nebulosa
> mueve en el aire Santiago.
> Grave silencio, de espalda,
> manaba el cielo combado.

> El veinticinco de junio
> abrió sus ojos Amargo,
> y el veinticinco de agosto
> se tendió para cerrarlos.

> His misty sword
> St James moves in the air.
> Heavy silence, from the back,
> the curved sky was pouring forth.

> On the twenty-fifth of June
> Amargo opened his eyes,
> and on the twenty-fifth of August
> he lay down to close them.[59]

It is to Lorca's friend and enthusiastic apologist Rafael Martínez Nadal that we owe an elucidation of these lines.[60] The feast of Santiago (St James) occurs on 25 July, equidistant from the day the Amargo learns he is to die and opens his eyes, and the day he lies down to close them for ever. On this midway date St James moves in the sky his sword which is the Milky Way. Astrology, associated with Gypsies in fairs all over Europe, has thus also decreed that the young man must die: pagan and Christian faiths unite. Dying in Roman style, with a quiet stoicism, the Amargo passes out of this life in peace:

> su soledad con descanso.

> his loneliness with rest.

– a complete contrast to the opening line: '*mi soledad sin descanso*'. But ironically it may now be the poet who saw the wild boy, not the wild boy himself, who will know no quiet in his soul.

The 'Romance del Emplazado' forms an extended act of charity, reconciliation and grateful tribute on Lorca's part. He has followed that hostile, glaring-eyed apparition at the windows of Fuente Vaqueros to the moment of death and beyond, and shown how his independent Gypsy nature helped him to bear, perhaps even to transcend, inevitable mortal sufferings. The book in which the Amargo dies is a testimony to the assistance towards wholeness of vision – vision of life, vision of its concomitant, death – that Lorca received from *cante jondo* Gypsy culture with *pena*, grief, in a central position.

## 6

*Agitanización* of the universe is a comprehensive affair in the *Romancero gitano*. The moon haunts the entire volume, appearing in both the first poem and the last in an important role. Indeed the first poem – its very title, 'Romance de la luna, luna' ('Romance of the Moon, Moon') indicates through reduplication her terrible power – *personifies* the moon: as a chaste woman with tin breasts who kidnaps a little boy from a Gypsy's forge. The wind is personified too – as a satyr in 'Preciosa y el aire' – as well as being apostrophised as *verde*, green, and therefore laden with passion, in 'Romance sonámbulo'. We feel the presence of the sea and the reminders of death and infinity that its measureless expanse and ebb and flow constitute. Above this world are archangels, and we meet three of them in the book – San Miguel (St Michael) patron of Granada; San Rafael (St Raphael) who presides over Córdoba; San Gabriel (St Gabriel) whose care is Sevilla. These archangels, San Gabriel in particular, are described as Gypsies would describe idealised versions of themselves. In his tributes to the handsomeness of these Gypsy-archangels Lorca permitted himself, virtually for the first time in his poetry, that lyricism towards the male form which he felt personally – especially, one conjectures, in its Gypsy manifestations:

> Un bello niño de junco,
> anchos hombros, fino talle,
> piel de nocturna manzana,
> boca triste y ojos grandes,
> nervio de plata caliente,
> ronda la desierta calle. . .
> En la ribera del mar
> no hay palma que se le iguale,
> ni emperador coronado,
> ni lucero caminante.
> Cuando la cabeza inclina
> sobre su pecho de jaspe,
> la noche busca llanuras
> porque quiere arrodillarse.
> Las guitarras suenan solas
> para San Gabriel Arcángel. . .

> A handsome rush-like boy,
> broad shoulders, slim waist,
> skin of nocturnal apple,
> sad mouth and big eyes,
> nerve of warm silver,
> walks about the empty street. . .
> On the sea-shore
> there is no palm to equal him,
> nor crowned emperor,
> nor wandering star.
> When he inclines his head
> over his jasper breast
> the night looks for plains
> because it wants to kneel down.
> The guitars play by themselves
> for Archangel Gabriel. . .[61]

Later, when we read the 'Llanto por Ignacio Sánchez Mejías', we will be reminded of this controlled, tender-hearted hyperbole, perhaps inspired by some flesh-and-blood rather than celestial boy but by no means inappropriate to the last (assuming his existence). The *agitanización* here has for me an interesting parallel with a poem by W.B. Yeats, whose art has much in common with Lorca's; the poem in question is 'The Happy Townland' (*In the Seven Woods*, 1904) in which Yeats gives us an 'Irish-isation' of two archangels, Michael and Gabriel, and a picture of the end of the world as it must have been entertained by Irish country-folk:

> Michael will unhook his trumpet
> From a bough overhead,
> And blow a little noise
> When the supper has been spread.
> Gabriel will come from the water
> With a fish-tail, and talk
> Of wonders that have happened
> On wet roads where men walk,
> And lift up an old horn
> Of hammered silver, and drink
> Till he has fallen asleep
> Upon the starry brink.[62]

Lorca's archangels, like Yeats', possess human qualities that arouse very human responses in us. Similarly the Amargo – and the girl Soledad Montoya of 'Romance de la pena negra' ('Romance of the Black Grief'),[63] one of the volume's finest and best-known poems, a girl who also embodies that all-pervasive, all-dominant grief – are apprehendable *people* whose predicaments move us. The death of El Amargo succeeds not only on the symbolic level; it is a convincing portrait of the death of a lonely, wilful Gypsy outcast. Indeed one should, I think, invert this and say that the Amargo's death succeeds on a symbolic level only *because* it is so truly felt and described on a human. Similarly Soledad Montoya speaks to our hearts because we can see, feel and hear this Gypsy girl coming down the mountain and speaking to the poet, telling him how in her distress she paces the house, walking backwards and forwards from kitchen to bedroom with her tresses trailing on the floor. So when she says '*Vengo a buscar lo que busco*' ('I'm looking for what I'm looking for') the sentence stirs us as a crystallisation of that nameless longing of which we have already spoken, because it already has worked upon us as an entirely credible thought of a girl such as herself. At the same time Lorca puts her at the centre of that transmutation of essences so characteristic of his vision of the inspirited world. In 'Romance de la pena negra', '*las piquetas de los gallos/cavan buscando la aurora*' ('The beaks of the cockerels/dig in search of the dawn'), lines which can be taken literally or metaphorically. But later the girl's breasts deliver screams, her eyes weep lemons, the black grief of the title rises up from the land of olives from under the murmur of trees, and the river sings at the onset of day. Again this sense of the human being standing at the centre of emotional forces is successfully conveyed only because we care about the human being herself.

Indeed what makes us revere the *Romancero gitano* is precisely the extent and depth of Lorca's humanity. I have already remarked how in 'Preciosa y el aire' he enters the mind of a Gypsy girl terrified by the wind, in 'La casada infiel' that of a *macho* Gypsy tricked by a young married woman. Then there is the superbly drawn Antoñito el Camborio, the 'hero' of two poems, 'Prendimiento de Antoñito el Camborio en el camino de Sevilla' ('The Arrest of Antoñito el Camborio on the Road to Sevilla')[64] and 'Muerte de Antoñito el Camborio' ('Death of Antoñito el Camborio'). El Camborio was a real person who lived on the *vega* in the nineteenth century and one night tumbled off his horse, to be killed by falling on his own knife. Lorca presents him as he would have liked to have been, as he *was* according to his own imagination rather than according to the factual truth. In the 'Prendimiento' he is captured rather ignominiously by members of the Guardia Civil and thrust into the local gaol, no heroic fate. But in the 'Muerte' his sorry death is transformed into the valiant affair it surely should have been:

> Voces de muerte sonaron
> cerca del Guadalquivir.
> Voces antiguas que cercan
> voz de clavel varonil. . .

En la lucha daba saltos
jabanados de delfín.
Bañó con sangre enemiga
su corbata carmesí,
pero eran cuatro puñales
y tuvo que sucumbrir.

Voices of death rang out
near the Guadalquivir.
Ancient voices which surround
a voice of virile carnation. . .
In the struggle he gave the slippery
leaps of the dolphin.
He bathed in enemy blood
his crimson tie,
but there were four daggers
and he had to succumb.[65]

Antoñito may have been, may be even on the two poems' showing, a self-deceiving scallywag, but for Lorca he was:

one of [the *retablo*'s] purest heroes, the only one in the book who calls me by name at the moment of his death!† A true Gypsy, incapable of evil, like many who are now dying of hunger rather than sell their millenial voice to the gentlemen who have nothing except money, which is very little indeed. . .[66]

The Guardia Civil supply one of the principal themes of the *Romancero gitano*, and one can use 'theme' in the musical sense of that term; again and again we hear their menacing presence – ignoring the piteous plight of Preciosa, condemning healthily brawling youths, wounding and killing a gallant young smuggler ('Romance sonámbulo'), threatening that gallant's loved one (*ibid*), arresting Antoñito el Camborio – until they appear given full expanded treatment in the 'Romance de la Guardia Civil española', one of the finest poems of the entire sequence. They constitute a theme in the usual sense of the word, too: what the Guardia Civil stand for is the threat to the instinctual, atavistic life that the Gypsies represent – and not only for Lorca! It is worth dwelling on this point a moment; doing so will make us less surprised than people have been that a lyrical poet of the countryside and its denizens should produce a savage indictment of the American economic system or become a man literally marked by the Right of his own country.

---

†Lorca is here referring to his character's death-cry: '*¡Ay, Federico García/llama a la Guardia Civil!*' ('Alas! Federico García/call the Civil Guard!').

A contemporary of Lorca's who did not know him, Arturo Barea, produced a very interesting, if somewhat *cahier*-like book, *Lorca: the Poet and His People* (1944), in which he records reactions of ordinary Spaniards, particularly those he was fighting alongside in beleaguered Madrid towards the end of the Civil War, to poems of Lorca's, showing how these encapsulated profound popular sentiments. The 'Romance de la Guardia Civil española' is one he especially praises in this respect. His words on the significance of the Guardia Civil for most Spanish people, above all those fighting for the Republic, are well worth quoting here:

> It must be difficult for the non-Spaniard to understand why and to what degree the Guardia Civil of Spain had become the symbol for the oppressive force of a hated State. And thus it must be difficult to understand how much Lorca spoke from the depth of popular feeling whenever the three-cornered hats of the *Benemérita* – the 'Meritorious Institute' as the official title puts it [and Lorca himself uses, ironically, this euphemism] cast their shadow over his verse.
>
> Founded as the arm of the civil administration, the Guardia Civil was supposed to maintain law and order in remote villages and to keep lonely roads free from bandits. Its members were ex-servicemen and discharged NCOs schooled in the wars and willing to live in rural barracks with their wives and children. The whole body was under the Minister of Home Affairs, in practice under the orders and at the disposal of the Civil Governors of the provinces and their local henchmen. For generations, people in villages and small towns, who did not belong to the ruling caste, knew the Guardia Civil solely as the powerful and ruthless instrument of the *cacique*, the political bosses, the landowners and the usurers. Under the Monarchy, it was taken for granted that at election-time the commander of the Guardia Civil in each village would arrest the men known for their opposition to the reigning clique; the secretary of the local administration would make out a polling list complete with the names of all inhabitants, including some already in the cemetery; and on the day after the poll the Guardia Civil would release the arrested men. They hardly ever protested, for they knew the power behind the Corporal of the Guardia Civil and had no wish to feel the end of his rifle-butt. But they came to hate the Guardia Civil with that bitter personal hatred which it is difficult to feel for an impersonal system. To them the Guardia Civil *was* the system which made them work for 1.50 pesetas a day in the olive-field; it was the men of the Guardia Civil who shot at them when they dared to protest and who beat them lame when they had the misfortune to be arrested during a strike.[67]

The opening lines of that *romance* which has them as their subject have become famous: Lorca speaks of leaden skulls (*'tienen. . .de plomo las calaveras'*), of patent-leather souls (*'alma de charol'*) and concludes:

> Pasan, si quieren pasar,
> y ocultan en la cabeza
> una vaga astronomía
> de pistolas inconcretas.
>
> They pass, if they want to pass,
> and hide in their heads
> a vague astronomy
> of indefinite pistols.[68]

Lorca shows here that his understanding of humanity has not precluded, indeed has most definitely *in*cluded, realisation of the human capacity for evil. Not just capacity, but appetite! The men of the Guardia Civil have allowed their imaginations to be filled with images of destruction which will nag at them until they have been granted some sort of translation into reality. The ruling classes have, out of their own interests, given these men dispensation to indulge such appetites; it can always be excused with rhetoric about the feckless lawlessness of those who suffer at their hands (e.g. the Gypsies).

After this portrait of the mentality of the Guardias Civiles, Lorca then moves on to a city under the happy occupation of revelling Gypsies, in point of fact Jerez de la Frontera. It is Christmas, the whole place is full of flags and jollity and totally *'libre de miedo'* ('free of fear'), with even the Virgin and St Joseph (Gypsified) taking part. Upon this scene of joy the Guardias Civiles advance, and even the Holy Pair themselves can do nothing against their organised, physically articulated hatred. Precisely what this means is brought home to us in an unexpected and painful vignette in which we see a Gypsy girl, Rosa de los Camborios, kin to Antoñito, being mutilated, her breasts cut off out of sheer sadism. And still:

> . . .la Guardia Civil
> avanza sembrando hogueras,
> donde joven y desnuda
> la imaginación se quema.
>
> . . .the Guardia Civil
> advances sowing bonfires
> where young and naked
> the imagination is burned out.[69]

Read today, these lines seem terribly prophetic of Franco's Spain in which the Guardia Civil had such a key role.

Arturo Barea had a friend, Angel – 'almost illiterate, 46 years old, in the Republican militia from the first days of the struggle'[70] – who carried around with him a tattered copy of the *Romancero gitano*; he was moved by the 'Romance de la Guardia Civil española' and would ask Barea to unravel passages from it. Barea asked him whether he recognised himself 'and all Spaniards in those Gypsies whom the Guardia Civil assault and torture'. This was Angel's answer, and in reading it we come to realise how much Lorca had achieved his ambition for the *Romancero gitano* stated in a letter to Jorge Guillén: 'I want the pictures I draw of the characters to be *understood* by themselves, to be visions of the world in which they live':[71]

> 'Do you remember the Sunday in July last year, the 18th it must have been, the day after Franco proclaimed the insurrection in Morocco? We all went out of town as if nothing had happened, because it was very hot and a beautiful day, and we fooled around like children. I went to the Jarama to bathe and you went to the Guadarrama. . .he made me think of how the soldiers shot at us from the Cuartel de la Montaña. And since then it has been as if we were fighting against the Guardia Civil all the time, getting nearly as bad as they are, too. . .'[72]

★

I shall be returning to the *Romancero gitano* when considering Lorca's evolving attitudes to his art and his own emotional needs (which indeed find correlative expression in the book). But I could not leave this present survey of it without a brief examination of perhaps its most celebrated poem, the 'Romance sonámbulo'. In this piece all sides of the poet, as we so far have known him, come together in a miraculous whole: the mystical, the pantheistic, the empathic, the socially penetrating. In my experience its beauties of sound, imagery, feeling (and *articulation* of feeling) increase with every reading. Lorca himself felt that in *this* ballad he had truly attained another ambition of his: to fuse 'the narrative ballad with the lyrical without changing the quality of either'.[73] It is a poem which even when moving us baffles, and to no one were its mysteries greater than to Lorca himself, who wrote of it:

> one gets the sensation of anecdote in a poignant dramatic atmosphere and no one knows what is happening, not even me, for poetic mystery is also mysterious to the poet who imparts it, often unknowingly.[74]

The '*Romance sonámbulo*' opens with perhaps the most heart-felt tribute to the colour green ever written, green with its connotations of innocence, sexuality, fecundity:

> Verde que te quiero verde.
> Verde viento. Verdes ramas.
>
> Green, how much I want you, green!
> Green wind. Green branches.

Maintaining this hypnotic, somnambulistic rhythm Lorca continues:

> El barco sobre la mar
> y el caballo en la montaña.
> Con la sombra en la cintura
> ella sueña en su baranda,
> verde carne, pelo verde,
> con ojos de fría plata.
> Verde que te quiero verde.
> Bajo la luna gitana,
> las cosas la están mirando
> y ella no puede mirarlas.
>
> The ship upon the sea
> and the horse upon the mountain.
> With the shadow at her waist
> she dreams against the balustrade,
> green flesh, green hair,
> with eyes of cold silver.
> Green, how much I want you, green!
> Beneath the Gypsy moon
> things are looking at her
> and she cannot see them.[75]

The ship and the horse are, in the mythology of Lorca's poems – that organic blend of Gypsy, classical and personal – harbingers of death (c.f. their use in the 'Romance del emplazado'). Mountain and sea are the boundaries of Andalucía; they can also, with their respective qualities of height and measurelessness, be seen as suggesting what lies *beyond* life itself. These symbols of mortality are particularly effective when juxtaposed against the greenness that is impressed so musically upon us. We notice, however, that it is a quality *wished* for as well as, in some way, dominant on this night. It contrasts with the silver of the girl's eyes, a cold metal that again is death-connoting, and this while the flesh of her body is bathed in the very light of fertility. The fact that the girl cannot see that *las cosas* (i.e. the inspirited land around her) are looking at her shows us not merely her helplessness but the helplessness of all human beings, for all their sensory perceptions, trapped until death in a body. Girl, wind, sea, mountain and Gypsified moon – part of that grammar of images – have all been brought together in a new and poignant order.

It should perhaps be said here that the whole poem has – perhaps construed from the above lines – been interpreted as being about Granada. Lorca refers to this view in his lecture on the *Romancero gitano*:

> [It] is thought. . .to be a ballad expressing Granada's longing for the sea and the anguish of a city that cannot hear the waves and seeks them in the play of her underground waters and in the undulous clouds with which she covers her mountains. This is so, but this poem is also something else. It is a pure poetic event of Andalusian essence, and will always have changing lights, even for me, the man who communicated it.[76]

As we shall see, to confine it to a poem of, as it were, geographical anguish is to limit it unduly.

The poem's next section is a development of what has been stated in the first; the landscape receives further animation, attributable to that transmutation of essences which Lorca found so much part of the Gypsy *cantaor's* mind. Stars come at one like a fish, a fig-tree rubs the air as if its leaves were pieces of sandpaper, the mountain is likened to a thieving cat. And Lorca (or is it the Gypsy girl, dreaming there?) asks the urgent question:

> ¿Pero quién vendrá? ¿Y por dónde?

> But who will come? And from where?[77]

Into the girl's head the distant sea breaks; it is bitter (*amarga*) with its suggestion of infinitude.

Rhythm, mood and scene now change; we move from the feminine to the masculine, from the slow evocations of green, night and dream to an urgent exchange between two men linked by an obviously very close bond. One of the two men is dying, bleeding to death from a wound; we are in the world of an earlier poem, 'Reyerta', already alluded to, but with a significant emotional addition. *Love* is now present – passionate and several-faced:

> Compadre, quiero cambiar
> mi caballo por su casa,
> mi montura por su espejo,
> mi cuchillo por su manta.
> Compadre, vengo sangrando,
> desde los puertos de Cabra.

Si yo pudiera, mocito,
este trato se cerraba.
Pero yo ya no soy yo.
Ni mi casa es ya mi casa.
Compadre, quiero morir
decentemente en mi cama.
De acero, si puede ser,
con las sábanas de holanda.
¿No veis la herida que tengo
desde el pecho a la garganta?
Trescientas rosas morenas
lleva tu pechera blanca.
Tu sangre rezuma y huele
alrededor de tu faja.
Pero yo ya no soy yo.
Ni mi casa es ya mi casa.
Dejadme subir al menos
hasta las altas barandas,
¡dejadme subir!, dejadme
hasta las verdes barandas.
Barandales de la luna
por donde retumba el agua.

'Comrade, I want to exchange
my horse for your house,
my saddle for your mirror,
my knife for your blanket.
Comrade, I come bleeding
from the passes of Cabra.'
'If I could, young lad,
this bargain would be closed.
But I am no longer I.
Nor is my house my house.'
'Comrade, I want to die
decently in my bed.
Of steel, if it's possible,
with my sheets of holland.
Don't you see the wound I have
from my heart to my throat?
'Three hundred dark roses
your white shirt-front bears.
Your blood seeps and oozes
around your sash.
But I am no longer I.
Nor is my house my house.'

'Let me climb at least
as far as the high balustrades,
let me climb, let me,
up to the green balustrades.
Little balustrades of the moon
where the water resounds.'[78]

These lines surely possess a Shakespearean quality: they are a dramatically stirring expression of a particular predicament yet set up deep psychic resonances. The simple yet pregnant antitheses of objects associated with a lawless life and objects associated with domesticity and decency are both *of* the situation here and of entirely universal application; the repeated apology '*Pero yo ya no soy yo*' has something of the magic directness of Antony's 'I am dying, Egypt, dying.' Echoes are sent from this interchange back to earlier poems, forward to later ones – by the charged words *caballo* and *cuchillo*, for example. The *sábanas* the dying youth here would so like upon his last bed (in this case they should be of holland-cloth) will appear again in the 'Romance del emplazado' where another doomed wild man – the Amargo in person – has upon *his* death-bed '*la sábana impecable/ de duro acento romano*' ('the impeccable sheet/ of hard Roman accent').[79] The high balustrades, towards which the two men are climbing with such difficulty and by which the Gypsy girl is dreaming, are suffused by that greenness to which the opening sections of the *romance* paid homage. This colour contrasts ironically with the *morena* of the youth's oozing blood and with the blackness of the night on which his death is taking place. The balustrades, furthermore, are hailed as '*barandales de la luna*' reminding us of that baleful power established in the first lines of the book's very first poem.

And who are these two men, these *compadres*? What has befallen them and what is their relationship to each other and to the girl of the high balustrades? Lorca sets up a mystery here; overt statement would impair the emotional atmosphere, one which is thick and fragrant with confusions the poet sees as inextricable from the human lot. Nevertheless answers to the questions I have just posed *are* to be found by careful reading of the text.

Andalusians would at once connect the place the youth has just come from, '*los puertos de Cabra*', with brigands, smugglers. (Lorca himself at one time took a keen interest in the lives of nineteenth century men of this type. They feature, among other places, in the 'Canción de jinete', *Canciones 1921–1924*).[80] At the end of the poem drunken Guardias Civiles are banging on the door, out to get somebody; these two facts make us realise that certainly the younger man, and probably the older one too, associated with smugglers and earned the aggressive disapproval of the Guardia Civil – who presumably have given the younger his mortal wound. The two men are therefore bound one to another by common activities which have engendered the tenderest comradeship. But there is another bond too – this bond is through the distant girl. The shifting use of the second person, from the formal to the intimate, culminating in the sudden impassioned reference to '*tu niña*' ('your girl') make us realise that the older man is her father, the other her lover or fiancé.

The *romance* ends without the reconciliation so desired and striven for between the men and the girl. The young man dies, a long way from the steel, holland-sheeted bed he'd yearned for. And the girl herself seems also to pass into the realm of death. She stands over a cistern of water and is held above this by *un carámbano de luna* ('an icicle of moon'). The Guardia Civil in all its debauched murderousness arrives, and Lorca repeats those opening invocations to *verde* and, too, the contrasting deathly images of ship-on-sea and horse-upon-mountain.[81]

The emotional legacy of this *romance* is, first, a harrowing sense of loss. The implied love of the girl for the two men, the love of the two men for each other, the respective loves of the men for the girl – none of these prevails against a harsh destiny in which nature and brutal authority, for the first time in the book, can be seen as having colluded. And this loss, this helplessness are both surely implicit in the title; the somnambulist has lost the peace of real sleep and is peculiarly vulnerable to both his own and others' acts. But if the Gypsies are the victims, they are the victors too, since what else does the poem communicate but an awed regard for their capacity for passion and bravery and for the value they put on freedom? And this leads me to another point: though the young man does *not* die with any of the desired accoutrements of the domestic life around him, perhaps in not having them he is being truer to himself. Lawlessness can have its own vindication and moral victory.

Truth – truth to self – is indeed an overriding concern of 'Romance sonámbulo', for all its seeming strangeness and quasi-deliberate mystery. The plights of the people, the immanence of emotions in the natural world about them – taken together these form a metaphor which both *is* and illuminates. Lorca himself said, and à propos of this poem: 'By means of poetry a man more rapidly approaches the cutting edge that the philosopher and the mathematician turn away from in silence.' It was by means of poetry too, poetry as mastered in the inspirited land of Andalucía, that Lorca approached the cutting edge of modern life as manifested in the confusions of New York on the eve of the Depression.

## Chapter Three
# Light Buried by Chains and Noise

Lorca's complaint against New York revolved round the divorce from Nature that life in that great city of 'extra-human architecture and furious rhythm'[1] seemed to him not only to involve but to impose. But before considering this complaint in any detail one should perhaps say that the New York of the poems – especially for us now, reading them over fifty years after their composition – is not only the city itself but an embodiment of general American social and cultural values, and, beyond this, stands for *any* megalopolis of the capitalist world.

The 'geometry and anguish' of the city triumph, even if ultimately doomed, over all elements of existence, whereas in the organic community which has made no breach with nature it is the other way about: elements govern living beings and impose patterns upon their desires and yearnings. *Cante jondo* sang in the night and in doing so reminded its listeners of the tragic nature of man's lot, but these reminders were salutary, spiritually healthy, linking us all more nearly together and relating us too to members of the creature and plant worlds. Night in New York, on the other hand, is blighted, the sky is tainted, the moon frequently obscured. '*No duerme nadie*', Lorca insists in 'Ciudad sin sueño (Nocturno del Brooklyn Bridge)' ('City without Sleep (Nocturne from Brooklyn Bridge)'). 'No one sleeps '– that is, in any proper meaning of the world 'sleep'; for the city cannot even provide rest for its dead:

Hay un muerto en el cementerio más lejano
que se queja tres años
porque tiene un paisaje seco en la rodilla;
y el niño que enterraron esta mañana lloraba tanto
que hubo necesidad de llamar a los perros para que callase.

There's a dead man in the most distant cemetery
who's been complaining for three years
because he has a dry countryside on his knee;
and the little boy they buried this morning was crying so much
that they had to call the dogs in order to quieten him down.[2]

Maybe, though, it is as well that rest is so difficult – for the living if not for the dead – because everybody should be constantly aware of the monstrous cruelties of urban life.

'No duerme nadie,' the penultimate section of 'Ciudad sin sueño' reminds us again:

> Pero si alguien cierra los ojos,
> ¡azotadlo, hijos míos, azotadlo!
> Haya un panorama de ojos abiertos
> y amargas llagas encendidas.
>
> No one sleeps.
> But if anyone closes his eyes,
> flog him, my boys, flog him!
> There should be a panorama of open eyes
> and bitter inflamed wounds.[3]

To have open eyes in New York is to suffer a burning wound, but surely this is preferable to joining the vast army of the insensible and blind – 'Panorama ciego de Nueva York' ('Blind Panorama of New York') – who make up so many of the city's inhabitants.

Night gives way to day. In the dimness of the oncoming light two voices can be heard. They talk of a murder committed – or at any rate a case of man's inhumanity to man that is tantamount to murder, to a violation of the natural order of things:

> Una uña que aprieta el tallo.
> Un alfiler que bucea
> hasta encontrar las raicillas del grito.
> Y el mar deja de moverse.
>
> A thorn that harasses the stalk.
> A pin that dives
> till it meets the little roots of the scream.
> And the sea ceases to move.[4]

Dawn, when it arrives, only emphasises the city's general contamination of life. Lorca, who in the *Romancero gitano* had celebrated the sun's triumph over the moon and darkness, like the priest of some ancient religion (c.f. 'Romance sonámbulo' and 'Thamar y Amnón'), now mourns on its behalf in one of the most successfully elegiac poems of the whole sequence, 'La aurora' ('Dawn'):

> La aurora de Nueva York tiene
> cuatro columnas de cieno
> y un huracán de negras palomas
> que chapotean las aguas podridas.

La aurora de Nueva York gime
por las inmensas escaleras
buscando entre las aristas
nardos de angustia dibujada.

La aurora llega y nadie la recibe en su boca
porque allí no hay mañana ni esperanza posible.
A veces las monedas en enjambres furiosos
taladran y devoran abandonados niños.

Los primeros que salen comprenden con sus huesos
que no habrá paraíso ni amores deshojados;
saben que van al cieno de números y leyes,
a los juegos sin arte, a sudores sin fruto.

La luz es sepultada por cadenas y ruidos
en impúdico reto de ciencia sin raíces.
Por los barrios hay gentes que vacilan insomnes
como recién salidas de un naufragio de sangre.

Dawn in New York has
four columns of mud
and a hurricane of black doves
who dabble in the putrid waters.

Dawn in New York moans
on the immense stairways
searching among the pebbles
for tuberoses of outlined anguish.

Dawn arrives and nobody receives it in their mouth
because here there is neither morning nor hope possible.
From time to time coins in furious swarms
perforate and devour abandoned children.

The first people to go out on the street understand in their bones
that there won't be paradise or unleafed loves;
they know that they're going to the slime of numbers and laws,
to games without art and sweat without fruit.

Light is buried by chains and noise
in the brazen threat of science without roots.
In the suburbs there are people who totter sleepless
as if recently escaped from a shipwreck of blood.[5]

The mud, the blackened doves, the putrid waters, these concomitants of daybreak in New York testify to the pollution, literal and metaphoric, of the city. The doves, however, have further connotations: a dove appeared to Noah after the flood as a promise of God's good will, and has been used as a symbol of peace and of the Holy Spirit from the early church onwards. But in New York morning and promise, as later lines tell us, have been, as it were, cancelled out by the materialistic immersion in the present that capitalist society imposes on its members. Hence the black colour of the usually pure white birds. However, as we shall be seeing shortly, their blackness is significant in another way, since the only sign of hope that Lorca finds in the city is in the Black community. The Blacks are the dove and the rainbow of a sick society that Lorca can compare only to slime, less politely, to shit, made up of figures and regulations, a society whose pleasures and whose tasks alike (because so polarised) are sterile and joyless.

Note the pervasive religious imagery in this poem. I shall be exploring more complex instances of this in Chapter Five, when examining the 'Grito hacia Roma (Desde la torre de Crysler Building)' of which 'Aurora' can be seen as a herald, a warning. '*La aurora llega y nadie la recibe en su boca*' – isn't this a comparison of dawn to the holy sacrament, to the dispensation of God's body in the form of the bread/wafer? For all the power of the monster-like city the sun *does*, of course, come in its glory into the sky, but the separation between man and nature has become so complete that no one appreciates the fact, let alone rejoices in it, God's great daily blessing. Only the Blacks, Lorca suggests in the final section of 'El rey de Harlem', are capable of proper concentration on the sun. Maintaining the religious imagery, Lorca speaks of the men and women out on the streets as if they were exiles from Eden (and it is surely the earthly preservations of Eden such as the inspirited land of Andalucía of which Lorca is thinking here).

The surrender to Mammon, to money, is what has brought about this terrible state of affairs. Even small children are perforated and consumed by coins. Earlier in the sequence, in 'El rey de Harlem' ('The King of Harlem') we have read:

> Las muchachas americanas
> llevaban niños y monedas en el vientre. . .

> The American girls
> carry coins and children in their bellies. . .[6]

We have already observed how the young Lorca was first moved to express his sense of communion with nature through lyrical salutations to the innumerable small creatures who share existence with us. 'The kingdom of plants and animals is near at hand; though Man forgets his Maker, plants and animals are very near the light' (*El maleficio de la mariposa*). Maybe, but in New York man has so thoroughly suppressed the plants and animals that even *they* are starved of their usual spiritual properties. This condition is often symbolised by details of wicked mutations or mutilations; throughout the poem-cycle we encounter creatures suffering from afflictions through no fault of their own, victims all of New Yorkers' prostration to a false economic god. A few examples will have to suffice:

. . .los escarabajos borrachos de anís
olvidaban el musgo de las aldeas.

. . .the scarab beetles drunk on anis
were forgetting the moss of the village.[7]

. . .la mujer gorda
que vuelve del revés los pulpos agonizantes.
La mujer gorda, enemiga de la luna,
corría por las calles y los pisos deshabitados
y dejaba por los rincones pequeñas calaveras de paloma . . .

. . . the fat woman
who turns upside down the suffering octopuses.
The fat woman, enemy of the moon,
was running in the streets and the empty apartments
and leaving in the corners small skulls of doves . . .[8]

¡Esa esponja gris!
Ese marinero recién degollado. . .
   Cantaba la lombriz el terror de la rueda
y el marinero degollado
cantaba el oso de agua que lo había de estrechar;
y todos cantaban aleluya,
aleluya. Cielo desierto.

This grey sponge!
This sailor recently beheaded. . .
   The earthworm was singing the terror of the wheel
and the beheaded sailor
was singing of the bear of water who had to hold him tightly;
and all sang alleluia,
alleluia. Empty sky.[9]

. . .algunos niños idiotas han encontrado por las cocinas
pequeñas golondrinas con muletas
que sabían pronunciar la palabra amor.

. . .some idiot–children have met in the kitchens
little swallows with crutches
who knew how to pronounce the word love.[10]

The word love is not easy to pronounce in this loveless megalopolis. And the reality behind the word is not easy to discern either. Few
of the poems are more desolate – or more moving in their desolation –
than 'Nocturno del hueco' ('Nocturne of the Void'), one of the
'Poemas de la soledad en Vermont'. In the quiet of the countryside
Lorca can address a loved one and speak out his sense of despair at all
the multiple blighting of life he has so recently seen:

Mira formas concretas que buscan su vacío.
Perros equivocados y manzanas mordidas.
Mira el ansia, la angustia de un triste mundo fósil
que no encuentra el acento de su primer sollozo.

Cuando busco en la cama los rumores del hilo
has venido, amor mío, a cubrir mi tejado.
El hueco de una hormiga puede llenar el aire,
pero tú vas gimiendo sin norte por mis ojos.

No, por mis ojos no, que ahora me enseñas
cuatro ríos ceñidos en tu brazo,
en la dura barraca donde la luna prisoniera
devora a un marinero delante de los niños.

Look at the concrete forms that are searching for their
        own voids.
Mistaken dogs and bitten apples.
Look at the anxiety, the anguish of a sad fossil world
that doesn't find the tone of its first sob.

When I search in the bed for the murmurs of the thread
you have come, my love, to cover my roof.
The void of an ant can fill the wind,
but you go on moaning without goal before my eyes.

No, not before my eyes, for now you show me
four ashen rivers on your arm,
in the uncomfortable hut where the prisoner-moon
devours a sailor in front of the children.[11]

Here truly is a déréglement of Lorca's former and trusted grammar of
images. In the world of transmuting essences in which he had rejoiced
back in Andalucía, inanimate and animate beings alike seemed in
touch with the primeval era in which they originated. Indeed

maintenance of kinship with the primeval had been a major factor in the young Lorca's reverence for insects and reptiles. In 'El lagarto viejo' ('The Old Lizard') – in *Libro de poemas* – the lizard *'gota de cocodrilo'* ('drop of crocodile') is called *'dragón de las ranas'* ('dragon of the frogs')[12] and carries the poet's mind back to the beginnings of life. New York had sundered this atavistic sense of community, and the 'Nocturno' written in the pastoral peace of New England is perhaps the most powerful testimony to the imaginative loss this severance involves. The apple of Eden has become a bitten fruit; ants, who once saw heaven from a bough of a tree ('Los encuentros de un caracol aventurero'), now are mere cavities in the wind; forms cannot even find the empty spaces they once evolved in but are set, imprisoned in their moribund existences in time, in a pointless quest for these. The moon, which as Death provided the eventual acceptable home for the boy Amargo, now – anthropomorphised, as in the *Romancero gitano*, but morbidly, horribly – performs an act of cruelty upon a free-ranging human being to ensure the defilement of the innocent.

The position of the bucolic interludes in *El poeta en Nueva York* as we now have it is, it will be remembered, misleading where the actual chronology of Lorca's New World experiences is concerned. In his lecture on the New York cycle – as much a poem in its way as those that comprise the sequence – Lorca said:

> Green lake, landscape of hemlocks. . .I live with some farmers. A little girl, Mary, who eats maple syrup, and a little boy, Stanton, who plays a Jew's harp, keep me company. . .I run, I drink good water, and my mood sweetens among the hemlock trees and my little friends. . .In such surroundings, of course, my poetry took on the tone of the woods.† Tired of New York and yearning for the least significant, poorest living things, I wrote an insectary. . .I wanted to sing to the insects who spend their lives flying and singing to our Lord with their little instruments.[13]

And so he did – 'Luna y panorama de los insectos' ('Moon and Insect Panorama'), one of the most tender and haunting poems of the entire sequence. But its nature, and the emotional effect it has upon us, aren't really what Lorca's description of the piece would suggest. Here, as elsewhere, we receive the feeling that the *un*naturalness and *in*human-ity of New York life have been too much for him. Even lyrical

---

†In other words, that partly Platonic, partly Christian (Franciscan) pantheism so natural to him and which he had admired in the *cantaores*, had returned to him temporarily, though it rather resembles a limb that hasn't recovered from the injury it has received!

apprehensions of the wonders of the natural world exist in the midst of an unremitting disquietude. In italicised lines, after he has sung to the insects, Lorca emphasises:

*la luz tiene un sabor de metal acabado*
*y el campo de todo un lustro cabrá en la mejilla de la moneda.*

*the light has a taste of worn-out metal*
*and the extent of a whole chandelier will fit into the cheek of a coin.*[14]

Everywhere the ceremony of innocence, to borrow Yeats' phrase, is seen to be drowned – literally so in the case of the little girl Mary who in the touching 'Niña ahogada en el pozo' ('Little Girl Drowned in the Well')[15] dies – in poetry as, it would seem, she did not in life – to represent the fate of so many guileless souls in the New World.

The whole business of transmutation which afforded Lorca so much numinous joy fills him now – even in a country setting where belief in it seems possible again – with a sense of weariness that is a grim analogue to death ('Muerte'):

¡Qué esfuerzo!
¡Qué esfuerzo del caballo por ser perro!
¡Qué esfuerzo del perro por ser golondrina!
¡Qué esfuerzo de la golondrina por ser abeja!
¡Qué esfuerzo de la abeja por ser caballo!

What an effort!
What an effort for the horse to be a dog!
What an effort for the dog to be a swallow!
What an effort for the swallow to be a bee!
What an effort for the bee to be a horse![16]

Doesn't this depressed mutatory round read like a blasphemy coming from the poet we know from other works? In the poem that follows this – the 'Nocturno del hueco' at which we've already glanced – the poet, speaking as he only rarely does in full *propria persona*, doesn't conceal the distressing disorientation he is suffering from and which at present is conditioning his life:

Yo.
Con el hueco blanquísimo de un caballo,
crines de ceniza. Plaza pura y doblada.

Yo.
Mi hueco traspasado con las axilas rotas
Piel seca de uva neutra y amianto de madrugada.

*Toda la luz del mundo cabe dentro de un ojo.*
*Canta el gallo y su canto dura más que sus alas.*

I.
With the whitest void of a horse,
mane of ash. A pure and doubled square.

I.
My void criss-crossed with debauched armpits.
The dry skin of a neuter grape and asbestos of dawn.

*All the light of the world fits in behind an eye.*
*The cock sings and his song survives longer than his wings.*[17]

The horse (c.f. 'Canción de jinete' and 'Diálogo del Amargo') always connoted death in the Lorquian mythology, but *natural death*, a sense of which harmonious living in the countryside could grant one. Now the horse has become a white void with an ashen mane. Village squares – symbol to Lorca of the organic rural community (c.f. 'La balada de la placeta' and its account of the poet's moving encounter in the square with the village children)[18] – has now been distorted as if by double vision: at the time of writing, so to speak, Lorca can neither see nor think straight! His sense of his corporeal identity becomes impaired by preying images of socially ostracised parts of the body, of neuterdom, of minerals being substituted for light and the plant-life which light feeds. Yet hope is not altogether absent. . .

'*Toda la luz del mundo cabe dentro de un ojo*' seems on one level to be an expression of those solipsistic feelings common to people in states of breakdown: existence seems entirely contained in the body confronting it, and without external independence. It also is implicitly a cultural comment on America and the American *weltanschauung*, and I cannot clarify this statement better than by quoting from Stephen Spender's *Love-Hate Relations: a Study of Anglo-American Sensibilities* (1974). Under the chapter heading 'Subjective America; Objective Europe', a phrase we shall do well to remember when we look at Lorca's confrontation with Whitman in his great ode, Spender says:

> Objective Europe was the historical reaching back to the past within which the individual could escape from his personality into the tradition crystalised in libraries, museums and architecture, greater than the life of any single living genera-tion.† Subjective America was geographical, the identification of the single separate American with. . .the whole continent and beyond the continent, the whole earth. . .The unexplored

†And one could add to this loss the whole inspirited European countryside with its centuries of human associations and relationships.

continent spoke in the present tense. . .

The subjective consciousness, shut off from the past and tradition, is of the inner world of the self, dreams, physical and spiritual life, the subconscious; and of things immediately present which it can receive into its isolation. Such receptiveness also implies its opposite, expansiveness passing through the doors of the senses into the world beyond, with a sensation of becoming another person, the atmosphere, perhaps the whole universe. Through empathy, the subjective can enter into the objectivity of things; but does so moving as it were from inwards outwards, not as though the outward world, existing authoritatively, independently and indifferently, pressed inward upon it.[19]

Surely, in the light of the above so perceptive analysis, what had happened to Lorca intellectually and creatively while in America was that he had become *subjectivised* in the double sense perhaps inherent in that word. The alarming riotous world around him – promoting alarming riotous images in his poetry – had drawn him into its self; the lines just quoted show that he felt he lacked any strength, any capacity for establishing dialogues, let alone relationships with the *monde visible* as he had done back in Spain. At the same time it seemed almost to him as if the world itself now lacked objective reality, that all its light could indeed be gathered behind the eye.

*Canta el gallo y su canto dura más que sus alas.*

This line, however, could have been written by the Spanish Lorca, the 'other Federico', to use terminology from that sad letter to Carlos Morla Lynch. It must have had a punning significance for him – *Gallo* had been the name of a literary review founded and edited by himself and friends, and Salvador Dalí had been a contributor. The line says that the song survived the bird, is stronger even than its most energetic strivings. This reads to me like an indirect tribute to the friend with whom relations had recently been so exceedingly painful, but who stands behind the entire New York corpus of work – his spirit, his art, Lorca is surely saying, transcend the limitations of the man himself. The poem in which this line appears – and its fellows – irresistibly recall the Daliesque surrealist world. Indeed images that they contain can be encountered in Dalí: dead horses, clusters of ants, shit, eyes both whole and mutilated, even armpits (c.f. *Le chien andalou* where we move from close-ups of armpits to close-ups of sea-urchins).

Dalí was, of course, celebrated for the way in which his art attempted those regions of the human personality which Freud insisted were opened up. When Dalí at the Residencia de Estudiantes in Madrid read Freud's *Interpretation of Dreams*, his enthusiasm knew no bounds. 'This book presented itself to me as one of the capital discoveries of my life, and I was seized with a real vice of self-interpretation, not only of my dreams but of everything that happened to me, however accidental it might seem at first glance.'[20]

With him indeed the subjective entered into the objectivity of things, the movement was from inwards out. (Hence perhaps his great popularity in America, particularly in the Thirties and Forties.) Daliesque and American-induced subjectivity resulting in the welling-up of images from his unconscious forced Lorca to look at himself as a *whole*, as an ontologically placed, bodily housed and conditioned personality from which he could no longer withhold analytical understanding. These poems of solitude in the New England countryside are transitions of the utmost importance in Lorca's development. After them he moved back to New York to offer it the most vehement denunciation in 'New York (Oficina y denuncia)' ('New York (Office and Denunciation)'). There is an increase in sharpness in this poem and its successors. If these first person accusations lack the imaginative richness or suggestion that are normally associated with Lorca's poetry, one must also say that with hindsight they seem completely necessary for that fusion of the subjective and the objective that is to distinguish the great odes, and for that matter all Lorca's important later work. For in 'New York (Oficina y denuncia)' Lorca is ripping open that envelope of American subjectivity, searching the light that lies beyond or outside his own eyes:

> He venido para ver la turbia sangre,
> la sangre que lleva las máquinas a las cataratas.

> I have come to see the turbulent blood,
> the blood that carries the machines to the cataracts.[21]

In a sequence of lines that suggests an anguished twentieth-century Whitman, he tells us:

> Todos los días se matan en New York
> cuatro millones de patos,
> cinco millones de cerdos,
> dos mil palomas para el gusto de los agonizantes,
> un millón de vacas,
> un millón de corderos
> y dos millones de gallos,
> que dejan los cielos hechos añicos.

> Every day there are killed in New York
> four million ducks,
> five million pigs,
> two thousand doves for the pleasure of suffering people,
> a million cows,
> a million lambs
> and two million cocks,
> who leave the skies broken into pieces.[22]

Lorca's anger at the quality of life in New York extends even to the more enlightened sections of society because they have acquiesced in all the brutality:

> Yo denuncio a todo la gente
> que ignora la otra mitad,
> la mitad irredimible
> que levanta sus montes de cemento
> donde laten los corazones
> de los animalitos que se olvidan
> y donde caeremos todos
> en la última fiesta de los taladros.
>
> I denounce all people
> who ignore the other half,
> the irredeemable half
> who build their mountains of cement
> in which beat the hearts
> of the little creatures who are forgotten
> and where we will all fall
> in the last festival of the drills.

And later:

> Yo denuncio la conjura
> de estas desiertas oficinas
> que no radian las agonías,
> que borran las programas de la selva.
>
> I denounce the conspiracy
> of these empty offices
> which don't shine forth their agonies,
> which efface the designs of the forest.[23]

This last line is a very reverberative one, since the whole sequence is much occupied with the idea of Nature taking a savage revenge upon megalopolis and those who made it possible. According to the poet himself the denunciations owe their courage and force to that period in New England and upstate New York:

> And then once again [i.e. after this] the frenetic rhythm of New York. But it no longer surprises me. I know the mechanism of the streets and talk to people and penetrate a bit deeper into social life. And I denounce it. Denounce it because I have come from the countryside and do not believe that man is the most important thing in the world.[24]

All this is true, no doubt. And that Lorca did not believe man to be the most important thing in the world is evidenced in all his poetry, including what he had written so far in America, a belief which paradoxically increases his humanity of vision because he sees man as part of the totality of creation. Nevertheless I don't think that Lorca is telling the entire truth here. The intensity, the spiritual accuracy of his later work comes, rather, from the honesty and completeness of self-knowledge he attained in this period of withdrawal and imposed subjectivity. . .'*Canta el gallo*' – Lorca cannot have been unmindful of the phallic association of the bird in almost all cultures. Only out of unity with his own cock could major appraisal and artistic expression of the spiritual and cultural problems facing him come. And *gallo*, as I have already intimated, must have brought him back to Salvador Dalí and to the whole question of his crisis of 1928–29.

★

For what *was* Lorca doing in New York, in America? His easy abandonment of his English studies and his failure to resume them when the winter semester started tells us that, whatever his purpose, it was not to master the English language.

Lorca had quite clearly come to get away from Spain, to get away from a hell of suffering which he felt unable to discuss fully even with very close friends. (They were not, however, ignorant of its reasons, as later comments from them have made clear.) The period of depression began, by common consent, some time in 1928, its roots obviously reaching much further back in Lorca's past.

No one reading through Lorca's published letters can fail to notice the change – in style as well as content – that occurs in the late summer of 1928; a gloom, a restlessness of soul prevail which last, as we have already seen, until well after his arrival in New York. He expresses dissatisfaction with his art, not merely with his early productions but with his greatest success to date, the *Romancero gitano*. Anxiously he essays new manners, new matter. He encloses two prose-poems in a letter to his friend, the art critic Sebastian Gasch. 'They answer to my new *spiritualist* manner,' he says, 'pure disembodied emotion, detached from logical control, but – careful! careful! – with a tremendous poetic logic. . .the clearest self-awareness illuminates them.'[25] While neither piece, 'Suicidio en Alejandria' ('Suicide in Alexandria') nor 'Nadadora sumergida' ('Submerged Girl Swimmer'), seems to me at all satisfactory in itself, they do show Lorca's determination for his art to take a new direction, as well as the inner disquiet that was prompting this determination:

> When they placed the severed head on the office-table, all the glass-panes of the city were broken. . .
> After the terrible rite, everyone was raised to the topmost blade of the thistle; but the ant proved so mighty, so mighty, it had to keep to the ground with the hammer and the threaded eye of the needle.[26]

> I abandoned the old literature I had cultivated with great success.
> It's necessary to break it all up so that the dogmas are purified and the norms have a new tremor.
> The elephant must have eyes of a partridge and the partridge hooves of a unicorn.
> Through an embrace I know all these things, and through this great love that has slit my silk waistcoat.[27]

And to Jorge Zalamea Lorca wrote:

> I am fashioning now a sort of VEIN-OPENING poetry . . .[28]

Lorca's language here is very reminiscent of Dalí's own. When at work on the (now lost) painting 'Honey is Sweeter than Blood' (the title has, it seems to me, a somewhat Lorquian flavour), Dalí wrote (autumn 1927) to his friend:

> Federico, I am painting pictures which make me die for joy, I am creating with an absolute naturalness, without the slightest aesthetic concern, I am making things that inspire me with a very profound emotion and I am trying to paint them honestly. . .[29]

Lorca and Dalí had become friends in 1923. Lorca would go to Cadaqués on the Catalonian coast to stay with Dalí and his family; indeed a very tender and special friendship grew up between Lorca and Dalí's sister Ana, as his letters to her, full of touching affectionate nonsense, show. Of the great admiration Lorca had for Salvador Dalí himself, six years his junior, there is the most ample evidence. Letter after letter pays tribute to his gifts; they shared many interests and friends (Luis Buñuel, for instance) and, at that time, philosophic and political tenets. Only a month or so after their friendship started, the military dictatorship of Primo de Rivera began. Dalí's protests against the regime and the orthodoxies that propped it up were more audacious than Lorca's own – interesting in the light of the volte-face he was to make to a Rightist, Catholic position. Dalí designed costumes and decor for Lorca's play *Mariana Pineda* (June 1927); Lorca, for his part, tried to learn Catalan, actively associated himself with Catalan artists and artistic movements and pursued further his own talents as a painter and draughtsman, Dalí's encouragement here going as far as helping to arrange an exhibition of Lorca's work in a Barcelona gallery. Perhaps the most sustained evidence of Lorca's regard for Dalí, however, is the 'Oda a Salvador Dalí' published in the *Revista de occidente* in May 1926. '*O Salvador Dalí,*' he hails him, '*de voz aceitunada*' ('of the olive-hued voice'):

> No alabo tu imperfecto pincel adolescente,
> pero canto la firme dirección de tus flechas.
>
> Canto tu bello esfuerzo de luces catalanas,
> tu amor a lo que tiene explicación posible.
> Canto tu corazón astronómico y tierno,
> de baraja francesa y sin ninguna herida.
>
> I don't praise your imperfect adolescent paint-brush,
> but I sing the firm direction of your arrows.
>
> I sing your beautiful strength of Catalan lights,
> your love for that which has possible explanation.
> I sing your astronomical and tender heart,
> of French playing-cards and without any wound.

And a stanza later on he emphasises:

> Pero ante todo canto un común pensamiento
> que nos une en las horas oscuras y doradas.
> No es el Arte el luz que nos ciega los ojos.
> Es primero el amor, la amistad, o la esgrima.
>
> But before everything I sing a common thought
> that unites us in the dark and golden hours.
> It isn't Art the light that blinds our eyes.
> It is first of all love, friendship or the art of fencing.[30]

Love is surely what it was. In the ode the image of the direction of arrows, the qualification of love as a fencing-game, both would seem to me to suggest a physical fascination in the poet for the painter who is the subject of his poem. The biographer of Lorca has much to illuminate here. What we are concerned with in this critical study, however, is to appreciate how inextricably Dalí was connected with Lorca's crisis, the apotheosis of which was the New York poem-cycle.

Letters of 1928–29 show to what extent, to use the language of 'Nadadora sumergida', his love had slit the waistcoat of Lorca's emotional equilibrium. The estrangement between the two men began some time in 1928; Dawn Ades in her exemplary study tells how Dalí had felt for some time that he must free himself from the spell of Lorca's personality, interesting for those of us who have read Lorca's correspondence and ode and have therefore come to see Lorca prostrating himself before Dalí (as in that famous photograph of the two men on the beach at Cadaqués). And then there was Dalí's growing involvement with Paul Eluard's wife Gala, whom later he married; their lifelong companionship began in 1929.

So far I have spoken of the personal feelings that Lorca entertained for Dalí. His admiration for his art was intense – for all that in the ode he called his paint-brush *imperfecto* and *adolescente*. Maybe it was Dalí's views about art as much as the productions themselves that filled Lorca with such excitement, for, as Dawn Ades points out, Dalí was very much the painter of an Idea; his pictures (c.f. Freud's opinion of them) primarily exist to serve his mental obsessions. Be that as it may, Lorca, never given to understatement, revered his friend's art in such terms as the following:

> Everyday I appreciate Dalí's talent even more. He seems to me unique and he possesses a serenity and a *clarity* of judgement about whatever he's planning to do that is truly moving. He makes mistakes and it doesn't matter. *He's alive*. His denigrating intelligence unites with his disconcerting childishness, in such an unusual combination that it is absolutely captivating and original. What moves me most about him now is his *fever* of constructions (that is to say, creation), in which he tries to create out of *nothing* with such strenuous efforts and throws himself into the gales of creativity with so much faith and so much intensity that it seems incredible. . . .Dalí inspires the same pure emótion (and may God Our Father forgive me) as that of the baby Jesus abandoned on the doorstep of Bethlehem, with the germ of the crucifixion already latent beneath the straws of the cradle.[31]

It must be pointed out that these lines were written before Dalí's most celebrated excursions into Freudian-influenced surrealism, before 'Dismal Sport' or 'The Great Masturbator', before his most provocative anti-art statements. All the same, even in the rather De Chiricoesque productions from the time of the two men's greatest friendship, it is a little hard to work outwards from these praises to the actual works themselves.

A later letter (to Jorge Zalamea) brings the admiration of the man and the admiration of the artist together, and also alludes to the stresses of the relationship:

> Dalí is coming in September [1928]. In his last letter he told me: 'You are a Christian tempest and have need of my paganism. This past season in Madrid you gave yourself to something you should never have given yourself to. I'll come to get you to give you a sea cure. It will be winter time and we will light a fire. The poor beasts will be nearly frozen. You will remember that you are an inventor of marvels and we'll live together with a camera.'
> He's like that, this marvellous friend.[32]

Probably what Dalí is referring to here is Lorca's having assembled for publication the *romances* that form the *Romancero gitano*. The Lorca who rejoiced so in popular art, and who through Falla's influence became learned in folklore, found no sympathy in Dalí. The work of the Old Masters, particularly the Spanish, and the new movements in the arts, especially those centring on Paris – these are what interested the younger man. 'Folkloric' was a term wholly of abuse where he was concerned, and he even went so far as to think that the Catalans should give up dancing the *sardana*.

When the *Romancero gitano* came out to such general applause, it was all too obvious that many liked it for the picturesque-romantic associations that Gypsies and their doings have for the bourgeoisie (*los putrefactos* as Lorca and Dalí and their friends called its members). Lorca was somewhat upset that this should be the case; he wanted his poems to be taken seriously, and enough has surely been said about them here for it to be clear that they deserved this, that they were the result of deep emotion and intense application to art. Nevertheless Dalí wrote Lorca a long letter in which, among many things, he said that the *Romancero gitano* was chained to the forms and conventions of the past, that it was 'incapable of moving us or of satisfying our contemporary desires'.[33]

Lorca must have been very hurt, though the high regard in which he held Dalí – combined perhaps with more intimate and passionate feelings – seem to have rendered anger and defence of his own art impossible for him. As he wrote to Sebastian Gasch on 8 September 1928:

> Yesterday Dalí wrote me a long letter concerning my book. . .A sharp, arbitrary letter that sets forth an interesting poetic problem. Of course the *putrefactos* do not understand my book, although they say that they do.

In spite of everything, it holds no interest for me any more, or hardly any. It died on my hands in the most tender way. My poetry takes an even keener flight. A personal turn it seems.[34]

But that keener flight, that personal turn was not to be vindicated, nor indeed was in any proper way apparent, until the poems of New York. Lorca began many projects which only later, the crisis resolved, were worked up into interesting artefacts; in particular he re-applied himself to the theatre. Valuable though they may be as psychological stepping-stones, I cannot find anything in 'Suicidio en Alejandria' or 'Nadadora sumergida' that distinguishes them from countless other – to us today, pretentious – excursions into the then fashionable surrealism. Lorca was at this time too engulfed in what his admired St John of the Cross called the dark night of the soul to be wholly creative – for him a strange fate since fecundity of invention and ability to convert ideas into works of art had been a pre-eminent characteristic of his ever since adolescence.

All Lorca's friends have testified to the darkness of the poet's mind and heart in 1928–29, though later they were reticent about its causes, at least as far as public utterance went. Lorca himself left them in no doubt of his continuing misery:

In spite of everything, I'm neither well nor happy. . .It's necessary to be happy, a *duty* to be happy. Take it from me, I who am passing through one of the saddest and most unpleasant moments of my life.[35]

I also have a great desire to write, an unstoppable love for poetry, for the pure verse that fills my soul, still shuddering like a little antelope, from the last brutal arrows.[36]

In the spring of 1929 one of Lorca's closest friends, Rafael Martínez Nadal, received during the hour of the family meal a visitor, an elderly gentleman unknown to him but with certain features unmistakably '*garcíalorqueño*'. It was Don Federico, Lorca's father, and he had come simply to ask Martínez Nadal: '*¿Qué le pasa a mi Federiquito?*' ('What's the matter with my little Federico?')[37]

Excitement, Nadal tentatively suggested, depression. Would Federico, his father asked, be the better for a spell outside Spain? Nadal thought this would be the case. Some days later he heard that Lorca was sailing to New York with his loved former teacher, Fernando de los Ríos, who, so many years ago, had first saluted the young Federico's prodigious gifts when he heard him playing Beethoven sonatas.

But even at that time, in fact – when to make Federico's acquaintance seemed to enhance life for so many, young and old – the seeds of the later anguish, of the breakdown of 1929, were burgeoning. The great contemporary Lorquian Ian Gibson, who has so revolutionised approaches to the poet (see Introduction), speaks of a whole cache of adolescent poems, all still unpublished, which express awareness, guilt and angst about his sexual orientation.[38] Guilt is not in any real measure apparent in the published writings, even those of an early age, but awareness and angst – the latter invariably presented in oblique or translated forms – undoubtedly are. To be homosexual in conservative provincial Spain can have been no easy matter, and by the time Lorca left Granada for New York it seems that most people of his acquaintance knew – to some extent or other – the truth about his nature.

For a mind as piercing and as honest as Lorca's, full appreciation of his sexuality and its implications was both inevitable and certain to be difficult – for the analytical and imaginative person is obviously going to see all manner of consequences and attendant problems of stance that a more phlegmatic temperament will not. Lorca was ever anxious to attain wholeness of vision, ever anxious to see human relationships and behaviour *sub specie aeternitatis*. His own homosexuality he would have to fit into this. And in the wake of the crisis he clearly felt that he must, at whatever level of overtness he could attain, try to use his sexual orientation as the base from which to survey life and its complexities.

Dalí's rejection of him and his most popular book clearly brought about a truly agonising scrutiny in Lorca of his nature and his art. In *El poeta en Nueva York* as much as in those unsuccessful prose-poems, we often have the feeling that Lorca is trying to produce work Dalí would not despise him for, work that he could not castigate as irredeemably tethered to an outdated world. The kind of Dalí-approved art on which he'd embarked – with its obsessive and prolix use of Freudian associations – would, whatever the emotional situation of the recent past, have been bound to bring forth from Lorca more overt presentation of his homosexual position than his earlier art could have allowed.

But in fact right from the *Libro de poemas* on Lorca's work is full of references to his sexual orientation, mostly indirect, full also of images whose vitality derives from their homosexual content. In the next chapter, then, I am considering such instances, such pieces, and also reviewing what is inseparable from Lorca's attitude to his sexuality, his (developing) attitude to art. We shall see that, splendid leap forward though it is, *El poeta en Nueva York* is – contrary to what was thought at the time – organically related, in craft, images, sexual emotion and ideas, to Lorca's work before he left in such depression of spirits for America.

## Chapter Four
# Honey and the Honeycomb

## 1

Of the greatest interest to the student of Lorca's psychological and spiritual progress is a letter he wrote shortly before his twentieth birthday to the futurist poet, Adriano del Valle. The letter is headed 'PAZ' ('PEACE') and in it he plunges almost immediately into a most revealing, if at times rambling, presentation of himself. If we want to get a lively picture of Lorca's predicament as he embarked on his life's work of writing poems and plays, we cannot do better than attend to the letter, even to its inconsequentialities:

> I am a poor impassioned and silent fellow who, very nearly like the marvellous Verlaine, bears within a lily impossible to water, and to the foolish eyes of those who look upon me I seem to be a very red rose with the sexual tint of an April peony, which is not my heart's truth. . . I feel like a Chopinesque Gerineldo in an odious and despicable epoch of Kaisers and La Ciervas . . .† My image and my verses give the impression of something very passionate. . .and, yet, at the bottom of my soul there's an enormous desire to be very childlike, very poor, very hidden. I see before me many problems, many entrapping eyes, many conflicts in the battle between head and heart and all my sentimental flowering seeks to enter a golden garden and I try hard because I like paper dolls and the playthings of childhood . . . but the phantom that lives within us and hates us pushes me down the path. One must move along because we must grow old ´and die, but I don't want to pay attention to it. . .and, nevertheless, with each day that passes I have another doubt and another sadness. Sadness of the enigma of myself! There is within us, Adriano my friend, a desire not to suffer and an innate goodness, but the external force of temptation and the over-whelming tragedy of physiology insure our destruction. I believe that everywhere around us is full of souls that passed on,

†La Cierva was the Spanish Minister of War of the time, who became virtual head of government.

that they are the ones who provoke our sorrows and that they are the ones who enter the kingdom inhabited by that white and blue virgin called Melancholy. . .or, in other words, the kingdom of Poetry (I have no conception of poetry other than the lyric). I entered it a long time ago. . .After I entered the kingdom of Poetry, I ended by anointing myself with love for everything. To sum up, I'm a good boy, who opens his heart to the whole world. . .Of course I'm a great admirer of France and I hate militarism with all my heart, and feel only an immense desire for Humanity. Why struggle with the flesh while the frightening problem of the spirit exists? I love Venus madly, but even more I love the question, Heart? And most of all, I keep to myself, like that rare and true Peer Gynt with the Button-Moulder. . .I want me to be myself.[1]

Lorca says here that it's obvious both from his external character and his poems that he is a passionate person, and yet that passion is other than people suppose. It is impossible, I think, that Lorca did not use Verlaine here quite deliberately as a representative (with his desperate love for Rimbaud) of the homosexual.† If one takes Verlaine in this sense the entire passage quoted reads like a confession of sexual heterodoxy: the foreseeing of problems ahead; the statement that the desire to be good and the desire to meet one's physical yearnings are not, as the *bien-pensants* hold, incompatible; the 'belief' in a mystical communion of souls who have been through the same pains as we have; a hope that poetry redeems, because it fills one with love for the entire human race, a love that surely can include the sexual love of male for male; the thought that anyway, beside the terrible problems inherent in being alive as a responsible human, one's sexual choice, even if 'wrong', is something that should not detain one with fruitless guilts; a conviction that ultimately one must be true to oneself. 'Know thyself,' the oracle's dictum to Oedipus, must be followed and acted upon for any self-fulfilment. And while one is not being true to oneself, one is living dishonestly and so cannot, on any important level, be of help to others.

†In the section 'Tres retratos con sombra' ('Three Portraits with Shadow') of the *Canciones* Lorca includes a poem on Verlaine whose 'shadow' is 'Baco' (Bacchus). It significantly opens with words which will receive development during the lyric's course:

| La canción, | The song |
| que nunca diré | that I will never say |
| se ha dormido en mis labios. | has been asleep on my lips.[2] |

Doesn't this suggest the euphemism of 1890s parlance, 'the love that dare not speak its name'?

Peer Gynt, it will be remembered, stands, with his braggings and self-love, for fallen humanity in all its most foolish – if lovable – manifestations. The Button-Moulder would seem at first to be the embodiment of some sterner morality, the imperative to be good and not merely to seek self-gratification. Yet it is through *his* merciful offices that Peer is united with his childhood sweetheart, Solveig. And he will stand beside Peer in the next world. Clearly Lorca saw the story of Peer as a metaphor for himself, determined to be faithful to his sexual nature, to be happy, while accepting misery as inevitable to the human lot, and, in the face of all this, even *via* all this, to be good, to live in charity and, as the heading of the letter suggests, peace.

And the word 'peace' leads on to another aspect of the letter both important and interesting: Lorca shows himself fully cognisant of what is happening in the world outside Granada. He loathes the quasi-dictatorship of La Cierva with its military intervention in civil matters. He expresses, in the most forceful terms, his deep detestation, to last all his life, for everything military: later in this very letter he speaks of living in a 'century of zeppelins and stupid deaths'. In this hatred he may well have been educated by Manuel de Falla who, in articles on musical subjects for *Tribuna* and *Revista musical hispanoamericana* went out of his way to attack the War, blaming it, however, exclusively on the Central Powers: 'a cruel and unjust war'; 'the horrible war that Europe is going through'. His own love for France was very deep, and this, one presumes, he also communicated to Lorca. For Falla France was simply 'the highest musical centre in Europe',[3] and the disseminator of the arts of peace. Of Lorca's indebtedness to French culture (or French culture as transmitted to him by Falla) more presently.

That Lorca did not see himself (unlike Falla here) as committed to any religious orthodoxy is evident in some sentences – perhaps rather youthfully florid – that occur a little further in the same letter:

> I sob at my piano dreaming of the Handelian mist and I create verses very much my own, singing the same to Christ as to Buddha, to Mohammed, and to Pan. For a lyre I have my piano and, instead of ink, the sweat of yearning, yellow pollen of my inner lily and my great love.[4]

'instead of ink. . .yellow pollen of my inner lily': what does this remind us of? In *El maleficio de la mariposa* – to be produced in a Madrid theatre some twenty-two months later – the character nearest to Lorca himself, the poet Boybeetle, was, we recall, described as:

> a trim and refined little boy whose distinction derives from painting the tips of his antennae and his right leg with lily pollen.[5]

It is to *El maleficio*, the first full-length imaginative work of Lorca's to be offered to the public, that we must now turn again for further light upon Lorca's development as a gay person.

The very opening of the play is instructive. The dramatist himself speaks a prologue, the first of many deliberate intrusions of the author into/upon his plays. Lorca tells the audience that what they are going to see is:

> of no great importance, and yet, disturbing. A kind of defeated comedy about someone who, reaching for the moon, reached only his own heartbreak.[6]

He then proceeds to adumbrate the theme (as opposed to the mere story) of the work:

> Love, that love which with its ironies and its misfortunes occurs in the world of men, here occurs in a deep meadow populated only by insects – a meadow where life, but that was a long time ago, was serene and undisturbed. These insects led lives of contentment. They had nothing to worry about except peaceful-ly drinking their dewdrops and bringing up their children in the saintly fear of their gods. They made love to each other out of habit, without worrying about it. For love was given from father to son like a jewel old and exquisite, a jewel which had been passed to the first insect by the hand of God. With the same calm and certainty with which a blossom surrenders its pollen to the wind, they enjoyed making love to each other under the lush green grasses.
> Ah, but one day there was an insect who attempted to go beyond this love. He formed an attachment for something quite far away from his mode of living.[7]

Significant confusions are present in this address, verbally so clear; they increase as the play goes on. On one level the love that is 'given from father to son' could be interpreted as ordinary procreative sex, against which the Boybeetle (the insect of the second paragraph) stands apostate; he shuns the Girlbeetle proffered him with her paraphernalia of conventional femininity (e.g. her dainty daisy parasol) and becomes infatuated with a being (the Butterfly) with whom procreative sex will not be possible. On another level, though, the lines decribing the passing-on from generation to generation of the gift of sexuality seem to be informed by a prelapsarian vision. In this meadow of long-ago all manner of sexual communication was joyfully acceptable. The insect who attempts to go beyond this easiness – and dies as a result – may have been (so Lorca suggests in somewhat over-whimsical sentences) corrupted by a poem he'd found lying in the meadow, a poem beginning 'O, Woman Unattainable, you I love'. According to *this* reading the Boybeetle's story represents the perversion of guiltless, guileless sexual communication into idealised, i.e. romantic and frustrating 'love'. This reading seems to me borne out by the flowery effusions of the poems the Boybeetle writes to the Butterfly, pastiches amounting to parodies of conventional and 'unreal' late romantic stuff. The Butterfly is female, it must be remembered, and therefore perhaps the first of Lorca's women who are imprisoned by the conventions of male courtship and love. Nevertheless we are not on her side in the play: the title would suggest that the spell she exerts over the poet-protagonist is baleful, evil, and when she speaks we feel this ourselves:

> que la gota de lluvia se asombre
> al resbalar sobre mis alas muertas.
> Hilé mi corazón sobre carne
> para rezar en las tinieblas
> y la muerte me dió dos alas blancas,
> pero cegó la fuente de mi seda.
> Ahora comprendo al lamentar del agua,
> y el lamentar de las estrellas,
> y el lamentar de viento en la montaña,
> y el zumbido punzante
> de la abeja.
> Porque soy la muerte
> y la belleza.

> let the drop of rain become dark
> on slipping upon my dead wings.
> I span my heart over flesh
> in order to pray in the darkness.
> and death gave me two white wings,
> but dried up the source of my silk.
> Now I understand the lamentation of the water,
> and the lamentation of the stars,
> and the lamentation of the wind in the mountain,
> and the stinging hum
> of the bee.
> Because I am death
> and beauty.[8]

There is a strange religious sub-text to *El maleficio* which accords with the young Lorca's declaration that he sang alike to Christ, to Buddha, to Mohammed, to Pan. We have already seen (p. 34) that the

Boybeetle was a disciple of San Cucaracho whose words are a sort of homely, pastoral fusion of the Sermon on the Mount and St Francis' *Canticle to the Sun*. But, in fact, the Boybeetle's mentor where the doctrine of San Cucaracho is concerned, the Curiana Nigromántica (Witchbeetle) says – in some of the most powerful lines the young Lorca had so far written:

> Mi alma tiene gran tristeza, ¡vecina!
> Me dijo ayer tarde una golondrina:
> 'Todos las estrellas se van a apagar.'
> Dios está dormido, y en el encinar
> ví una estrella roja toda temblorosa
> que se deshojaba como una enorme rosa.

> My soul is full of great sadness, neighbour.
> Yesterday evening a swallow told me:
> 'All the stars are becoming extinguished.'
> God is asleep, and in the wood
> I saw a red star all trembling
> that was dropping its petals like a huge rose.[9]

In terms of the play's action the fall of the star turns out to be the death of a fairy – of just such an *hada* as Lorca claimed to have seen clinging to a curtain – and it is this event that brings about the descent of the Butterfly and the Boybeetle's surrender to her spell. But obviously behind these lines there is the poet's own sense of the possibility of God's retreat, if not abdication from His world. It is Nietzsche's 'God is dead' burgeoning in the mind of one reared in a tradition-consecrated Catholicism. Later the Boybeetle, brooding over his doomed infatuation, ruminates:

> Pero pienso en el mundo con que mi madre sueña,
> un mundo de alegría más allá de esas ramas,
> lleno de ruiseñores y de prados inmensos:
> el mundo del rocío
> donde el amor no acaba.
> ¿Y si San Cucaracho no existiera? ¿Qué objeto
> tendría mi amargura fatal?

> But I think of the world of which my mother dreams,
> a world of happiness further than these branches,
> full of nightingales and immense meadows:
> the world of dew
> where love doesn't come to an end.
> And if the Holy Beetle doesn't exist? What point
> would my ill-fated bitterness have?[10]

We are surely not so very far here from the state of mind that produced a 'Nocturno del hueco'.

★

I have said that for Lorca psychosexual and artistic questions are inextricably woven together, and a way into appreciating this is to see how *El maleficio*, which *does*, however ambivalently, tackle and present a difficult sexual-emotional situation, relates to cultural movements of its times. To see also how it shows Lorca's precociously developed attitude to them.

I have related how to the first audience both setting and cast of *El maleficio* appeared so outlandish that they greeted the play with a terrible violence of derision. But we must also remember that it was put on by one of the most eminent men of the theatre of the day, Gregorio Martínez Sierra, a friend of and collaborator with Falla himself – producing the scenarios for *El amor brujo* and *El sombrero de tres picos* – and *he* must have seen what we can see today: that the play for all its imperfections and whimsicalities is strong in feeling, characters and plot, that it is not an eccentric sport but a work showing its author as sensitively attuned to the vanguard culture of his day – as well as independent and original.

Francisco García Lorca suggests as an antecedent of his brother's play one by the French dramatist, Edmond Rostand – *Chantecler* (*Chanticleer,* 1910) – which a Madrid theatre had put on a little while before.[11] Set in a farmyard this is an allegory in which the cockerel stands for the Orphic truth always under threat from crass normality. Of this cockerel Lorca's Boybeetle could be a descendant. Possibly, but a far stronger influence must have been Maurice Maeterlinck, Nobel Prizewinner for 1911, whose work Martínez Sierra had both staged and translated. Maeterlinck represented one of the triumphs over the naturalism then being contested by artists and intellectuals all over Europe. Maeterlinck's use of dream and fairytale elements, his symbolic quests in which mysterious figures embody psychic forces – they don't seem to have stood the test of time well – had an immense impact on sensitive young writers of the day, and it is not hard to see how and why Lorca responded to them. Think only of the stage sets he demanded for his first dramatic work: Act Two takes place in a twilight-bathed forest of gigantic daisies, somewhere in which glints the waters of a spring.

And, significantly, Maeterlinck had – with his *La vie des abeilles* (1910, translated as *The Life of the Bee*) – made the subject of insect-life both popular and appealing to intellectuals. Maeterlinck must surely have inspired, for example, the insect-ballet of Albert Roussel, *Le festin de l'araignée* (*The Spider's Feast,* 1913) – another possible antecedent for *El maleficio*, for even if he never saw the score itself Lorca could have been told about the work by Falla or by Falla's pianist friends Viñes and Rubenstein – sources, I suggest, for much of

Lorca's knowledge of international cultural matters. Roussel's score is at once delicate and precise, and suggestive in its rhythms and jagged melodies of primordial savagery. In the ballet itself the fall of a butterfly determines the action as in *El maleficio*, beetles represent us humans, and there is poignant use of an ephemera (c.f. the Boybeetle) doomed to a life of passivity and brevity despite his complex sensitivity. Both works show through the beauties and cruelties of the insect microcosm (beyond which move beings they have not even guessed at) the beauties and cruelties of the human macrocosm (beyond which – what?).

Another possible influence on the Lorca of *El maleficio* is André Gide, who in his hymnings of the sensual wonders of the entire created world (e.g. in *Les nourritures terrestres* of 1897) did not forget the insects (just as he did not forget Lorca's own Granada!). In his great *Journals* he spoke of his admiration for the French entomologist Jean-Henri Fabre, and was to allude to him at an important point in *Corydon*, his dialogues about homosexuality.[12] Fabre is often called 'the insects' Homer' and is rightly thought of as a particularly fine example of that French tradition of patient objective pursuit of truth – c.f. Bouffon, Pasteur, Pierre Curie. Lorca could have known of Fabre from his contacts with French life, and when reading *El maleficio* it is tempting to think that he did. Fabre's wonderful accounts of experiments he made with moths and butterflies certainly remind us of the Butterfly of Lorca's play and her effects on other insects. E.g. – in response to a superb Great Peacock moth born in the morning Fabre observed forty or more great moths invading his study in the evening. The naturalist placed another female moth, a rare Banded Minim, in a glass bell and was able to watch male butterflies, allured by her presence but not perceiving her whereabouts, making love instead to pieces of cotton-wool and slips of oak-leaves.[13] A *maleficio* at work indeed!

Rostand, Maeterlinck, Gide, Fabre, Falla (in his first real creative period, his Paris years of 1907–14), Falla's mentors and associates: Debussy, Ravel, Satie, Roussel, Dukas – and to this list we must add Russian Igor Stravinsky and Spanish Pablo Picasso – all bring us to France, to Paris in particular. And what did Lorca say in that letter of May 1918 to Adriano del Valle but: 'Of course I'm a great admirer of France'?

Let us remind ourselves of some outstanding and characteristic artistic and intellectual achievements of these years.

In 1917, the year of Falla and Lorca's friendship, Falla's masterly ballet *El sombrero de tres picos* was staged in Madrid; while in Paris that extraordinary fusion of the geniuses of Satie, Diaghilev, Cocteau and Picasso – *Parade* – was given its memorable first performance. 1917 was also the year of Stravinsky's haunting tableau for voices and instruments *L'histoire du soldat*, of Valéry's philosophic poem 'La jeune parque' ('The Young Fate'), of Ravel's *Tombeau de Couperin*, of

Apollinaire's *Les mamelles de Tiresias*, of Max Jacob's *Le cornet à dés*, and Debussy's violin and piano sonata. Jung produced his major work on the unconscious and Freud gave his *Introductory Lectures on Psychoanalysis*. The great Spanish poet Juan Ramón Jimenez, with whom Lorca was to enjoy friendship, produced in his American exile his *Diario de un poeta recién casado (Diary of a Poet Newly Married)* and renounced all his work done before 1916; he began writing the kind of poetry dissolving and resolving experiences into the elements of light and water of which the *Eternidades (Eternities)* of 1918 is perhaps the first major manifestation.

Of these artists the majority produced further seminal and distinguished work by the end of 1920: Stravinsky *Les noces, Ragtime, Le chant du Rossignol* and *Pulcinella*, Satie that so individual, so captivating work *Socrate*, Cocteau *Le coq et l'harlequin*, Valéry 'Le cimetière marin', Falla himself his major work for solo piano, *Fantasia Baetica*. Other cultural events or productions that seem worth citing are Pirandello's *Sei personaggi in cerca d'autore (Six Characters in Search of an Author)*, the concerts of the Original Dixieland Jazz Band, Blok's symbolic narrative poem born of the Russian Revolution, *The Twelve*, and the foundations of the Bauhaus (1919) and 'Les Six' (1920).

What most of the works have in common, and what was certainly a characteristic of the mentality of their creators, is an unprecedented fusion of artifice and atavism. The sophisticated stylisations of the ballet, the night-club cabaret and the avantgarde atelier receive African masks, Black jazz-players and rites adapted from primitive religion or arcane rural communities. Stravinsky and Falla – great admirers of each other's work – used advanced musical techniques to put forth ancient Orthodox liturgical material (as in *Les noces*) or the agonised cries of *cante jondo*. In literature and in the realm of ideas we can see a desire to free human beings from the bondage of conventions, to insist on the depths within their personalities which relate them to earlier societies, to a whole community of humans and living beings, past and present, and which contemporary society has failed to understand or do justice to. In *Sei personaggi in cerca d'autore* Pirandello shows how too often we move through life tethered to roles written for us by others; there should be an imperative to break through these and attain – to use the language of a later movement – authenticity. There is little interest among the writers in surface realism or social observation, but a great deal of concern with masks, puppets (a love of the *saloniste* Princesse de Polignac who commissioned work from both Falla and Stravinsky), clowns and circuses, dolls and minstrels.† All these seem,

†Almost all Lorca's drawings (*dibujos* – see *Obras Completas*) make use of this iconography. Clown and Harlequin occur in them in many forms, and even figures such as St Sebastian irresistibly recall *saltimbanques*. Almost all the cultural observations that follow are true of Lorca's excursions into the visual

and often at one and the same time, both symbols of what we are too often reduced to by socialisation *and* representations of our basic drives and urges concealed by the elaborate network of disguises that comprise social life. The media themselves – puppet-theatre, dance-stage, circus – both put us in touch with more instinctive audiences (for are they not beloved by children and primitive peoples?) and allow the artist to pursue to logical and beautiful conclusions aesthetic ambitions untrammelled by the claims of bourgeois society with its dulling rules and materialist concerns.

The animating spirit behind these cultural productions is surely not hard to seek and can be stated quite simply. It is a reaction against the civilisation that had culminated in the vast carnage of the Great War; a protest against a reduction of humans to numbers, shadows, corpses; a dislike of the approaches to life – including artistic ones – that had served such a civilisation; a return to the wisdom of ancient or primitive peoples who had not deployed such energy and ingenuity on mutual destruction; a delight in exercising imagination and technical skills on creations of 'alternative' artificial worlds; a determination to practise the arts of peace.

Three further features of this culture should be noted: first, its centre, its *fons et origo* was France, the country on whose soil 'half the seed of Europe' (to use Wilfred Owen's haunting phrase)[14] had for four years been bled to death in the service of callous governments and armaments manufacturers. Second, the gay element is not just very considerable, it is indispensable to it. Leading figures, Gide, Cocteau, Diaghilev, Satie, Max Jacob, Proust (parts of whose great novel were appearing at this time and were read eagerly by members of Lorca's *tertulia*, El Rinconcillo) and Ravel† were all homosexual. And Stravinsky and Picasso – who were not gay – associated with, and drew inspiration from, intimate gay friends and their creations; their own art is frequently concerned, and at profound levels, with transpositions of accepted sexual roles and androgyny. Again the reason is not difficult to arrive at: homosexuals of the kind associated with these arts were free (often defiantly so) from both the aggression and the domesticity of a certain heterosexual male stereotype appealed to and made rhetorical use of in the Great War. The times had therefore peculiar need of their artistic contribution.

Third, almost every aspect of the cultural movement that I have been discussing is present in the art of Manuel de Falla – who, it must be said, learned much from the (younger) Stravinsky. Stravinsky's music, he proclaimed in *La tribuna* in June 1916, 'is imbued with

† It is usually thought that Ravel was non-practising. There are stories, which may or may not be apochryphal, to the contrary.

---

arts, which show – perhaps a little too evidently – the fashionable influences of Picasso and Cocteau.

sincerity; the kind of brave, unbowed sincerity of one who says what he thinks fearless of what those who do not think or feel like him might say'.[15] He compared his music to a poster 'shouting defiance at timid people',[16] referred admiringly to *Petrushka* and *Le sacre du printemps*, and then, coming on to his more recent works-in-progress *Renard* and *Les noces*, said:

> . . .in both the instrumentation is completely new. Each instrument has its own tonal and expressive function, and each string instrument has a separate part, never playing in unison. The dynamic impetus comes from those instruments that are by nature dynamic, for example trumpets, trombones and timpani. The other instruments create a web of pure melodic lines without the need for any support. It could be that in this work the idea of so-called pure music has come to life. . . Stravinsky employs means of expression that are completely new, and which exactly produce the effects he wants. Stravinsky's sincerity contains two qualities which determine the unity of his whole work: a very conspicuous national character, rhythmic and melodic, and the attainment of new sonorities. Let us follow this example, which is more valuable for Spain than for any other country, since the popular elements – traditional and religious – of Russian music are the same as those that have given rise to the songs and dances of our people.[17]

Those who are familiar with the works of Falla's maturity, *El retablo de Maese Pedro* (*Master Peter's Puppet-Show*, 1923), *Psyche* (1924), the *Concerto for Harpsichord* (1926), will see how much Falla himself accomplished what he praises in Stravinsky's work. And so – making suitable and obvious adjustments – did Lorca, most particularly in his plays from *El maleficio* on to the masterpieces written after his return from New York. Thus Lorca's work can be said to owe enormously to Paris and the arts of peace being practised there, and a line can be drawn from Stravinsky to Falla to Lorca. This matter needs expanding on – for Falla's influence on the young Lorca was, in my view, by no means confined to helping him to immerse himself in *cante jondo*.

## 2

By an interesting coincidence Falla had also, as a boy, been a devotee of puppets and toy-theatres; indeed he constructed an entire one himself, with puppets worked by his brother and sister.[18] Like Lorca too, he did not turn his back on this interest with age; both his absorption in folkloric studies *and* his enthusiasm for the modernist movements in France would have confirmed him in the rightness of fidelity to his boyhood passion. How delighted he must have been to find that Lorca shared it!

On 6 January 1923, just six months after the *cante jondo* festival, Falla and Lorca organised another feast of ancient art, one attended – as was only proper for Twelfth Night – by the children of the city.[19] A stage was set up in the doorway between the two main reception-rooms of the García Lorca family's house, and memorable entertainment produced. An *entremés* (interlude) by Cervantes was the first item to be performed; Cervantes had himself been a great lover of puppets and the puppet-theatre, as the 'Retablo de Maese Pedro' chapter of Don Quixote testifies (it was the basis, of course, of Falla's own later masterpiece). The musical background for this work was an arrangement by Falla of Stravinsky's *L'histoire du soldat*, and not only can this marvellous composition be seen as standing behind Falla's *Retablo*, but it can be felt, or so it has long seemed to me, as an ancestor for much that is valuable in Lorca's oeuvre: the use of archetypal figures; the insistent repetition of a theme that nevertheless undergoes meaningful metamorphoses; the sense of dialogue as a pitting of wills that achieves but a tragic resolution; the personification of Death; the combination of the mythic and the 'cabaret'. Surely, to take an instance from the poetry rather than the plays, and one which will be familiar already to the reader of this book, the 'Diálogo del Amargo' derives from *L'histoire du soldat*, results from this charming Epiphany entertainment.

Next came a now lost puppet-play by Lorca himself, *La niña que riega la albahaca y el príncipe preguntón (The Girl Who Waters the Basil Plant and the Inquisitive Prince)*. This was performed to music by Albéniz, Debussy and Ravel. Third was the principal piece of the evening, a thirteenth-century miracle play, *The Three Wise Men*. The characters of this play were large figures cut out of heavy painted cardboard moved by Federico and other members of the household along wooden tracks. In between the three plays the Spanish equivalent of Punch, Don Cristóbal, made enthusiastically greeted appearances. These are best described by Lorca's brother in his introduction to the volume of English translations entitled *Five Plays: Comedies and Tragi-Comedies*:

> [Don Cristóbal] addressed himself to his young and delighted audience, calling the children by their first names and carrying on an impromptu dialogue with them, a practice also in the tradition of Spanish hand puppets. Don Cristóbal was manipulated and impersonated by Federico García Lorca so naturally that one could suspect that Federico was animated by the puppet.[20]

The fruits of the evening would seem to us, looking back upon it from the perspective of Lorca's entire work, to have been many and good. Lorca later wrote poems about Albéniz and Debussy, he himself declared that *Así que pasen cinco años* was a sort of medieval miracle/mystery play, he continued to write for children (mostly poems), and toyed with the idea of creating pieces for big cardboard figures which were to represent characters from popular photography/iconography.[21] Don Cirstóbal did not desert him, but continued, so to speak, to animate him into the writing of two plays (one of which may indeed have already been begun before the Epiphany night performances): *Los títeres de cachiporra* (*The Billy-Club Puppets*) and a minor piece, *El retablillo de Don Cristóbal* (*The Little Puppet-Show of Don Cristóbal*). Falla was probably inspired to pursue the work that became *El retablo de Maese Pedro*, which in turn – whether in inception or in some executed form – seems to me to have influenced Lorca's *La zapatera prodigiosa* (*The Shoemaker's Prodigious Wife*) – the first act of which was probably finished by the end of July 1923.

The chronology of Lorca's plays is – if anything – even more difficult than that of the poems; he would often write one act (as in the case of *La zapatera prodigiosa*) and not resume work on the piece until much later; he would conceive a play (e.g. *Doña Rosita la soltera* (*Doña Rosita, the Spinster*) in the autumn of 1924) and then let years elapse before turning idea into the written word (*Doña Rosita* was actually *written* in 1934–35, being performed in the latter year). Also versions of the plays vary considerably, the one finally put on the stage probably relating only partially to the first draft. In this chapter, as indeed elsewhere in the study, I am interested in the development of Lorca's thinking, and so the fact that a play did not know final and satisfactory form until *after* the period here covered does not seem to me to render it less relevant. I propose now to discuss the following plays and in this order; *Los títeres de cachiporra*, *La zapatera prodigiosa*, *El amor de don Perlimplín y Belisa en su jardín* (*The Love of Don Perlimplín and Belisa in the Garden*), returning after these to poems which deal with comparable themes and reveal similar preoccupations. All these plays seem to me to come out of the genre celebrated on that surely magical Twelfth Night. The puppet-theatre, stylised masque, etc. would appear – like the ballet to which they are obviously related – to have a particular appeal for the homosexual. We have noted that Hans Andersen was a devotee of this art-form and that his profoundest productions – his fairy-tales – can be proved to have a kinship with his childhood delight. Perhaps the interplay of archetypes has a life-enhancing allure for those who find the traffic of the persona difficult and oppressive.

It is therefore not surprising that we can find in the pieces cited – worked into their delicate, small-scale art – correlatives for Lorca's homosexual situation.

The story of *Los títeres de cachiporra* has already been briefly told, to illustrate how, like Andersen in fairy-tale, Lorca managed to make a miniature art-form encapsulate important and consequential human concerns. The play positively rejoices – as indeed do all the pieces under review here – in the stylised conventions and limitations of the folk-theatre. It is introduced, like *El maleficio de la mariposa*, by someone confronting the audience; in this case Mosquito: 'a mysterious personage, part ghost, part leprechaun, part insect. He represents the joy of a free life and the wit and poetry of the Andalusian people.'[22] Later he interposes himself in the little drama he is presenting, thus compounding the sense of illusion imparted by the play. What he says by way of preface is interesting in that it shows us how right from the start Lorca wanted his work to be of both the widest and the deepest address:

> My company and I have just come from the theatre of the bourgeoisie, the theatre of the counts and the marquises, a gold and crystal theatre where the men go to fall asleep and the women to fall asleep too. My company and I were prisoners there! You can't imagine how unhappy we were. But one day, through the keyhole, I saw a star twinkling like a little fresh violet of light all aglow. I opened my eye as wide as I could (the wind kept trying to close it with its finger for me) and there, under the star, and furrowed by slow ships, a wide river smiled. Then I, ha!ha!ha! told my friends about it, and we ran away over the fields, looking for the plain people, to show them the things, the little things, and the littlest little things of this world, under the green mountain moon and the rosy seashore moon.[23]

Don Cristóbal – braggart and bully – wants Rosita despite the fact that her heart is elsewhere. At the end of the play he is revealed as being nothing but a puppet, Lorca here using the devices of artifice for a very serious purpose. For the tyranny of machismo is dehumanising both to the man who exercises it and to its victims male and (pre-eminently) female. This is vividly brought home to us here by the demonstration that the one character who embodies machismo is a simulacrum of a human being, not a real and feeling one. (It is unclear whether Lorca intended *Los títeres de cachiporra* to be acted by puppets or by people; it would, however, be effective with either.) The amusing – and farcically dextrous – denigration of Don Cristóbal is the first instance in Lorca of an intense hatred of the swagger traditionally expected of the conventional male in too many societies, rural Andalucía among them. We shall meet it again, above all perhaps in *Así que pase cinco años* (*When Five Years Have Passed*) where the Friend and the Rugby-Player are unfavourably contrasted with the hero and his delicate second self, the Second Friend.

But Rosita, the pretty heroine of *Los títeres de cachiporra* is not the only victim in the play, and in my earlier summary I referred to the poetic character of Currito from the Harbour, thrown over – or rather forgotten – by Rosita. He enters the play cloaked, disguised, and though it is he who first seriously assaults the malevolent Cristóbal – an assault which because of the bully's true identity has curious results – it is difficult initially to see quite why he was needed as far as plot is concerned. The answer is, of course, that he was needed *emotionally* by the dramatist, is one of the figures of his carpet, representing sensitive man spurned by role-engendering and -expecting woman, and we will meet him again in other plays, most fully once more in *Así que pasen cinco años* where he is given the central part, El Joven, the hero. In this context his cloaking of himself – i.e. hiding his real identity – acquires a real significance.

Before coming on to *La zapatera prodigiosa* I want to turn momentarily to Falla's masterwork *El retablo de Maese Pedro*, a puppet performance of which was given in the house of the famous patroness of the arts, the Princesse de Polignac, on 25 June 1923. Its setting is the stable of an inn, where the trestle theatre of an itinerant showman, Maese Pedro, has been erected. Here Maese Pedro directs a puppet-play dealing with courtly love at the time of Charlemagne, while his Boy interprets the action for the audience among whom we find Don Quixote and Sancho Panza. Maese Pedro, the Boy, Don Quixote and Sancho Panza all have sung parts and are played by large puppets (as opposed to the small ones of the drama itself). Don Quixote is from time to time moved to comment upon both the Boy's commentary and upon the subject of this commentary, a play dealing with a theme dear to his heart, romantic love. Falla's score, which is one of singular mystery and beauty, does full justice to the very Spanish theme of illusion versus reality, presented in the equally Spanish way of putting one artefact inside another and making one reflect the other (c.f. Velásquez's *Las meninas*).

The climax of *La zapatera prodigiosa* seems to me to bear the closest resemblance to *El retablo de Maese Pedro* and to suggest that Lorca and Falla had often discussed – and come to agreement about – the symbolic properties of puppets. We are given a warning about the artistic and, so to speak, philosophic nature of this climax in the Prologue, once again a speech delivered in personal terms to the audience, this time by the Author himself:

Everywhere walks and breathes the poetic creature that the author has dressed as a shoemaker's wife with the air of a refrain or a simple ballad, and the audience should not be surprised if she appears violent or takes bitter attitudes because she is ever fighting, fighting with the reality which encircles her and with fantasy when it becomes visible reality.[24]

And – like Mosquito in *Los títeres* – he communicates with the subject of the play, with indeed the Wife herself.

She is a pretty young woman married to a much older man (18 to his 53), a familiar enough subject of folk-drama. Her pertness, flirtatiousness and capriciousness – her erratic housekeeping and extravagance, her emotional reminders that she is young and he old – these all drive the Shoemaker out of his own house. In fact, tiresome though she seems, the Wife is – to use traditional vocabulary – an innocent and virtuous girl, and any suspicions of her infidelity, even after her desertion, are totally unjustified. To keep herself while he is away (four months) she turns the house into an inn, but the village gossips are wrong who accuse her of receiving men by night as well as by day. She has plenty of opportunities: the conceited Mayor whose seasoned machismo brings Don Cristóbal to mind, the seductive Youth with Sash and the even more seductive Don Merlo (Don Blackbird). But loving thoughts of her husband and remembrance of the promises she made him render any sexual relations with these men impossible for her.

A visitor comes to the inn that the cobbler's house has become: a puppeteer who stages a violent little drama dealing with the cuckolding of an elderly tanner by his attractive and much younger wife. The drama has the greatest effect on its audience, upon the wife most of all. Of course the puppeteer is none other than the Shoemaker himself, and after a long and charged exchange when they are alone together, he reveals his identity, but only because he has perceived that his flighty wife really loved him, indeed still loves him. The play ends ironically and convincingly: the gossips of the village continue their insulting song about the Wife's alleged misdemeanours. She, on hearing it, turns furiously to her husband, for isn't *he* responsible for *her* humiliation? Then she realises that he stands beside her both literally and figuratively and that from now on they can face the community, including its most unpleasant and jeering members, *together*.

Thus *La zapatera prodigiosa* uses both the play-within-a-play *and* the reacting audience to make its points, just as *El retablo de Maese Pedro* does. The idea of the participant audience clearly had great fascination for Lorca, and this idea controls Lorca's most ambitious work for the theatre, the extraordinary *El público (The Public)*, significantly his most explicitly gay play.

Lorca called *La zapatera prodigiosa* a 'violent farce'. Its use of disguise, its energetic entrances and exits, its controlled mayhem give it its farcical quality; the 'violence' is in the strength of feeling that the play both shows and imparts. Once more Lorca has availed himself of the circumscription of a theatrical convention to show the passions that inform and dominate the ordinary people he wanted to address. The Shoemaker's age, his feeling of impotence, not so much sexual as spiritual, in the face of his lively partner, his wistful memories of himself when young, and his almost incredulous gratitude when he finds out what his wife's attitude to him really is – these are movingly done. Similarly we have access to the understandable impatience that the wife experiences, her boredom with the domestic duties expected of her, and her moments of heartfelt tenderness for the ageing man who is her husband and whom she does not treat as well as she'd like to. The completest revelation of her warmth of heart, her goodness, comes however in the scene between her and the Boy. In a letter to his friend, Adolfo Salazar (of August 1921) Lorca had written:

> Here in the village I'm very much loved by the labourers, especially by the boys, with whom I walk and talk and everything.[25]

Certainly – they appear too in his early poems – *los niños* of the villages and countryside have a very important contribution to make to the Lorquian landscape; invariably they are spontaneous, kindly, tender-hearted, truthful. The Boy in *La zapatera prodigiosa* is all these things; devoted to the Shoemaker's Wife, as she is to him, he alone among all the village has the courage to tell her that her husband has left her, and the courage to make her face up to the evil slanders being spread about her. (He is alone also in recognising the Shoemaker in the Puppeteer.) Before the Boy can break the news of her desertion to the Wife, however, he catches sight of a butterfly, and so lovely is it that he feels he must direct her attention to it. The uniting delight of the two in the insect – harbinger of the world of the Platonic Ideal, illustrator of the transitoriness of both sorrow and joy – confirms us in our admiration for them, for all who let instinctual tenderness be their mentor. The loving creation of the Boy is, no doubt, the result of Lorca's gratitude to his village companions. It will be paralleled elsewhere many times in Lorca's work of the Twenties, and will receive its fullest expression in the 'Little Boy Stanton' poem of *El poeta en Nueva York* and in *Así que pasen cinco años*.

★

If *La zapatera prodigiosa* was a 'violent farce', *El amor de don Perlimplín y Belisa en su jardín* is an 'erotic lace-paper valentine'. Immediately to our mind comes an image of a heart, imposed large and vulnerable, on a delicate background, and this could indeed serve as a description of the play, the shortest, the most concentrated and the profoundest of the three under discussion. In *Los títeres de cachiporra* we saw a young girl victimised by a rapacious and self-centred older man – who, in the end, lost the battle for her. In *La zapatera prodigiosa* we had a young girl tied to an older man and loving him but finding the situation painfully hard to cope with; sympathies were fairly evenly distributed, though I think finally Lorca comes down on the side of the Wife. The ending, as will be clear, is ambiguous by intention, but it would not be untrue to say that, in *this* play as well, the man loses: he has regained the woman, yes; had his love for her vindicated, certainly; but we have little doubt that she will continue to plague him with her wilfulness until the end of his days. Now in *Perlimplín y Belisa* we have a very disturbing and strange variation on the theme of young girl and older man, one which, in my opinion, tells us much about Lorca's psychological condition.

Perlimplín, like the Shoemaker, has decided to marry, partly because he is getting on and lonely; his bid for the hand of Belisa, a beautiful young girl, is accepted according to the conventions of the old-fashioned society in which he lives. A more inadequate husband-to-be than Perlimplín could scarcely be imagined, and lest we should be in doubt of his total sexual inexperience, two Sprites appear – interjected into the action like Mosquito in *Los títeres* – to emphasise it. Not that Perlimplín is immune to sexual attraction. On their wedding night Perlimplín tells Belisa:

> I married. . .for whatever reason, but I didn't love you. I couldn't have imagined your body until I saw it through the keyhole when you were putting on your wedding dress. And then it was that I felt love come to me. Then! Like the deep thrust of a lancet in my throat.[26]

His words fail to move Belisa who resents her enforced marriage. That very night she cuckolds him five times – each man represents one of this world's races. Perlimplín – realising that he fails to interest her amorously – decides to have recourse to a trick. He disguises himself as a young man and woos her in his own garden. The plan works; Belisa is fascinated by the mysterious gallant. By no means wholly deceitful by nature Belisa confides her predicament to her husband:

> BELISA. I love him! Perlimplín, I love him! It seems to me that I am another woman!
> PERLIMPLÍN. That is my triumph.
> BELISA. What triumph?
> PERLIMPLÍN. The triumph of my imagination.
> BELISA. It's true that you helped me love him.
> PERLIMPLÍN. As now I will help you mourn him.
> BELISA, *puzzled.* Perlimplín! What are you saying?. . .
> PERLIMPLÍN. Well, since you love him so much, I don't want him ever to leave you. And in order that he should be completely yours, it has come to me that the best thing would be to stick this dagger in his gallant heart. Would you like that?
> BELISA. For God's sake, Perlimplín!

PERLIMPLÍN. Then, dead, you will be able to caress him in your bed – so handsome and well groomed – without the fear that he should cease to love you. He will love you with the infinite love of the dead, and I will be free of this dark little nightmare of your magnificent body. [*Embracing her.*] Your body. . .that I will never decipher![27]

Killing her loved one means, obviously, killing himself – though in fact the audience have not been made party to his secret. (The play gains rather than loses from the reader/spectator being in the know.) Perlimplín leaves the garden, then returns, dressed as Belisa's young inamorato and mortally wounded with a dagger in his chest. Only gradually, as she listens to the difficult speech of the dying man, does Belisa understand what has happened.

PERLIMPLÍN. Perlimplín killed me. . .Ah, Don Perlimplín! Youngish old man, manikin without strength, you couldn't enjoy the body of Belisa. . .the body of Belisa was for younger muscles and warm lips. . . . I, on the other hand, loved your body only. . .your body! But he has killed me. . .with this glowing branch of precious stones.
BELISA. What have you done?
PERLIMPLÍN, *near death.* Don't you understand? I am my soul and you are your body.[28]

The greatest expression of the soul in this life is commonly belived to be in the love of man and wife for which mutual sexual attraction is a prerequisite. Perlimplín was denied the satisfaction of the body and thus the only intense soul-like possibility for him is its translation into death.

Two differences between *Perlimplín y Belisa* and the other two plays will be apparent: the girl's cruelty is stressed, though her grief at the end of the play is redemptive; and the older man, while he loses in life, has the final victory, in his terrible apotheosis through suicide.

I have said that of the three works this is the most concentrated; Francisco García Lorca sees it as a 'kind of concerto grosso for four instruments'.[29] Its filigree, baroque perfection stylistically should not prevent us from perceiving the real agonies within the author that are implicit in it: indeed in this most artificial of works we come the closest perhaps to angers and hatreds that Lorca – a gentle and good young man – was perhaps reluctant to express in life or – with his dislike of the confessional mode – in art. (The angers and hatreds of *El poeta en Nueva York* are quite other, though perhaps they have distant antecedents in these that I am alluding to now.) What *Perlimplín y Belisa* expresses is a loathing for the whole world of courtship, sexual parrying, 'attractiveness', and for all the predatory, censorious, dismissive attitudes that it produces in both men and women. Because a man is the principal (though not the only) victim here, we feel for him and thus experience wrath towards females for their ability to castrate men through contempt. I believe that in *Perlimplín y Belisa* Lorca's resentment at having been placed outside the 'normal' world of Granadine people, at being – possibly – mocked by girls for his failure to correspond to their images of malehood is for the first time, and almost morbidly, articulated. *He*, though young not old, is the spurned Perlimplín, and the hideous fusion of murder and suicide is his act of revenge upon stupid, judgemental, conventional society. We shall find echoes of this situation, more universalised, in *Así que pasen cinco años*. *Perlimplín y Belisa*, then, may certainly correspond to an erotic valentine, but the heart upon it is a homosexual's, bleeding cruelly to an accompaniment of screams.

Early poems too suggest a world of isolation and sadness; Lorca's progress towards the richness of understanding and sense-of-life that makes his major works so valuable was often extremely painful.

## 3

Of particular importance to our theme are the following poems in the *Libro de poemas*: 'Canción menor' ('Minor Song'); 'Balada triste' ('Sad Ballad'); 'La sombra de mi alma' ('The Shadow of My Soul'); 'Si mis manos pudieran deshojar' ('If My Hands Could Strip Leaves'); 'El canto de la miel' ('The Song of Honey'); 'Cantos nuevos' ('New Songs'); 'Preguntas' ('Questions'); 'Balada interior' ('Interior Ballad'); and the two poems both from May 1919 and entitled 'Sueño' ('Dream'). Not one of them is an entire success; there is a diffuseness about some – e.g. the 'Balada triste' – that is wholly uncharacteristic of Lorca at his best even in his youth, and, corresponding to this, many lack shape. But almost all contain lines or images of striking effectiveness, and the majority of these concern an inner agony Lorca was never quite to voice again in so frankly, ingenuously personal a way.

The 'Canción menor' would appear to describe the poet's rejection by girls (not in itself, of course, a homosexual predicament); he compares his sadness to that of Quixote and Cyrano de Bergerac (cut off from the world of courtship by eccentricity and ugliness respectively) – and most interestingly of all describes his burgeoning art as follows:

> . . .mi voz
> manchada de luz sangrienta,
> y en mi lírica canción
> llevo galas de payaso
> empolvado.

> . . .my voice
> stained with blood-coloured light,
> and in my lyrical song
> I wear the trappings of a clown
> covered in dust.[30]

Lorca is attaching himself to that world of Petrushka and 'Les saltimbanques' which he was to present so memorably in his plays.

The 'Balada triste' compares his heart to a butterfly drinking the fatal pollen of disillusionment; he refers to the *'ella impenetrable del romance'* ('the impenetrable *she* of romance'), and as in *El maleficio* one can sense a bitterness at the concealment of the real person, the real girl, in all the paraphernalia of stylised romantic love. The poem addresses itself in an often reiterated refrain to the *'niños buenos del prado'* ('good boys of the meadow') from whom Lorca perhaps – for all his affection for them – feels cut off; they would not have his particular brand of loneliness.[31] 'La sombra de mi alma' describes a state of mind in which an old life is abandoned and a new one must be embraced – but rather disjointedly, so any more exact knowledge of what had been happening to the poet is not attainable. He has, he says, arrived at the line where nostalgia must cease and lamentation turn itself into the alabaster of the spirit – which, of course, conjures up a whole host of romantic and late romantic poets, Becquer perhaps pre-eminently.[32] Better, though not what we think of now as really Lorquian, is 'Si mis manos pudieran deshojar', a lyric of the despair that afflicts the young lover through the sleepless watches of the night. The closing lines do, I think, give us a hint of the poet's apprehension of his sexual heterodoxy (though his broodings may well have had a girl as their subject) and contain an image which the later Lorca will develop with idiosyncracy and intensity:

> ¿Qué otra pasión me espera?
> ¿Será tranquila y pura?
> ¡¡Si mis dedos pudieran
> deshojar a la luna!!

> What other passion awaits me?
> Will it be tranquil and pure?
> If only my fingers could
> strip leaves off the moon!![33]

'El canto de la miel' is not really a good poem at all, and far too long. We do, however, appreciate as a result of it how the Catholicism surrounding Lorca in his earliest years was a not inconsiderable factor in that sacramental attitude towards both art and the natural world so characteristic of him later. And one stanza placed in parenthesis seems to me as good a summary of his art as any he was to make:

(Así la miel del hombre es la poesía
que mana de su pecho dolorido,
de un panal con la cera del recuerdo
formado por la abeja de lo íntimo.)

(Thus the honey of man is poetry
which flows from his afflicted breast,
from a honeycomb with the wax of memory
formed by the bee of intimacy.)[34]

The 'Cantos nuevos'[35] is a more closely worked piece, and, together with the 'Balada interior',[36] shows the beginning of Lorca's ability to fuse his Platonic sense of transmutations and echoes of perfect form with presentation of an emotional plight. In 'Cantos nuevos', for instance, the afternoon thirsts for shade, the moon for stars, the fountain for lips, and the poet for songs that will be free of moons and lilies, without dead loves. One cannot but read the deeply felt ambition to create a new kind of love-song as a protest against the hegemony in this domain of the conventional, the heterosexual. Certainly the *Libro de poemas* gives enough indication of the poet's apprehension of himself as different from the 'normal', convention-approved young man and enough disquiet of soul for us not to be surprised that it has turned out to be the first book of someone who went on to do remarkable things. The unhappinesses of the 'Sueño'[37] poems are so clearly not rhetorical mouthings even though their language is not yet that which Lorca was eventually to master, at once direct and allusive. 'Preguntas' is interesting in its revelation of the intellectual debates of the young man; against a background of cicadas he thinks of Marcus Aurelius, by running water of Socrates, by roses de-petalling into the mud of St John the Divine; interestingly it is he who earns the compliment of the last line:

¡Chico es tu corazón!

Dear is your heart![38]

The kind of tension that informs the above poems – and others like them – is surely alluded to in a (roughly) contemporaneous letter to the famous guitarist, Regino de la Maza. One is surely justified in seeing sexual disquietude and frustration as the essential subject here:

Now I've discovered something awful (don't tell this to anyone). *I haven't been born yet.* The other day I studied my past attentively. . . and none of the dead hours belonged to me because it wasn't I who had lived them, neither the hours of love, nor the hours of hate, nor the hours of inspiration. There were a thousand Federico García Lorcas, stretched out forever in the attic of time and in the storehouse of the future. I contemplated another thousand Federico García Lorcas, very tightly pressed, one on top of the other, waiting to be filled with gas in order to fly off without direction. This moment was a terribly fearful moment, my mother Lady Death had given me the key of time and for a second I understood everything. I'm living on borrowed time, what I have within is not mine; let's see if I'm going to be born.[39]

Some of the dislocation expressed here must have come from the conflict between his outer, agreeable social self which Granada and the family could approve of, and his inner yearnings and concerns. Not that this conflict always revolves round sexuality; there are also intellectual and religious departures from orthodoxy. We can see these in what is for me, and for many critics, his earliest completely successful poem, the 'Balada de la placeta' ('Ballad of the Little Square'). Here the poet is accosted by some children in a village square, and – the opening four lines and the closing four lines excepted – the 'Balada' takes the form of a dialogue between them and him. The first attribute that the children accord him is happiness. They ask:

> ¿Qué tiene tu divino
> corazón en fiesta?

> What does your divine
> rejoicing heart hold?

But then, on inquiring what the poet feels in his mouth, they are told that it is:

> El sabor de los huesos
> de mi gran calavera.

> The taste of the bones
> of my big skull.

The children ask him whether he is going far. Lorca replies:

> más allá de esas sierras,
> más allá de los mares,
> cerca de las estrellas,
> para pedirle a Cristo
> Señor que me devuelva
> mi alma antigua de niño,
> madura de leyendas,

con el gorro de plumas
y el sable de madera.

farther than those hills,
farther than the seas,
close to the stars,
to ask Christ
the Lord to give me back
my ancient soul of a child,
ripe with legends,
with the feathered cap
and the wooden sword.

The poet's pining for the harmonious life of childhood suggests the neo-Platonism that animates those English masterpieces, Vaughan's 'The Retreat' and Wordsworth's 'Ode: Intimations of Immortality'. But in fact, the tone of the poem, especially that of the above lines, is such that one is left in no doubt that Lorca does not subscribe to any orthodox Christian faith, and that even his natural neo-Platonism is offset by a strong private awareness of the void. While valuing the enhancing beauty of the mental images these philosophies engender, he feels himself compelled to confront mortal existence with a naked eye, to face mutability and death in all, including himself. And the poem ends with a brief and affecting evocation of the sufferings that extend – beyond the poet and children in the little square – even to the vegetable world:

Las pupilas enormes
de las frondas resecas,
heridas por el viento,
lloran las hojas muertas.

The enormous pupils
of the parched fronds,
wounded by the wind,
weep dead leaves.[40]

The more elliptical form of presentation, the creation of metaphors, of objective correlatives for his preoccupations – these were far more suited to Lorca's creative personality than the directly autobiographical articulation. Even the most personally charged of all his poems – those of *El poeta en Nueva York* and the *Sonetos del amor oscuro* – work on us according to their complex ordering, disordering and consequent re-ordering of images and scenes, and are no mere spontaneous overflows of feeling.

★

I want now to turn to three poems in the *Canciones 1921–1924* which, mysterious artefacts susceptible to many different interpretations, seem to me to constitute a presentation of Lorca's homosexual position.

First two poems placed in the book next to each other: 'El niño mudo' ('The Little Dumb Boy') and 'El niño loco' ('The Little Mad Boy'):

EL NIÑO MUDO

El niño busca su voz.
(La tenía el rey de los grillos.)
En una gota de agua
buscaba su voz el niño.

No la quiero para hablar;
me haré con ella un anillo
que llevará mi silencio
en su dedo pequeñito.

En una gota de agua
buscaba su voz el niño.

(La voz cautiva, a lo lejos,
se ponía un traje de grillo.)

The little boy is looking for his voice.
(The king of the crickets had it.)
In a drop of water
the little boy was looking for his voice.

I do not want it to speak with;
I shall make with it a ring
that my silence will wear
on its little finger.

In a drop of water
the little boy was looking for his voice.

(The captive voice, in the distance
was putting on a cricket's clothes.)[41]

EL NIÑO LOCO

Yo decía: 'Tarde'.
Pero no era así.
La tarde era otra cosa
que ya se había marchado.
    (Y la luz encogía
sus hombros como una niña.)

    'Tarde.' ¡Pero es inútil!
Esta es falsa, esta tiene
media luna de plomo.
La otra no vendrá nunca.
    (Y la luz como la ven todos,
jugaba a la estatua con el niño loco.)

    Aquella era pequeña
y comía granadas.
Esta es grandota y verde, yo no puedo
tomarla en brazos ni vestirla.
¿No vendrá? ¿Cómo era?
    (Y la luz que se iba dio una broma.
Separó al niño loco de su sombra.)

I said 'Afternoon.'
But it was not so.
The afternoon was something else
which had already gone away.
    (And the light was shrugging
its shoulders like a little girl.)

    'Afternoon.' But it is useless!
This is false, this has
a half-moon of lead.
The other will never come.
    (And the light as all see it,
was playing at 'statues' with the mad little boy.

    That girl was small
and was eating pomegranates.
This one is enormous and green, I am not able
to take her in my arms nor dress her.
Will she not come? What was she like?
    (And the light which was passing away played a joke.
It separated the mad little boy from his shadow.)[42]

These two lyrics both have as their subject boys isolated from their fellows, from conventional life by an infirmity (dumbness, madness) not of their own causing and which others are not able to remove.†
The little dumb boy, we observe, is actively looking for his voice though he doesn't find it and will never do so. Voice is the instrument of communication with another and in his case has disappeared from his possession into the keeping of the king of the crickets. Later this voice, a being with a life of its own, puts on a cricket's clothes. We have already explored the relation between insects – above all, crickets, cicadas and grasshoppers – and blissful sexuality. The voice in the poem can surely be read as an analogue for another instrument of communication, the sexual parts, which, in their heterodox inclination, have left the boy bereft and joined a domain where notions of conventional right and wrong don't exist.

This reading receives confirmation from the middle section of the poem. The *yo* (I) who may or may not be the eponymous little boy declares that he doesn't want his voice to talk with (e.g. to do the conventional thing with) but for his silence to wear (i.e. defiant quiet assertion of his own proclivity) like a ring on his little finger, an image with delicate but obvious phallic implication.

Much of the initial effect of 'El niño loco' derives from its magical evocation of the time of day, the ebbing of daylight that can't quite be described as 'twilight' but which marks the end of the afternoon ('*La tarde era otra cosa*') – *tarde* being used in Spain from lunch-time on to nightfall, and thus carrying atmospheric ambiguities not possible in any English rendering of the word. Such conditions always both deceive and enhance the vision with their rendering of figures or objects as changeable or uncertain. The hour conjured up for us here has clear metaphorical connotations – of shiftable and shifting identity. The little mad boy appears at one point like a statue in a game – momentarily transfixed and seemingly motionless. But the final lines of the poem part him from his shadow; thus he stands in a state of temporary severance from the human norm.

The tenderness of presentation here must be inextricably associated with the *yo* figure, himself in a state of uncertainty since he bids someone (the mad boy himself) 'afternoon' when this is visibly not quite the case. The third stanza appears to describe hesitancy and lack of success where a girl is concerned; indeed she comes to lack substance and even personality for the speaker: '*¿Como era?*' All that remains for him at this point, then, is the irregular little boy lacking a normal human property and eliciting through his vulnerable eccen-

---

†Related is the little boy in the poem 'Canción del muchacho de siete corazones' (Song of the Boy with Seven Hearts') in *Suites* (*Obras completas*, p. 726). Though he has seven hearts, he can't find his own – '*¡Pero el mío no lo encuentro!*'

tricity a curious and very articulate solicitude.

Linked to 'El niño loco' in imagery and ideas is 'Suicidio' ('Suicide') which bears an intriguing parenthetical title: ('Quizá fue por no saberte la geometría') ('Perhaps for not knowing your geometry').

> El jovencito se olvidaba.
> Eran las diez de la mañana.
>
> Su corazón se iba llenando
> de alas rotas y flores de trapo.
>
> Notó que ya no le quedaba
> en la boca más que una palabra.
>
> Y al quitarse los guantes, caía,
> de sus manos, suave ceniza.
>
> Por el balcón se veía una torre.
> El se sintió balcón y torre.
>
> Vio, sin duda, cómo le miraba
> el reloj detenido en su caja.
>
> Vio su sombra tendida y quieta
> en el blanco diván de seda.
>
> Y el joven rígido, geométrico,
> con un hacha rompío el espejo.
>
> Al romperlo, un gran chorro de sombra
> inundó la quimérica alcoba.

> The lad was becoming unconscious.
> It was ten in the morning.
>
> His heart was passing away filling
> with broken wings and rag-flowers.
>
> He noticed that there did not remain
> in his mouth more than one word.
>
> And on taking off his gloves, there fell
> from his hands a soft ash.
>
> From the balcony a tower was to be seen.
> He felt himself balcony and tower.

He saw, without doubt, how the clock
was watching him motionless in its case.

He saw his shadow spread out and quiet
on the white silk divan.

And the rigid youth, geometrical,
broke the mirror with an axe.

On shattering it, a great jet of shadow
inundated the chimerical room.[43]

First let us remark Lorca's use in the first and second couplets of the imperfect tense: we are being taken into the whole frightening process of the lad's dying. In the visible world, however – in contrast to his slipping-away into eternity (nothingness) – time can be measured, named ('*Eran las diez de la mañana*'), a significant detail which presages other obsessions with the exact moment of death and its ironic relation to death's own measurelessness (c.f. the end of *Bodas de sangre* and the 'Llanto por Ignacio Sánchez Mejías' with its insistent reiteration of the time of the bullfighter's death: '*las cinco de la tarde*' ('five o'clock in the afternoon').

All the unsatisfactory matter of his brief life, those romantic longings which will now never know any kind of realisation fill the boy's ebbing being, together with the sense that they are now but broken toys:

Su corazón se iba llenando
de alas rotas y flores de trapo.

And now the tense changes. For an event occurs in the dying mind which necessitates the preterite. And the preterite is to persist for the duration of the poem:

Notó que ya no le quedaba
en la boca más que una palabra.

But what this word is Lorca never tells us, leaving us to puzzle over it after the agony of the subsequent verses and to connect it – somehow – with the geometry of the title's parenthetic qualification and of the poem's penultimate line.

It is not the only thing that we are not told in this strange piece. We never know how the boy killed himself or what were the circumstances leading up to his death:

Por el balcón se veía una torre.
El se sintió balcón y torre.

Balconies and towers are, of course, places which suicides could use for their purpose, but there is no reason to suppose that the youth of the poem has done so. Rather he appears to be dying in his bedroom (the clock in its case, a view presumably to be seen from the balcony window, the white silk divan). The point of the balcony and the tower, so patently important, must therefore be quite other. The resemblance of tower to penis scarcely needs commenting on; but if one envisages the balcony in terms of old Spanish houses, as a small, arcane receptacle for the sun, it can be seen as a correlative of the vagina or anus. The youth felt himself to be both tower and balcony, in other words he partook of male and female, took a double sexual role. In the seventh couplet Lorca develops further the picture of the boy looking down on his body as he quits it, and we notice another use of shadow as detached and separate from the flesh-and-blood entity that produces it: symbol as in 'Narciso'[44] and 'El niño loco' of a departure between actual and societal selves.

The seventh and eigth couplets are, it must be conceded, very hard to comprehend even when we realise that they contain the key to the tragic death. Though before the poem began we were told that perhaps the suicide did not know his geometry, it is only now, at this late stage, that the idea is turned to. In the last seconds of his life (in which he passes from being *jovencito* to the dignity of *joven*) the subject of the poem is suddenly called *geométrico*. So what is this geometry that the lad, so intimately addressed in the subtitle, once might not have known and now apparently does?

Could it not be the fitting together of human bodies in sexual positions? Perhaps the lad had never been able to know the conventional procreative position, and maybe shame at his inability led him to take his life. But now – and he is after all tower and balcony in one – he appreciates that another kind of fitting-together, two male bodies with interchanging roles – is possible, is beautiful even. And now resolute before extinction he shatters the mirror (life, distorted, as he has known it), and great shadows proceeding from the real world – the domain of death – invade the room, engulfing him and it, and making 'chimerical' the whole ordinary world in which he had lived so unhappily that he decided to put an end to things. Reality can best be achieved through fidelity to one's own deepest desires.

'Suicidio', it will be evident, can be viewed as an indirect narrative, a 'secret narrative' as the contemporary poet Andrew Motion would say, a concealed or transposed ballad. Speaking on the ballad in his lecture on the *Romancero gitano* Lorca said:

From my very first steps in poetry, in 1919, I devoted much thought to the ballad form, because I realised it was the vessel best shaped to my sensibility. The ballad had gone nowhere from the last exquisite little ballads of Góngora until the Duque de Rivas made it sweet, fluent, and domestic and Zorrilla filled it with water lilies, shades, and sunken bells . . .†

The typical ballad had always been a narration, and it was the narrative element that made its physiognomy so charming, for when it grew lyrical without an echo of anecdote it would turn into a song. I wanted to fuse the narrative ballad with the lyrical without changing the quality of either, and this is achieved in some of the poems of the *Romancero gitano*, for example the 'Romance sonámbulo', where one gets the sensation of anecdote in a poignant dramatic atmosphere and no one knows what is happening, not even me, for poetic mystery is also mysterious to the poet who imparts it, often unknowingly.[45]

This description of 'Romance sonámbulo' is equally applicable, I think, to the three poems we have been dealing with – though of course Lorca is being somewhat disingenuous in his disavowals of comprehension of his work and does not, I believe, mean us to abandon attempts at attaining this ourselves. The 'Romance sonámbulo' is in fact, as we have seen, a far richer, more complex production even than 'Suicidio', but perhaps its success and that of its fellows in the *Romancero gitano* owe a good deal to these ventures.

Whatever his later resentments against it, whatever his attitude towards the turn that came in his poetry after the publication and enormous success of the *Romancero gitano*, there is no doubt that the poems which constitute that book seemed to Lorca as he was working on them the most exciting, the most artistically *whole* works of his to date.

## 4

Before considering the artistic aspects of the *Romancero gitano* that give it its unassailable place in the earlier Lorquian canon, one must pay homage to Lorca's membership – however loose – of the group of Spanish poets who, a year before the publication of Lorca's most successful book so far, declared themselves the *Generación del '27* in homage to the great Spanish poet Luís de Góngora whose tercentenary fell in 1927. Lorca, like several other poets of his circle, gave a

---

†Here Lorca refers to two famous European–influenced figures of the romantic movement, Angel de Saavedra Remirez de Baquedano (1791–1865) and Jose Zorrilla y Moral (1817–1893).

lecture on Góngora, and what he says in it is very relevant to the direction his art was taking:

> The metaphor is an exchange of clothes, ends, or occupations among natural objects or ideas. It has its planes and orbits. The metaphor unites two antagonistic worlds by means of an equestrian leap of the imagination. The cinematographer Jean Epstein says that it is a 'theorem in which one jumps directly from the hypothesis to the conclusion'. Exactly.
>
> The originality of Don Luís de Góngora, apart from grammar, is in his method of *hunting* images, which he invented. He studied these images using his dramatic powers of self-criticism. A man with an amazing capacity for myth, he studies the beautiful conceptions of the ancients and, fleeing the mountains and their luminous visions, he sits down on the shores of the sea where the wind
>
> > le corre, en lecho azul de aguas marinas,
> > turquesadas cortinas.
> > (draws round him on the blue couch of the sea,
> > turquoise curtains.)
>
> And there he ties down and bridles his imagination, as though he were a sculptor, in order to begin his poem. So greatly does he want to dominate it and round it off that he unconsciously loves islands, for he thinks, with good reason, that a man can possess and govern, better than any other piece of land, the defined, visible orb that is limited by water. His imaginative machinery is perfect. There are times when each image is a created myth.[46]

These words seem eminently applicable to the metaphors that fill *El poeta en Nueva York*, and are not inappropriate – comparatively easy of access though it is – for the *Romancero gitano* itself.                              .

Lorca's fellow poets of the *Generación del '27* would also have contributed through the stimulus their company provided to the artistic sophistication of his work in the latter half of the Twenties. Apart from the roughly contemporaneous Nashville Fugitives† no more distinguished group of friendly, mutually helpful poets has existed anywhere this century. One can find cousinships between Lorca and almost any of the inner circle of the *Generación*: Vicente Aleixandre shares his metaphysical/ontological preoccupations, and his ability to create an imagistic paradise as a place of constant

---

†These young writers, mostly from Vanderbilt University, followed the lead of John Crowe Ransom. They espoused their native South in its rich traditional culture – from an Agrarian standpoint – and sought to give it a literary expression that brought it into the contemporary world.

reference; Rafael Alberti has an idealistic quality, a directness, that makes his work kin to Lorca's, though he is far more overtly political. His ambitious excursion into surrealism *Sobre los ángeles* (1929) is thought by some to have spurred Lorca towards *El poeta en Nueva York*. Then there was Luis Cernuda who like Lorca was homosexual, and made the complications and anguishes of his loves – as well as their existential significance – the subject of poems of a sombre loveliness. And to these poets we must add the influences of Salvador Dalí and Luis Buñuel.

Two features of the *Romancero gitano* which were not commented on in any detail in Chapter Two need mentioning here. One is the artistic unity of the work which points towards that symphonic nature of *El poeta* which I have already been remarked. The second is the emergence of heterodox desire as a subject demanding serious and exacting poetic treatment.

When discussing the *Romancero gitano* – both in letters and in the *conferencia* of 1935 – Lorca was always insistent upon the book's organic unity. He gave the *romances* which comprise it not only names but numbers, and would take the audience of the *conferencia* through them in sequence. To follow Lorca's own approach to his work is to appreciate more easily and fully that overall imaginative design, that closely worked development of interrelating themes, of which he himself was so proud and to which readers have perhaps been insufficiently attentive. It must always be remembered that Lorca himself spoke of the *Romancero* as a *poema* in the singular, also, as we have noted, as a '*retablo* (altar-piece or puppet-show) of Andalucía' with 'figures of millenial depths, and just one character': *pena*, grief. A poem, an altar-piece and a puppet-show have this in common: each is made to be regarded as an entity, an entirety.

Inspection will reveal the volume as balancing very carefully the male and the female, the dark and the light, the moon and the sun. Appropriately it opens with a poem about what so many ancient cosmologies have thought of as the supreme feminine constituent of the universe, the moon: 'Romance de la luna, luna'. (In Greek mythology in which, as has already been noted, Lorca was immersing himself at the time of composition of these *romances*, the moon antedates the sun; Diana/Artemis was born before her twin, Apollo, at whose birth indeed she assisted.) And the *Romancero* ends with the most turbulently passionate of its poems – that on the Biblical story of incest, 'Thamar y Amnón'; this gives the moon a dominating role, responsible perhaps for the deviant emotions depicted with such force, but in the final lines she gives way to the sun. This splendidly emerging sun heralds the Apollonian qualities the poet wished to inform his subsequent work. (And while it was not until after the New York period that they were fully to do so, there are important Apollonian injunctions in 'El rey de Harlem' and at the very conclusion of 'Oda a Walt Whitman'.)

If we think of the *Romancero gitano* in musical terms, there is a break in movements, so to speak, after the stark 'Romance de la pena negra' at which we have already looked. Lorca in his *conferencia* on the work himself remarked on the caesura that occurs in it: 'Suddenly the archangels that express the three great Andalucías burst into the poem:'[47]– San Miguel of Granada, San Rafael of Córdoba, San Gabriel of Sevilla.

We are back in the world of *El poema del cante jondo* with its apostrophes to the respective merits of the three Andalusian cities, and of certain of the *Canciones*, for instance the lyric 'Arbolé' ('Tree'), in which representatives of Granada, Córdoba and Sevilla tempt – unsuccessfully – a girl picking olives to leave her work and sample their various joys.[48] And interestingly, with this return to the three loved cities, with this *agitanización* of their patron archangels, for the first time in the book – indeed, to any proper extent, for the first time in Lorca's work to date – the homoerotic sounds bold and undisguised. And by 'homoerotic' I mean a frank and patently sexual delight in the male form. Archangels are by their very nature heralds, bringers of glad tidings, and San Miguel, San Rafael and San Gabriel fanfare in a gay treatment of men that will persist for the rest of the *poema* and for that matter of Lorca's oeuvre.

But before considering this properly let us just clarify that point about balance between male and female that has been effected in the *Romancero gitano* up to the archangelic entrance. 'Romance de la luna, luna' presented a chaste woman and a small boy; 'Preciosa y el aire' a chaste girl and a cruelly lascivious male. 'Reyerta' took us into a male world but one without (named) sexual passions; in 'Romance sonámbulo', on the other hand, there were many passions, none shown in any realised form, all connected to death, and established with the sexes separated from each other by a symbolic and actual tract of mountainland. In the wistful 'La monja gitana' ('The Gypsy Nun') a girl sits alone but with her thoughts upon men; in 'La casada infiel' a man and a woman make sexual use of each other, while in the 'Romance de la pena negra' a girl gathers into her being all the merits and mysterious apprehensions attributed severally to the female Gypsy protagonists of the other poems. There is a palpable tenderness in her portraiture. But now, and onwards, the poet exercises this tenderness upon the male figures. Maybe the unearthly status of the heroes of the next three poems enabled Lorca to release his lyrical grateful responses to earthly male charms.

With San Rafael and San Miguel, Lorca draws our attention to a homosexuality *outside* himself, and present in conventional religious ritual and iconography. The relation between San Rafael and the little boys making their prescribed fun of him is undoubtedly pederastic, but the pederasty has been so long absorbed in traditional rite that it is not acknowledged for what it is.[49] San Miguel – of Granada itself[50] – provides an even more interesting occasion for Lorca to connect his own homosexual feelings with those accepted, but not named, by an Andalusian community. The archangel is evoked for us in terms of the statue to him which stands in a chapel on the Sacro Monte in Granada and which, on his *romería* (festal pilgrimage), 29 September, is adorned with lanterns.

Lorca – who actually calls the whole poem a *romería* – hails San Miguel as '*efebo de tres mil noches*' ('ephebe of three thousand nights'), '*fragante de agua colonia*' ('fragrant with eau-de-cologne'); he stays serenely in his alcove with his swirl of petticoats; he is '*rey de los globos*' ('king of the balloons') and possesses '*el primor berberisco*' ('the berber elegance'). Editors Allen Josephs and Juan Caballero have detected irony here; I do not.[51] That 'camp' element in Lorca, so strong as a boy when he would have delighted in the dressing-up and general festivities of the *romería* to his city's patron saint, is surely asserting itself here. The term *efebo* has pejorative connotations only for those hostile to trans-sexual behaviour.

Just as in that earlier poem of the sequence, 'La monja gitana', Lorca pointed out how traditional pious practice incorporates maidenly fixations upon certain aspects of male sexuality,[52] so in 'San Miguel (Granada)' he draws attention to a relish in male effeminacy present in much time-hallowed religious ceremonial. In doing so he is both linking himself to and getting his own back on his own city where he had had – with less than relish – to accept being branded effeminate.

The last poem of the *Romancero gitano*, the powerful 'Thamar y Amnón', asserts, for all the tragic fate of the protagonists, the compulsive force of sexual desire – whatever the official attitude of society to the legitimacy of its object. In his wonderful descriptions of Amnón burning with forbidden passion Lorca must have been releasing from his memory similar occasions of his own – the moral validity of which would have been questioned by the *bien-pensants* of his society, questioned and condemned. And in the emotive heat of his work Lorca achieves a Daliesque release of images from his unconscious. This indicates that when he will take his own unorthodox nature as a central subject he will deepen and extend this process. Thus in the *Romancero gitano*, particularly in 'Thamar y Amnón', the Rimbaud-like déréglements of *El poeta* are presaged. These occasions should have warned the percipient reader that, faced with a crisis in which his sexuality played a key part, the poet would be unable to check a veritable tempest of unconscious symbolism, such as he unleashes in his New York poem-cycle. Occasions such as this:

> Amnón a las tres y media
> se tendió sobre la cama.
> Toda la alcoba sufría
> con sus ojos llenos de alas.

La luz, maciza, sepulta
pueblos en la arena parda,
o descubre transitorio
coral de rosas y dalias.
Linfa de pozo oprimida
brota silencio en las jarras.
En el musgo de los troncos
la cobra tendida canta.
Amnón gime por la tela
fresquísima de la cama.
Yedra del escalofrío
cubre su carne quemada.

Amnon at half-past three
stretched himself upon his bed.
The whole bedroom suffered
with his eyes full of wings.
The unassailable light buries
villages in the brown sand,
or reveals transitory
coral of roses and dahlias.
Oppressed water from the well
blossoms silent in the jars.
In the moss of the trunks
the cobra stretched-out sings.
Amnon moans in the very cold
sheets of his bed.
The ivy of a shudder
envelops his burned flesh.[53]

To *El poeta en Nueva York* we must now return. That social indignation and that love of people close to the atavistic which haunt the *Romancero gitano* are transferred onto the victims of the Depression and, in particular, onto the Black community of New York. That awareness of the strength of brute nature shows itself in the many anticipations of the eventual subjugation of the city by rebellious plant and animal life – and the lines which describe this process are decidedly surrealist, Daliesque, and connote the cataclysms that had already taken place within Lorca's psyche. The sense of people against a background of death and eternity – fortified by his realisation of his religious heterodoxy as expressed in the moving and reverent 'Oda al santísimo sacramento del altar' ('Ode to the Holy Sacrament of the Altar')[54] which shocked its dedicatee, the devout Manuel de Falla – becomes a vision of man versus the void, to which we have already paid tribute. And for reasons which I have tried to make clear, homosexuality could now emerge from the tacit or the indirect and become a major theme and vantage-point.

It is now time to examine the three great climaxes of *El poeta en Nueva York* – 'El rey de Harlem' (originally called 'Oda al Rey de Harlem') and the two odes: 'Grito hacia Roma (Desde la torre del Crysler Building)' and the 'Oda a Walt Whitman'. These are labyrinthine honeycombs for the finest honey.

# Chapter Five

# Towards the Kingdom
# of the Ear of Corn

There is no doubt that the Blacks exercise great influence in
North America, and, I don't care what anyone says, they are the
most delicate and spiritual element of that world. Because they
believe, because they hope and they sing, and because they have
an exquisite religious purity that saves them from all their
dangerous present-day troubles.[1]

The first poem in the cycle to celebrate the spiritual zest of the Blacks
does so in terms highly reminiscent of those in which Lorca had
apostrophised the Andalusian Gypsies:

> Con la ciencia del tronco y del rastro
> llenan de nervios luminosos la arcilla
> y patinan lúbricos por aguas y arenas
> gustando la amarga frescura de su milenaria saliva.

> With the science of tree-trunk and pathway
> they fill with luminous nerves the clay
> and skate lubricious on waters and sands
> tasting the bitter freshness of their millenial saliva.[2]

And when in the dives of Harlem he heard the Blacks singing and
making music, he was irresistibly reminded of the Gypsy *cantaores*, for
like the Andalusian musicians, they were charged with atavistic forces
from an earlier, freer life, forces their performances not merely
expressed but served:

In one cabaret – Small's Paradise . . . I saw a naked dancer
shaking convulsively under an invisible rain of fire. But while
everyone shouted as though believing her possessed by the
rhythm, I was able, for a second, to catch remoteness in her eyes
– remoteness, reserve, the conviction that she was far away from
that admiring audience of foreigners and Americans. All Harlem
was like her.[3]

For, despite the exuberance of its inhabitants, Harlem – Lorca's favourite quarter of New York – did not impart a sense of happiness. It was not like Jerez de la Frontera at Christmas-time when the Gypsies were in possession (c.f. 'Romance de la Guardia Civil española'), though it amply had the capacity to be like it; it was:

> the most important Black city in the world, where lewdness has an innocent accent that makes it disturbing and religious. A neighbourhood of rosy houses, full of pianolas and radios and cinemas, but with the *mistrust* that characterises the race. . .I wanted to make the poem of the Black race in North America and to emphasise the pain that Blacks feel to be Black in a contrary world. They are slaves of all the white man's inventions and machines. . .[4]

This 'poem of the Black race' is 'El rey de Harlem', this eponymous character being the 'spirit of the Black race'. Just as the Gypsy was 'the loftiest, most profound and aristocratic element of my country. . .the very keeper of the glowing embers, blood, and alphabet of Andalusian truth', 'but was in danger (c.f. description of Antoñito el Camborio) of having sell his 'millenial voice to the gentlemen who have nothing except money, which is very little indeed',[5] so the Black in New York can be described by Lorca, when addressing Harlem, as:

> . . .tu gran rey prisionero con un traje de conserje!

> . . .your great king prisoner with a janitor's suit![6]

'*¡Ay Harlem! ¡Ay Harlem! ¡Ay Harlem!*' Lorca gives the cry of the *siguiriya* on behalf of this captive, tragic, inspirited city-within-a city. The Black man, inheritor of a culture that awedly accepted its determination by Nature, is now forced to be, in V.S. Naipaul's phrase, a 'mimic man', and a subservient one at that, moving among man-made things not of his own devising. His own rites and enthusiasms too often can find expression only in acts of destruction (including self-destruction).

The poem opens with lines that will be repeated:

> Con una cuchara,
> arrancaba los ojos a los cocodrilos
> y golpeaba el trasero de los monos.
> Con una cuchara.

> With a spoon
> he scooped out the eyes of the crocodiles
> and spanked the behinds of the monkeys.
> With a spoon.[7]

The Black king should, of course, have a golden sceptre or some such object. In his African life he could either have dominated the beasts or established communion with them; in this present fettered life of his he has to be content with mutilating one creature and coarsely sporting with another – though both actions do suggest a certain magic power inaccessible to the white. (Surely the strange stone-like eyes of the crocodile and the vivid-hued erogenous behinds of the monkeys are chosen by the poet to suggest the wondrousness of primeval Nature.) It is only fair to say here that Rafael Martínez Nadal – who heard Lorca himself read this poem – takes the spoon as a huge ritual instrument, part of an authentic African chief's 'arsenal'.[8] But in fact this doesn't change the essential point of the lines, which is that *el rey de Harlem* is not in his rightful kingdom.

His humiliation fills Lorca with rage. Only violence, he feels, can bring an end to it. Throughout the poem there is – what has already been alluded to – an insistence that the vegetable and animal worlds will take appalling, justified revenge upon this Nature-spurning society. In humans too there is a surge of energy which the materialist world cannot satisfy:

> Sangre furiosa por debajo de las pieles. . .
>
> Blood furious underneath the skins. . .[9]

Only force of some kind will end the reign of anti-Nature which has made water pestilent, spread slime and shit everywhere, filled up the wombs of American girls with coins and emasculated the white youths, and has given power to worthless, cruel people who traffic in health-destroying liquor and other alleged, commercially productive restoratives.

It would be dishonest, in this context, not to mention one of the most disturbing passages of the poem:

> Es preciso matar al rubio vendedor de aguardiente,
> a todos los amigos de la manzana y de la arena,
> y es necesario dar con los puños cerrados
> a las pequeñas judías que tiemblan llenas de burbujas,
> para que el rey de Harlem cante con su muchedumbre. . .
>
> It's necessary to kill the fair-haired seller of liquor,
> all the friends of the apple and sand,
> and it's necessary to hit with clenched fists
> the little Jewesses who tremble full of bubbles,
> so that the king of Harlem may sing with his multitude. . .[10]

It's not difficult to see why corrupting bootleggers should be killed –

or people who support mistaken condemnations of sexual freedom tantamount to recommendations of aridity (*los amigos de la manzana y de la arena*). But why should the little Jewesses be hit? Some translators have hesitated over these lines, bowdlerising them (for *judías* can also mean 'beans'), but I think we must take the more probable reading and try to see what Lorca is getting at here.

There is, I think, no question of Lorca being anti-Semitic. What he dislikes are hegemonies and he is making here a rather dubious equation between the Jews and New York's rich business community – the New World's *caciques* represented by the most spoilt members of any oligarchy, the young marriageable girls. In fact Lorca was among the first signatories of a petition against Hitler's Germany, on 1 May 1933, and in a Buenos Aires interview of 25 December 1933 presented himself as 'un buen amigo de los judíos' ('a good friend of the Jews').[11] Increasingly, though, he was no friend to the rich!

And he *does* seem to me to suggest that some sort of revolution is the only way for freedom to be established, for the counterfeit death that has laid its hands on our society to disappear and natural life, natural death – familiars of the Blacks back in Africa – to be restored. The machine must be overthrown and the social hierarchy with it. Then the Black man can dance again, and with him all who are proud to belong to the inspirited world the Creator made. That is why Lorca exhorts the Blacks not to dally on the byways of Anglo-Saxon/Jewish life; not to imitate the habits of the hegemony; not to search for their age-old masks in the clefts of the great walls that are New York's skyscraper buildings, in some merely playful attempt at racial assertion. Rather they must concentrate on what they are all children of: the sun which Lorca can now celebrate (inspired by the people of Harlem) as he hadn't been able to since 'Thamar y Amnón':

> Buscad el gran sol del centro
> hechos una piña zumbadora.
> El sol que se desliza por los bosques
> seguro de no encontrar una ninfa,
> el sol que destruye números y no ha cruzado nunca un sueño,
> el tatuado sol que baja por el río
> y muge seguido de caimanes.

> Search for the great sun of the centre
> yourselves being made a humming pine-cone.
> The sun that glides through the forests
> certain of not finding a nymph,
> the sun that destroys figures and has never penetrated a dream,
> the tattooed sun that descends on the river
> and hollers followed by crocodiles.[12]

The sun – Apollo; God's eye – will bring about the Blacks' ultimate redemption.

★

When we read 'Grito hacia Roma (Desde la torre de Crysler Building)' we should envisage what was then the tallest building in New York City (for the Empire State Building had not been completed) matching itself against the greatest dome of Christendom: a dialogue adjudicated by a poet now under the shadow of the first but who had been brought up under the shadow of the latter. The poet's mind is as unhappy (it would at first seem) as at any other point in the cycle; images that have formerly sustained him, as they have sustained generations of mankind, know only fractured or travestied forms in his present imaginative weather: the apple is bruised; a coral hand bearing a chrysalis of fire tears apart the clouds; a rose wounds; a man pisses on luminous doves – neither the state of mental déréglement nor the empathy with the desolate inner world of Dalí need further comment here. The poet's distress is occasioned as elsewhere by the brutality of the life around him and by his feeling of a total absence of such a culture as Catholicism which, however inefficaciously, had at least counselled against materialism and its attendant woes.

> Porque ya no hay quien reparta el pan ni el vino,
> ni quien cultive hierbas en la boca del muerto,
> ni quien abra los linos del reposo,
> ni quien llore por las heridas de los elefantes.

> Because there is no one who might distribute the bread
>     and the wine,
> or who might cultivate grasses in the mouth of the dead man,
> or who might make ready the linen of rest,
> or who might weep for the wounds of the elephants.[13]

It is not just that there is no compassion in the society in which Lorca has found himself, it is that its whole business consciously tends *away* from humane activity, rendering it, in its *own* view, superfluous, though in the truly religious man's view, more obligatory than ever. The multiple activities of the city are likened to the forging of chains that everybody (including the still-to-be-born) must wear, to the making by carpenters of coffins, bleak, secular affairs which do not even have the traditional cross painted on them. The apportioning of bread and wine, the work of carpenters – these have the most obvious possible Christian reference. The refusal to bother about bread and wine (staple peasant fare in Lorca's southern Europe) for the poor who so badly need them is the same as refusing to administer the body and blood of Christ; the restrictive application of the carpenter's skills is analogous to a destructive restriction of the divine carpenter himself. This is made abundantly clear in the last lines of this section:

> Pero el hombre vestido de blanco
> ignora el misterio de la espiga,
> ignora el gemido de la parturienta,
> ignora que Cristo puede dar agua todavía,
> ignora que la moned quema el beso de prodigio
> y da la sangre del cordero al pico idiota del faisán.

> But the man dressed in white
> ignores the mystery of the ear of corn,
> ignores the moan of the woman giving birth,
> ignores that Christ can still provide water,
> ignores that money burns the prodigal's kisses
> and gives the blood of the lamb to the stupid beak of the pheasant.[14]

Though the 'Grito hacia Roma' is by no means free from obscurity, here there is surely none. The man who serves business – dressed in the then modish white suit – denies Christ in everything that he does, Christ being identified with all that is deep and quickening in life: corn, water, the uterus. The symbol of *la espiga* we will encounter again at the conclusion of the next ode – with which this should always be read in conjunction. Christ made use of the metaphor of corn for his kingdom many times; symbolically it was for plucking ears of corn on the Sabbath that the disciples were reprimanded by the Pharisees. Corn also has strong fertility associations (e.g. Ceres) and – as in the legend of John Barleycorn – stands for perpetual renewal/ rebirth through the male phallus. Money burning the prodigal's kiss suggests the cancellation of mercy embodied in the story of the Prodigal Son (surely the most powerful and persuasive of all the parables) and as for the last line it becomes meaningful at once if it is remembered that the pheasant is a promiscuous bird and connected with ideas of indulgence, conspicuous waste, etc. in folk bestiaries.

Lorca insists, however, that there *is* love everywhere and even in this blighted city, unknown to, or passed over by, those in powerful positions in it. There is love in hovels and ditches, and '*en el oscurísimo beso punzante debajo de las almohadas*' ('in the darkest kiss piercing underneath the pillows').[15] Bearing in mind the later, almost invariable, association of the adjective *oscuro* with homosexual,† it is, I think, tempting to read this line as a reference to the kind of sex (involving love) held in such neurotic horror by American conventional society. Wherever it exists, there will come an old man to

---

†Some of the *Sonetos del amor oscuro (Sonnets of the Dark Love)* may have been begun in New York.

announce it, to say '*Amor, amor, amor*' and '*Paz, paz, paz*' while crowds react in various ways, some people ecstatic, some hostile. But where, at their apocalyptic moment, will the old man come from? Not I think from Rome itself; the poem shows great sympathy for Christianity but not, in the end, for the Church. What the Church represents may be far more valuable than the materialism served by New York, but nevertheless the idea cannot be escaped that the Vatican as much as the Chrysler Building is a citadel of cruel authority, of domination over people – indeed peoples – and takes little heed of the intricacies of their lives as they have to live them. And so finally it is perhaps no more effective against misery than any more naked citadel of capitalism. Until that old man with his cries of peace and love arrives, the sufferings, alas, will continue: boys will be terrorised by bosses, women will figuratively (and maybe literally) drown in oil, people will scream out loud with their heads full of shit until the cities tremble like girls:

> porque queremos el pan nuestro de cada día,
> flor de aliso y perenne ternura desgranada,
> porque queremos que se cumpla la voluntad de la Tierra
> que da sus frutos para todos.

> because we want our daily bread,
> alder flower and perennial threshed tenderness,
> because we want the will of the Earth to be fulfilled
> that yields up its fruits for all of us.[16]

These last lines indicate the telluric and holistic philosophies with which, after this self-acknowledged disenchantment with official Catholicism, Lorca would wish to concern himself. America had, of course, produced such a philosophy of its own – that Jeffersonian belief in man and his harmonious relation with Nature which derives to some extent from Thomas Paine and from Jean-Jacques Rousseau. The fine Southern novelist Madison Jones, who has made Jefferson-ianism one of his principal fictional themes, puts it thus: 'Simply, it held that man in the state of nature is good, that evil is not a positive thing or force but simply a negation of good caused by the corrupt institutions of civilisation and the dead hand of the past.'[17] Most powerful of all the literary celebrants of this philosophy was America's first national bard, Walt Whitman. One can refer to him so because he was himself so obsessed by the vision of America as a society which could express and manifest a wholly new attitude to humanity. The self, not institutions or ossified custom, was to be the moral arbitrator, and poetic form and diction would have to be re-forged to champion this exhilarating credo, at once humanist and transcendental. And so now to Whitman it was that Lorca turned his attention.

★

'Good in all,' Whitman asserted in 'Song at Sunset':

> In the satisfaction and aplomb of animals,
> In the annual return of the seasons,
> In the hilarity of youth,
> In the strength and flush of manhood,
> In the grandeur and exquisiteness of old age,
> In the superb vistas of death.

And later in the same poem:

> To be conscious of my body, so satisified, so large!
> To be this incredible God I am!
> To have gone forth among other Gods, these men and women
>     I love![18]

Thus the Godhead was located in every human, and America was to be the first society to do this Godhead justice.

> Solitary, singing in the West, I strike up for a New World. . .
>
> Americanos! conquerors! marches humanitarian!
> Foremost! century marches! Libertad! masses!
> For you a programme of chants.[19]

Unfettered by the rituals and shibboleths of older society America could arise, the first true democracy on the face of the world. In the light of this hope, and in its furtherance, all activities could be seen as consecrated (and by a God, for Whitman seems to have acknowledged one, immanent in all creation). These activities could (perhaps should) include commerce, manual tasks, even (as in the case of the Civil War) fighting, because those engaged in them were bound to another in this great enterprise of joy; moreover all taking part were lovable in their fleshly forms (Whitman demanded as part of the new process that he was praising an unashamedly exultant attitude to the human body) and yet worthy of reverence as vessels of the eternal spirit:

> The soul,
> Forever and forever – longer than soil is brown and solid – longer
>     than water ebbs and flows. . .
> I will make the poems of my body and of mortality,
> For I think I shall then supply myself with the poems of
>     my soul and of immortality.[20]

Much of this Lorca, reading the poems in the Spanish versions of the socialist/humanist poet León Felipe, would have found intensely sympathetic. He was a natural democrat particularly attracted to peoples living an instinctive life; his vision of the whole natural world as inspirited would have encountered much that was sympathetic in the pantheistic/transcendentalist exultations of Whitman.

It is hard to think that Lorca would not have responded keenly to 'Out of the Cradle Endlessly Rocking', for instance, with its marvellous picture of love at work through all living things, epitomised by a pair of seabirds. But Lorca would have had another and still more important reason for ardent response to Whitman – the sexuality they shared. Homosexuality plays a determining and complex role in Whitman's work. His vision of a society in a state of creative flux, with an open road as its metaphoric and literal artery, made him espouse a camaraderie that becomes comradeshp, a universal generosity of gesture and salutation that does not exclude physical demonstration. Some of this has clear roots in the kind of *brüderschaft* needed in pioneer, expansionist activities inevitably carried on by men rather than by women. It is a philosophy for the most part deeply anti-domestic, though Whitman doesn't always face up to this; in historical terms Whitman saw how articulated friendship among men *had* been a unique constituent in the opening up and making of America; therefore he wanted to hail her as a country based, in a totally new way, upon a glorious male love, itself different in quality from any that had gone before:

> Come, I will make the continent indissoluble,
> I will make the most splendid race the sun ever shone upon,
> I will make divine magnetic lands,
>  With the love of comrades,
>   With the life-long love of comrades.
>
> I will plant companionship thick as trees along all the rivers of
>      America, and along the shores of the great lakes, and all
>      over the prairies,
> I will make inseparable cities with their arms about each other's
>      necks,
>  By the love of comrades,
>   By the manly love of comrades.[21]

But, of course, for Whitman it wasn't only a matter of entering into some joyous male communion – he was homosexual in the full sense of the word; he fell in love with members of his own sex and was drawn to them erotically. Of this his poetry – particularly the remarkable group called 'Calamus' – bears abundant testimony.

Calamus, a kind of rush, and the live-oak tree (growing sturdily in the Southern states) symbolise the men he loves:

> We two boys together clinging,
> One the other never leaving,
> Up and down the roads going, North and South excursions making,
> Power enjoying, elbows stretching, fingers clutching,
> Arm'd and fearless, eating, drinking, sleeping, loving. . .[22]

and, more passionately still, because more intimately:

> O camerado close! O you and me at last, and us two only.
> O a word to clear one's path ahead endlessly!
> O something ecstatic and undemonstrable! O music wild!
> O now I triumph – and you shall also;
> O hand in hand – O wholesome pleasure – O one more desirer and lover!
> O to haste firm holding – to haste, haste on with me![23]

Lorca in his own crisis of love must have found Whitman's proclamatory pride in his sexual condition both assuring and disconcerting. His ode to Whitman reveals this double attitude and helps to give the poem its haunting ambiguity.

Lorca opens up the 'Oda' with lines of a strong, surging rhythm that brings to mind both certain poems of his own *Romancero gitano* and works of Whitman's. The scene they depict certainly owes much to Walt Whitman. American place with its atmosphere of newness and American practical activity are saluted, and young men stand at the radiating centre:

> Por el East River y el Bronx
> los muchachos cantaban enseñando sus cinturas,
> con la rueda, el aceite, el cuero y el martillo.
> Noventa mil mineros sacaban la plata de las rocas
> y los niños dibujaban escaleras y perspectivas.

> By the East River and the Bronx,
> the young men were singing baring their waists,
> with the wheel, the oil, the leather and the hammer.
> Ninety thousand miners were extracting silver from the rocks
> and the boys were drawing ladders and perspectives.[24]

Here we see Whitman's vigorous, comradely mechanicals approached with something of the delight that Lorca manifested in Andalusian

Gypsy lads and country boys. But no sooner does that comparison register than one begins to object – and for reasons similar to the feeling that Lorca expresses in the powerful following lines:

> Pero ninguno se dormía,
> ninguno quería ser el río,
> ninguno amaba las hojas grandes,
> ninguno la lengua azul de la playa.

> But no one was sleeping,
> no one was wishing to be the river,
> no one was loving the great leaves,
> no one the blue tongue of the beach.[25]

That divorce from Nature that Lorca saw as such an unassailable feature of New York life makes these American boys – unlike their Spanish counterparts – unable to enter into the transmutations of all living beings that Lorca believed to be essential for a meaningful existence. Because what are these boys doing, for all their strength and camaraderie, but serving industry, the pursuit of money, the intensification of Mammon's sway? The next lines amplify this idea, and come to a climax in a familiar cry:

> Nueva York de cieno,
> Nueva York de alambre y de muerte.
> ¿Qué ángel llevas oculto en la mejilla?
> ¿Qué voz perfecta dirá las verdades del trigo?
> ¿Quién el sueño terrible de tus anémonas manchadas?

> New York of slime,
> New York of wire and death.
> What angel do your carry in your cheek?
> What faultless voice will speak the truths of the wheat?
> Who the dreadful dream of your stained anemones?[26]

The poet then turns aside from the New York in which the industrious and the squalid are so inextricably mixed to address the man who might constitute the answer to these questions, Walt Whitman himself. The lines in which he does so – and those which develop out of them – show how deeply and thoroughly Lorca had pondered the American poet's work; they show an intense familiarity with both his philosophy and its most characteristic articulations:

> Ni un solo momento, viejo hermoso Walt Whitman,
> he dejado de ver tu barba llena de mariposas,
> ni tus hombros de pana gastados por la luna,
> ni tus muslos de Apolo virginal. . .

> Not for a single moment, old beautiful Walt Whitman,
> have I ceased to see your beard full of butterflies,
> nor your corduroy shoulders worn thin by the moon,
> nor your thighs of virginal Apollo. . .[27]

Butterflies are a common and cherished symbol of Whitman's poetry (as of Lorca's); he too would appear to have been very influenced by Platonic ideas, and for him as for Lorca the butterfly is an emissary from the Ideal world. As for Apollo, we have seen that Lorca usually introduces him to provide cultural ballast for discussion of homosexual themes. He is virginal in that his sexual behaviour is free from any taint of sinfulness. Now Lorca can evoke Whitman in gay terms:

> amante de los cuerpos bajo la burda tela.

> lover of the bodies under the rough cloth.

> con aquel camarada que pondría en tu pecho
> un pequeño dolor de ignorante leopardo.

> with that comrade who would place on your breast
> the small pain of an ignorant leopard.[28]

Feeling Lorca going out to the old poet in gratitude and affection – he, unlike the boys, *did* dream and sleep as a river – one is then shocked by the change of tone that occurs in the next section, in which the argument of the Ode begins in earnest:

> Ni un solo momento, Adán de sangre, macho,
> hombre solo en el mar, viejo hermoso Walt Whitman,
> porque por las azoteas,
> agrupados en los bares,
> saliendo en racimos de las alcantarillas,
> temblando entre las piernas de los chauffeurs
> o girando en las plataformas de ajenjo,
> los maricas, Walt Whitman, te señalan.†

† Some editions have '*te soñaban*' ('were dreaming'). Essentially the meaning is unchanged.

> Not for a single moment, Adam of blood, male,
> lone man in the sea, old beautiful Walt Whitman,
> because on the terraces,
> grouped together in the bars,
> jumping in bunches out of the sewers,
> trembling between the legs of the chauffeurs
> or whirling on the platforms of absinthe,
> the pansies, Walt Whitman, point at you.[29]

The key phrase surely is '*Adán de sangre*'; partly this alludes to Whitman's status as father of American poetry, partly to his looks in later life (he bore a passing resemblance to Adam as depicted by Blake!), partly too to his being palpable ancestor for all those who believed in the validity of homosexual relations – the word *sangre* is especially pertinent here. But there is another meaning too: Adam in the garden male and alone (*macho* and *solo*) existed *before* the Fall. So too did Whitman in important ways which deserve to be considered. Whitman's sensibility was formed in an America which had not known the Civil War and in which industrialisation had not got under way to the extent that it so triumphantly did in the last part of his life. The vision of 'good in all' – close in so many respects to that of Whitman's contemporaries, the New England Transcendentalists – is much easier to arrive at, and act upon, in the looser-structured and still to a considerable extent 'virginal' world of pre-1860 America, though no doubt the signs of what was to come were there for the percipient to read.

But in Whitman – as in Emerson and Thoreau – there *is* something (and here we come even closer to Lorca's reason for reminding us of the story of Adam) prelapsarian in the whole outlook on life. Even though there are times when Whitman protests that there is of course evil in the world, that there is indeed evil even in himself; and in one of the loveliest of the 'Calamus' poems, 'Of the Terrible Doubt of Appearances', he reflects:

> Of the terrible doubt of appearances,
> Of the uncertainty after all, that we may be deluded,
> That may-be reliance and hope are but speculations after all,
> That may-be identity beyond the grave is a beautiful fable
>     only. . .[30]

The development of this is interesting – I was about to say 'resolution', but the fact is that no resolution exists:

> To me these and the like of these are curiously answer'd by my
>     lovers, my dear friends,
> When he whom I love travels with me or sits a long while
>     holding me by the hand. . .[31]

Evil, disquiet, they dissolve upon the air and seem unreal compared with the beauty of a moment with a friend. If only they did! But they don't, and to pretend otherwise is to come near to the Christian Science delusions of Mary Baker Eddy.

Lorca is thus rebuking Whitman (whom he continues to revere and love) on two accounts: that he didn't anticipate where he should have done the direction in which his society with its pioneering acquisitions and industry was moving; that he didn't properly acknowledge the wickedness and suffering that are part of life, even on the open road, even among the live-oaks and in the flowered fields and by the broad clear rivers! And if we come onto the important matter of homosexual life – which Whitman sang so continuously with such psalmodic ardour – we can see further limitations of the Whitmanesque viewpoint, ones which Lorca brings home to us in lines of a near-savage insistence. If one loves, has consistent sexual relations with someone, one inevitably enters into the world of that person's limitations, faults, problems, illnesses, etc., all of which challenge one while assisting towards a new, if painful self-knowledge. One finds little of this in Whitman, indeed there is in his poetry much sense of a crowd, of anonymous faces and bodies, but little sense of *another person*. Camaraderie along the open road may entail jubilant homosexual practices, but for the man who is homosexual by deep inclination – such as Whitman himself – the matter cannot be sensibly left at that. That Whitman in his exultations has liberated many people, has provided a kind of strident sexual pastoral which has given back to many gays a natural happiness in their sexual love and habits is indisputable. But no one leads a totally asocial life, and even less imaginable, at present, is a society that is itself asocial; acknowledgement of difficulties consequent on homosexual love of any intensity is made only very covertly in his poetry. Yet there *are* difficulties – though not insuperable ones – inseparable from being homosexual in modern western society. And without being too judgemental one must point out that these difficulties Whitman himself met with rather less than exemplary courage and honesty, encouraging untruths about a relationship with a woman and even amending certain poems so that heterosexual relationships could be attributed to him.

There is a further objection, one which touched a very exposed nerve in Lorca, particularly the Lorca of New York. Whitman's homosexuality does seem confined to a wonderful tribe of happy, healthy young men. Lorca, whose heart went out to the despised and rejected everywhere, whose recent poems had teemed with images of deformed children and animals, casualties of society, sick old men and bloated women, found this repellent. Is sexuality to be withheld from the ugly and the strange? Anyway – though it clearly appealed neither to Whitman nor indeed to Lorca itself – even homosexuality has a multiplicity of faces. In the 'Oda a Walt Whitman' we encounter them

– sado-masochists and transvestites, male tarts obsessed by lust, their own and others; all the greedy and neurotic riff-raff who form an important stratum of what is often called the 'gay scene', all a long way from two roughly-clad robust lads clinging together for a journey over virgin land. And so it should be. It is barbaric to reserve sexual satisfaction for the attractive and the well-adjusted.

The word *marica* still has a very pejorative flavour in Spanish – the more dignified 'male' form *maricón* being today preferred. Reading the poem one can often have a sense that Lorca – almost from his first use of the term onwards – is dissociating himself from the pansy/corrupt element of homosexual society. Certainly his imprecations against it are fervent; his anger is clearly not confined to Whitman's inability to see the complicated and the disagreeable aspects of being homosexual:

> Contra vosotros siempre, que dais a los muchachos
> gotas de sucia muerte con amargo veneno.
> Contra vosotros siempre. . .

> Against you always, who give boys
> drops of filthy death with bitter poison.
> Against you always. . .[32]

And then follows a Whitman-like list of names – which scarcely needs translation:

> *Faeries* de Norteamerica,
> *Pájaros* de la Habana,
> *Jotos* de Méjico
> *Sarasas* de Cádiz,
> *Apios* de Sevilla,
> *Cancos* de Madrid,
> *Floras* de Alicante,
> *Adelaidas* de Portugal.[33]

This list – made up indeed for the greater part of Iberian gays – does not only exist to counteract Whitman's vision of lovers of their own sex; it exists as a suggestive recital of people who seem to lack dignity or morality and who appear to be objects of opprobrium to the poet himself as well as to others. Death oozes out of their eyes, we are told, doors should be shut in their faces.

So while it is clear that Lorca chastises the prelapsarian vision, the refusal to look unpleasant truth in the face, perhaps his own attitude to homosexual life, to the consequences of being gay, is not so clear. Does he – like the Whitman for whom he so feels – really want only the cheerful, energetic elements and would prefer to shun the perverse, anti-social, disordered?

In trying to answer this we must *not* make the mistake of trying to force Lorca into positions pleasing to ourselves and more acceptable to the comparatively enlightened climate in which we live. This is a study of Lorca as he was, not Lorca as we would wish him to have been. The 'Oda a Walt Whitman' is, among other things, a document of an agonised state of mind. Does he not say in it:

> Agonía, agonía, sueño, fermento y sueño.
> Este es el mundo, amigo, agonía, agonía.

> Agony, agony, dream, ferment and sleep.
> This is the world, friend, agony, agony.

and a few lines later – using words startlingly reminiscent of Matthew Arnold's 'Dover Beach':†

> y la vida no es noble, ni buena, ni sagrada.

> and life isn't noble, or good or holy.[34]

★

I think repeated readings of the ode can bring us to the following understanding of Lorca's position in this, the most ambitious poem he had so far written:

1) Whitman, to be admired in so many ways for the nobility of his mind, is to be censured for his failure to do justice to the pain and evil in life. Sociologically his prognostications couldn't have been wider of the mark. This is symbolised in the image of the apple (fruit of Eden) tasting to the boy who bites it today of gasoline. The industry that Whitman found so impressive has resulted in a callous, inhospitable, structureless city deservant of the denunciations the Spanish poet has already abundantly heaped upon it.

2) The tender, hallowed manner of dealing with homosexual loving – Lorca's own kind – is similarly at once both admirable and culpably limited. Perhaps out in the freedom of the unclaimed country it is practically possible, but modern man is urban. If society could be de-industrialised, freed from the pressures of commerce, then indeed joyous love between men could flourish, but – as it is – in the jungle of the modern city even sex becomes distorted, twisted. Add to this the frequent need to use sexuality to get money; Lorca was writing in a

† . . .for the world, which seems
  To lie before us like a land of dreams,
  So various, so beautiful, so new,
  Hath really neither joy, nor love, nor light,
  Nor certitude, nor peace, nor help for pain . . .[35]

time of depression and unemployment. That Lorca found the whole business of rent-boys depressing, indeed repulsive, seems to me too apparent in this poem to need further commentary. The whole matter of appealing to (conjuring up) curious tastes which can be gratified – for cash, for a bed and a roof – is likewise abhorrent.

3) But diversity or singularity of taste is not: Lorca blesses the boy who dresses up like a bride for instance. Nothing that springs from deep inclination ' is to be censured. Here he cannot be linked to Whitman's preference for the 'normal'.

4) Therefore the failure of homosexual life to live up to the Whitmanesque image of it is inextricable from the failure of American society to live up to Whitman's social pastorals for it. What has gone wrong can be attributed to specifically American deficiencies of vision: a too easy equation of the material with the good; an inability not to be dazzled by industry per se to the exclusion of facing up to the ills concomitant with it; a reluctance indeed to accept, until too late, evil (however defined) as a reality, capable of self-engendered continuance.

The poem could, as its urgency of rhythm and image movingly demonstrates, have been written only by one who shared the sexual orientation of its ostensible subject, Walt Whitman; the very shifts and seeming contradictions in emotional mood that it contains make it indisputably a poem, a meditation, by one who stands before his public as a homosexual. This unequivocality of position enabled Lorca to speak uncompromisingly and honestly of his feelings towards western society, and American society in particular, its disastrous corruption of intimate (i.e. sexual) life. And if today we find those passages concerning homosexuals generically rather less than honest, we must also find them more than compensated for by the denunciations of capitalism's destruction of psychic health – in spite of all, a *gay* denunciation.

The ode does not leave us in a state of total hopelessness. In the wish with which it concludes we have an earnest of redemption from the quarter of American society which has best preserved the instinctual, anti-capitalist values, the Black:

> Quiero que el aire fuerte de la noche más honda
> quite flores y letras del arco donde duermes
> y un niño negro anuncie a los blancos del oro
> la llegada del reino de la espiga.

> I want the strong wind of the deepest night
> to remove flowers and letters from the arch where you're sleeping,
> and a Black boy to announce to the white people of gold
> the arrival of the kingdom of the ear of corn.[36]

Here is a veritable icon of hope; the Black boy carries that favourite Lorquian symbol of an ear of corn, and the New World will be new again with the harvest of unpolluted and life-giving crops.

The 'Oda a Walt Whitman' is, in its strength and width, a very complete poem. All the same it isn't complete as an expression of Lorca's vision of society and sexuality. He possibly wrote it when sailing away from America, in which case he was also preparing a major dramatic work, as unlike his other plays as *El poeta* was from his other volumes of poetry and for similar reasons: *El público* (*The Public*) which manifests and explores the widest variety of ways of being homosexual. Much of the manuscript of *El público* as it came into the possession of Rafael Martínez Nadal was written on notepaper from a hotel in Havana, Cuba where he had delivered his lecture on the *duende*.[37] *El público* also connects with another play on which he was working but which was not to be finished until August 1931, *Así que pasen cinco años* (*When Five Years Have Passed*). This play also exhibits Lorca's homosexual concerns, though more indirectly – and again has an acceptance of plurality which, even in the most generous reading, the 'Oda' does not quite possess.

I propose to take these three important works in the most probable order in which they came into the author's head: first *Así que pasen cinco años*, then *El público* and lastly what is perhaps Lorca's most famous non-dramatic prose work, 'Juego y teoría del duende' ('Play and Theory of the Duende')[38] – a lecture given in God's America, Spanish America before returning to the *fons et origo* of all the culture he deeply cared about.

## Chapter Six

# The Constant Baptism of Newly Created Things

## 1

Lorca styled *Así que pasen cinco años* a '*leyenda del tiempo*' (a 'legend of time').[1] He always chose descriptive phrases for his plays with care – c.f. 'erotic lace-paper valentine' for *Don Perlimplín y Belisa* – to tell us important things about their artistic natures and basic themes. So first why is this play called a *leyenda*?

A legend usually arises out of a puzzling feature of life which it either explains or illuminates by means of characters and events that do not conform to the rules of exterior existence but, on the contrary, are animated by forces from the interior, the unconscious. The protagonists of a legend, however – who can be both passive and yet engaged on an active quest – may bear recognisable kinship to ourselves, embodying as often as not particular problems of the persona – such as hesitation or the need for self-vindication.

In *Así que pasen cinco años* there is a young man at the centre – called simply El Joven – who closely resembles the heroes of legends and folktales. (Critics like Gwynne Edwards[2] and Reed Anderson[3] have indeed seen all the other characters of the play as projections of him, as his past, present or future avatars.) The predicament of El Joven which determines the entire course of the play has itself fairy-tale properties. He has fallen in love with a beautiful girl of fifteen, admiring her for her long tresses, but is to have nothing to do with her – and with his own full consent – until five years have passed. He even refuses to call her his *novia* (fiancée) – though this, by the beginning of the play, is what she is – preferring her to be simply his *muchachita*, his *niña*. Both these words, of course, imprison the girl – like some Sleeping Beauty or *princesse lointaine* of courtly love romance – keeping her fast in sweet nubile innocence. He is thus free to dwell on her charms without ever having to disturb the perfection of his image of her.

An extroverted friend calls on El Joven, hoping to budge him from this strange resolve by boasting about his own conquests and the fun they have been for him. To no avail! The youth's resolution is paralleled by his attachment to his house (itself like something out of folktale): he has had it isolated from the city streets whose noise and tumult he fears and detests. Five years must pass in tranquility, and at the end of them there will be further happy tranquility: *à deux*. Nobody else shares the optimism of El Joven, though, and as we listen to the remarks of the Old Man, the Friend, the Servant, we have a sense of foreboding. . .When the curtain goes up on the second act, however, the five years have passed – more or less in the way the young man expected.†

And now we have come to the second noun in Lorca's descriptive phrase, *tiempo*. *This* is the puzzling feature of life to which *Así que pasen cinco años* is addressed. It presents us with a desire common enough, and at once profound and foolish: to preserve against inexorable time one's personality, even one's person, to guard ideals, loves, values against its inroads. The majority of us employ ingenious mental subterfuges to disguise from ourselves the fact that we are being borne along by Time to what demonstrates its power incontestably: Death. One can no more fend off Time or defend others from it than one can possess a loved one by holding him/her in one's head rather than in one's arms. El Joven's decision to do the latter is in fact an image of his wish to defy Time and Death, and the legend that is the play shows what a tragically mistaken decision it is. Nevertheless El Joven is a sympathetic figure – nearer to Lorca himself, as I shall shortly intimate, than the protagonists of any of his other major plays – and he stands before us in all his equivocations and mistakes as a sort of Everyman in a mystery play.

He appears sympathetic because Lorca does *not* condemn him for his existential terrors. Though they may cause him to act wrongly, they reveal him as being quick to life, and able to apprehend what is tragic about it; those who rebuke him have often wilfully desensitised themselves to the problems inherent in being alive. That this is how Lorca sees him seems to me shown in the character of the Second Friend, who calls on El Joven in the first act. He is an obvious alter ego of the protagonist and stands in marked contrast to the swaggering First Friend with his hearty humour and girlfriends. This second young man tells El Joven about his own wish both to return to, and contain, the beautiful moments of his early childhood. He is articulating in even more extreme form the kind of fears and hopes that have led El Joven to pursue his chosen strategy. 'Quiero morirme,' he sings, 'siendo manantial/Quiero morirme fuera de la mar.' ('I want to die, being a spring/I want to die out of the sea.')[5] He adds to the Old Man: 'because I don't want to be full of wrinkles and pains like you'.[6]

---

†The play can, in fact, be read as if the five years are an illusion. The recurrence of the Dead Boy and the device of the striking clock unite the first act with the subsequent ones. Certainly Lorca's thinking is very much Eliot's 'Time present and time past/Are both perhaps present in time future,/And time future contained in time past'.[4]

The Old Man tells him that he is mad, and the first (extroverted) friend comments:

> Todo ese no es más que miedo a la muerte.

> All this is no more than fear of death.[7]

He may be right, indeed both these points may be valid. But only to a degree. For the Old Man *is* full of wrinkles and pain, and both Death and the fear of it *are* inevitable factors of human existence. While we must not behave like El Joven, trying to defy the march of Time, remaking the terms on which we move through life, we must work out our position with the Pauline 'fear and trembling'. Otherwise we end up with different but no lesser forms of evasion. For isn't the First Friend's womanising as much an exclusion of confrontation with reality as the strange acceptance of a five-year wait by El Joven?

The preoccupation with Time, and with the attitude we must adopt to it, that informs – more, animates – *Así que pasen cinco años* is intimately related to Lorca's feelings about American life. He believed, as we have seen, that Americans lived too wholly in the present, serving it in the delusion that it had the permanence it, by definition, cannot have. Wall Street epitomised this belief, the suicides caused by the crash its tragic folly. In the light of this American blindness to the past and future Lorca must have seriously scrutinised his own relationship to Time. Nobody could be less like a Lorquian New Yorker than El Joven, with his sensitivity and romanticism and detestation of coarseness and noise, yet he too, in his way, wants to live only in the present. His vow of keeping his love for five years is also a resolve to abolish the palpable future, and when the five years are over, he will deny the past as well. Further, the possibility of death – which defines past, present and future – is also not properly considered; significantly reminders of it and all that it entails come from the *other* characters, those emanations from his unconscious life. The emotional condition given dramatic expression here recalls that expressed in Stephen Spender's beautiful and courageous lyric, 'If It Were Not' (1971):

> If it were not for that
> Lean executioner, who stands
> Ever beyond a door
> With axe raised in both hands –

> All my days here would be
> One day – the same – the drops
> Of light edgeless in light
> That no circumference stops.[8]

But that lean executioner *does* await us, and, as *Así que pasen cinco años* hallucinatorily demonstrates, he *does* strike all of us without fail. El Joven himself is at the very end of the play his victim; he dies as the clock strikes twelve and the curtain begins to fall.

But to return to the situation as developed in the second act. The five years have passed and the young man comes – as in the veriest folktale – to claim his bride. The stage set is no longer the masculine library in the young man's house but a very feminine bedroom/boudoir. The bed itself is canopied and tasselled; the Bride's dressing-table resembles Belinda's in Pope's *Rape of the Lock*, and french windows give onto a balcony, the night and (female emblem of love and death) the moon. The Bride of course is no fifteen-year-old girl; indeed she corresponds in almost no way to the image of her that El Joven – and with him ourselves – has built up. She does not even have tresses! She is carrying on an affair with a young Rugby-Player whom she entertains in her room; the affair frankly centres on physical pleasure. This lover of hers represents – like the game he plays – all that is aggressive in the male personality – and, one must add, all that thrives on and needs aggression in the female. '*Dragón, dragón mío*' ('Dragon, dragon of mine')[9] the Bride calls him, and contrasts his vigour, his assertiveness with qualities of the young man who after five years is to come for her; 'What white-hot coal, what ivory fire your teeth give forth!' she compliments the Rugby-Player, adding sadly: 'My other groom had frozen teeth; he used to kiss me and his lips were covered with little withered leaves, they were like dry lips.'[10]

That when the young man and his Bride meet no relationship is possible has been prepared for us very skilfully by Lorca. Because hers has been the more truthful position of the two of them, it is the Bride who brings home to El Joven the reality of the situation *now*, including the presence of her other and *real* lover. El Joven is moved to exclaim in words at once poignant and indicative of the solipsism inherent in his position:

> It isn't your deception that hurts me. You aren't wicked. You don't mean anything. It's my lost treasure. It's my love without object.[11]

But if one is talking in terms of deception, then *his* is surely greater than hers, since his was *self*-deception, spreading outwards from self as that failing always does. Moreover the self-deception involved was indeed founded on lies about existence itself.

However there is more still to the predicament presented here than the confrontation (rich in suggestion though it is) between illusion and reality, defiance-of-Time and acceptance-of-Time. The whole interchange between El Joven and the Bride contains a discussion of role-imprisonment corresponding, and at a profound level, to Lorca's homosexual preoccupations of 1929–30.

El Joven is rightly censured for contracting in his mind a girl – in reality someone who grew, as is natural, from fifteen to twenty – into a pretty, only recently pubic miracle of fragrance; in exterior life she is, as we have seen, a robust, independent creature with strong sexual appetites. But equally El Joven himself – th ough one infers that he does not know this on a conscious level – is the victim of behavioural assumptions, of cruel role-expectations. (And if we step back from the play and try to examine the unconscious motivation for his decision to let five years pass before claiming his fiancée we can discover a multiplicity of fears about sex and gender.) El Joven is a delicate-spirited individual for whom assertion is not merely difficult but repellent; he reminds one in important respects of the Boybeetle of *El maleficio de la mariposa*, and just as that character must have stood for the gentle, artistic boy Lorca had been in Granada, so the equivocal, fearful yet imaginatively courageous Joven surely represents Lorca as he'd come to see himself in the years of his psychological crisis.

Certainly the contrasts made by the Bride between El Joven and the Rugby-Player will, as far as the play's audience is concerned, work wholly in the former's favour. (They are, in fact, pointed-up versions of the contrast between El Joven and the First Friend presented in Act One.)

> 'Have you played rugby?' the Bride asks El Joven, almost accusingly.'
> 'Never!'
> 'And have you carried off a horse with a mane and killed three thousand pheasants in one day?'
> 'Never!'[12]

We are not expected to feel any regret that El Joven has not indulged in these pursuits – only scorn that anyone could set them up as criteria for assessing another's value. The Rugby-Player does not come over as a sympathetic person; the First Friend to whom he bears some resemblance did not do so either, though he had a certain charm deriving from his evident delight in himself. We certainly felt more admiration for El Joven's Second Friend, embodiment of his own delicacy in its purest form, unsullied by any capitulation to convention. In contrast to the First Friend's vulgar boasts about his adventures with Matilde, we had the Second Friend's haunting memory of how when he was an infant he found a little woman made out of rain and cared for her for two days putting her in the safety of a goldfish bowl.†

---

†This, of course does have a parallel with El Joven's keeping his Bride safe in his head – a reprehensible act. *Así que pasen cinco años* is truly rich in ambivalence.

The relationship between El Joven and the Bride has a distorted reflection in that between El Joven and the Stenographer, of which something is seen in the first act. There we saw how greatly the Stenographer was in love with the hero – unrequitedly, because his thoughts were entirely upon the beautiful fifteen-year-old with tresses. Now, in Act Two, after his repudiation by the Bride, El Joven encounters a curious figure, a Mannequin wearing the Bride's wedding-dress and thus literally standing before him to represent what – through surrender to dream – he has lost. Through the offices of the Mannequin, El Joven is persuaded to return to his house and seek the girl who has *truly* been in love with him for so long – for the five years of the title, and more. (And here it is surely right to find the strongest echo of Maeterlinck – of his best-known play, *The Blue Bird*, where at the end of a long and difficult quest for it, the children find happiness to be located in their own home.) El Joven does indeed find genuine love in the Stenographer, a love he appears able to reciprocate. But in one of the many exchanges/transpositions of roles that we find in this play the Stenographer tells him that *he* now must wait, that consummation, marriage are not for the present but must be deferred, and she pronounces the actual words of the title. Softly she says to him, after he has expressed his wish to go away with her: '*Así que pasen cinco años*'.[13]

Shortly after this dialogue, in the second scene of the third and last act, the youth becomes party to a game of cards arranged by three professional sharpers. He loses, is granted a mysterious vision of the all-important card, the symbolic ace of hearts, which huge and luminous seems to stand behind the bookshelves of his library (an image fertile in symbolic properties). A few minutes later he dies.

So far discussion of the play has only *touched* on those elements in it which are not merely non-realistic, but fantastical, belonging to that domain of the extraordinary through which every legend travels. It is time now to think a little more extendedly about these. I had wanted to stress that, as in the strongest legends, *Así que pasen cinco años* is firmly rooted in vividly apprehended existence. Indeed, here again showing kinship with *El poeta en Nueva York*, no other play of Lorca's brings in so much of modern life – the confusions of the street, a stenographer, a fashion model, a rugby-player. Nevertheless its quest-like nature compels protagonist and audience to confront characters, witness events that act on him, and us, like fragments of épiphanic dream. We are introduced to a Dead Boy and his talking Cat, to a Harlequin, a Speaking Mask, a Clown and finally, at the moment of the hero's death, to an Echo. With the Dead Boy and his Cat we move, as the lighting suggests, through a strange world the other side of death. This is not the only phantasmagoric realm into which we are plunged. The first scene of the last act takes us to a forest made up of huge-trunked trees, anticipatory of that which we will find in *Bodas de sangre (Blood Wedding)*. Much use is made of a curious staircase which characters move down or climb up at emotionally significant moments. The dualistic Harlequin holds two masks behind his back when he first appears; with one held in front of him he speaks and acts in a happy manner, with the other in a sleepy one, reminiscent of night and all its attendant melancholy and perils. Later in the company of the Clown this apparition plays upon a white violin with golden strings, bringing into our mind images of Chagall. All these owe something, as I already have suggested, to Maeterlinck and *The Blue Bird*, something to the art of Stravinsky, Cocteau, etc. at which we looked in Chapter Four, something to the folklore in which these artists were so interested (pre-eminently in the use of Harlequin and Clown), something to the great German expressionists of the Twenties. As in an expressionist drama the characters here have no names, enormous attention is given by the writer to effects of lighting and stage – we are consciously, gleefully being presented with a *theatrical* event. *Bodas de sangre*, first of Lorca's 'classical masterpieces', will also show expressionist influence.

Each of the figures I have cited, each of the dream–like, dream–lit scenes in which they appear, constitute further stages in this version of Everyman's journey towards Death, that undeniable demonstration of Time's sovereignty. Those episodes which feature the Dead Boy and his Cat – who not only recur throughout the play but continually underpin it, providing in their strangeness a perpetual commentary on the action – are not only, in my view, the most poignant and original element in the play but are unsurpassed for these attributes in the entirety of Lorca's oeuvre. Again it is not hard to connect the pair to Lorca's imaginative concerns during his American year. We have already seen how wounded animals stalk through *El poeta en Nueva York*, and that children had important parts in the cycle too. The Dead Boy is cousin to Little Boy Stanton and – more obviously – to the small boy in 'Nocturno del Brooklyn Bridge' who was buried in the morning but who cried so loudly that dogs had to be called to quieten him down. (These *niños* had their own cousins, of course, *el niño loco* and *el niño mudo*, for instance, and perhaps the boy of 'Suicidio' who didn't know his geometry.)

The Dead Boy and the Cat first manifest themselves – quite unexpectedly – in the carefully sequestered atmosphere of El Joven's library. We are bemused by them, unable to see their connection with their surroundings; only later do we learn that the house-porter's son has died that day, also that a cat has been found stoned to death by some hooligans on the garden-roof. Further on in the play we discover other possible identities for the boy (curiously they do not seem mutually exclusive!) – he could be the child the young protagonist has never had and will never have, either from the Bride or from the Stenographer. (Here there is surely articulation, of an indirect kind, of the homosexual's inevitable childlessness; we shall encounter this more fully in *Yerma*.) The existence of the Dead Boy is emphasised by that figure from whom El Joven learns so much, the Mannequin, and it is implied that he is the son the two of them could have had. When the Mask speaks, however, we believe the Boy to be *her* child, by a treacherous Italian count. Above and beyond any of these identities, of course, the Boy is our inner self, screaming – as our persona will not allow us to do – against an even worse reality than Time, Death, whose sovereignty no amount of philosophic theories can diminish.

'*Y no quiero que me entierren*', calls out the Boy. ('I don't want them to bury me.')[14] His coffin is hateful and frightening to him. And more still the place where the coffin will be laid. The following lines, powerful enough in themselves, are echoed in one of Lorca's supreme productions, 'Gacela de la Muerte Oscura' ('Gacela of the Dark Death') in the *Diván del Tamarit*:

> No es el cielo. Es tierra dura
> con muchos grillos que cantan,
> con hierbas que se menean,
> con nubes que se levantan,
> con hondas que lanzan piedras
> y el viento como una espada.
> ¡Yo quiero ser niño, un niño!

> It isn't the sky. It's hard earth
> with many crickets that sing,
> with grasses that wriggle,
> with clouds that rise up,
> with slings that throw stones
> and the wind like a sword.
> I want to be a boy, a boy![15]

What a desperate cry that last line is! And how it should hurt us if we haven't – like the First Friend and the Rugby-Player – sealed ourselves off from honest awareness of the cruelties being alive entails. The Cat too has a major part to play in bringing these last home to us. In lovely lines he describes the freedom of his wild rooftop life, a freedom shattered by brutal ruffians' stones, which turn him into – as later lines disturbingly show – a mere bit of rubbish for the dustbin. The Dead Boy and Cat – and the poetry and light that accompany them – not only haunt and pervade the entire play but unify it, connecting the characters one to another, bringing together the diverse strands, Freudian, psycho-cultural, folkloric, expressionist.

Furthermore their desperation receives understanding from El Joven, as from the androgynous Second Friend and the also androgynous Mask. The gay sensibility – which does not shrink from tender confrontation of the painful – is now coming into its own, and when we realise how it is effected and effective here – through images of doves, oppressive street-noises, wounding grasses, buried boys and mutilated animals, already made familiar to us through *El poeta en Nueva York*, we see how legitimate it is to hail *Así que pasen cinco años* – wherever the bulk of it may have been written – as another masterpiece resulting from lessons harshly learned in the United States.

## 2

The title of Lorca's strangest and most ambitious play, *El público*, means both 'audience' and 'public', and of these two meanings the first is the one that we should primarily accord it (though out of the amorphous, heterogeneous public an audience comes). Possibly following Pirandello in *Sei personaggi in cerca d'autore* Lorca makes *El público* invert that sense of illusion customarily imparted by the theatre. Here, for much of the time, we *in* the theatre are looking *at* a theatre (indeed, in a deeper sense, we are doing this for the whole duration of the work); we are concerned with a director and his three actors, and we hear discussions, practical and theoretical, about the production of drama, the real nature of theatre; in particular we are occupied with a performance of *Romeo and Juliet*, an apotheosised scene from which we witness and the entirety of which haunts the play with all its complex symbolic overtones. Then, as the title would suggest, we are made aware of the imminence – and the dubious necessity – of an audience for the activities of the cast. The play both begins and ends with lines announcing the audience's presence and bidding them come in; like Godot in Beckett's play they, who never appear as such, could be said to constitute the real protagonist of the work.

During the play's course, however, we meet partial representatives of the audience, the four Horses (Scenes I and III), the discursive Students (Scene V). Lorca certainly saw the idea of the audience as not merely central to, but determining his play; any artist, however maverick, enters into a collusion with the outside world (if it is only in his own mind a very limited segment of it); more, he can be said to be its servant, even its creation, since the art-form in which he works (perhaps the drama pre-eminently) is an expression, an embodiment of the wishes of society. Lorca wanted to show in *El público* how art often, and at the highest level, mirrors thoughts, desires which we prefer not to admit to in our conventional social existences. And in particular he was intent on demonstrating the variety of homosexual desires that exists – particularly among men who would never admit

to this. As I intimated at the end of the previous chapter, *El público*
stands as both a complement and an antithesis of the 'Oda a Walt
Whitman'; what he castigated there, what he wanted to exclude even
from the homosexual fold (let alone from the fold of the generally
sexually 'saved') asserts itself in *El público* with a vengeance. Here,
forcing acknowledgement of themselves, are the outcasts of the ode:

> . . .maricas de las ciudades,
> de carne tumefacta y pensamiento inmundo,
> madres de lodo, arpías, enemigos sin sueño
> del Amor que reparte coronas de alegría.

> . . .pansies of the cities,
> of tumescent flesh and filthy thought,
> mothers of mud, harpies, enemies without dream
> of Love that apportions crowns of happiness.[16]

Here too are:

> ¡Maricas de todo el mundo, asesinos de palomas!
> Escalvos de la mujer, perras de sus tocadores,
> abiertos en las plazas con fiebre de abanico. . .

> Pansies of the whole world, murderers of doves!
> Slaves of women, bitches of their dressing-tables,
> available in the squares in a fever of fan. . .[17]

And there they all are, Lorca cries, inside every one of you who sits in
bourgeois comfort and pride in a theatre. Except that the vocabulary
of the ode – so vehement, so accented with some sexual Council of
Trent – is, in the play, only employed from time to time to suggest
wrong thinking, bad faith; *El público*'s purpose is to assert the
multiplicity and authenticity of all sexual desires, more precisely of all
homosexual desires.

There is a further sense in which the title is to be taken; all the
characters become, at some point or other, members of an audience.
They witness changes of role, discardings of clothes and masks (a
recurrent symbol), the takings on of different avatars, the epiphanic
presentations of true and hitherto concealed identities. And this in
addition to the use of *Romeo and Juliet* inside the play!

Of the characters that we actually do meet, the principal is the
Director. It is tempting to see him as a representative of important
aspects of Lorca himself – particularly where his artistic ambitions are
concerned – but he can also, it seems to me, be seen as an elder cousin
of El Joven in *Así que pasen cinco años*. He shares certain ambiguities,
certain reluctances to stand up before all in his true colours; at the same

time he has been far more emotionally adventurous than El Joven, and in a domain which perhaps the latter would never in his conscious self have admitted to be his. A number of the characters we meet are clearly – as in the other play – extended identities of the central figure's; as in *Así que pasen* the play ends with his death, with a dialogue of voices from the threshold of what lies outside life. Like El Joven, too, he would appear to have learned a lesson, and the play he dominates is like a medieval Morality, a dramatisation of that necessary and painful lesson.

In the first scene the Director is visited first by four mysterious Horses – who enter when he is expecting the audience, so that we can take them as epitomes of the love- and death-instincts within that body – and then by three Men, all looking alike with black beards. They praise the Director for his production of *Romeo and Juliet*: the Director comments a little sententiously that this is a play in which a man and a woman are in love. His sentence is to reverberate ironically throughout the work. Man 1 comments: 'Romeo could be a bird and Juliet could be a stone. Romeo could be a grain of salt and Juliet could be a map,'[18] the first of the suggestions of transmutation that is to become a truly obsessional motif in the play. (We note here that Romeo, the male, is seen as being changed into delicate, vulnerable forms, Juliet into stronger, larger ones.) The Director is proud of himself (and acknowledged by all) as the maker of a Theatre of Open Air; the term suggests daylight, reason, the public as opposed to the intimate/private. The opposite of the Director's Theatre of Open Air, which apparently has seen so fine a performance of *Romeo and Juliet*, is that suggested in a slow, deliberate voice by Man 1: the Theatre Beneath the Sand.[19]

Short though the exchange between the Director and the three Men has been, we have already had intimations of what this other theatre ('*el verdadero teatro*' – 'the true theatre') should concern itself with. Speaking of Romeo, Man 2 asks:

> How did Romeo urinate, Mr Director? Isn't it nice to see Romeo urinating?[20]

and later in the same speech:

> You could've seen an angel which was carrying off Romeo's sex while leaving him the other, his own, the one which suited him.[21]

Clearly the implications are that drama as conventionally produced – in some rationally controlled public way – doesn't do justice to the complications of flesh-and-blood people, its characters being mouth-pieces of rhetoric. The character Romeo, just like the actor who plays him, has a penis with which he pisses and fucks.

Man 1's declaration of his wish to inaugurate the Theatre Beneath the Sand brings forth from the Director the cry of 'Gonzalo'. So he knows him! More, it becomes apparent that the two of them have been lovers, and that the Director has had sexual relations with Man 2 and Man 3 as well. Among their other functions the three bearded Men stand for three different expressions of homosexual desire. The Director attempts to deny his own proclivities, declaring himself to be enamoured of Elena (Helen) who is stylised Woman, made in the image of romantic male expectations and who is soon to make an appearance. But not before – as in *Así que pasen cinco años* – a screen has been produced. To pass behind the screen is to pass into a form revelatory of the profoundest sexual needs/identities. The Director is pushed by Man 2 and Man 3 and appears as a very young boy dressed in white satin who must, Lorca specifies in the stage directions, be played by an actress. Similarly Man 2 comes out as a woman in black pyjamas and poppies upon her head, and Man 3 – after he has tried to make up to Helen – as a beardless, white-faced individual with a whip in his hand. Man 1 who directs the whole business of the screen does not go behind it himself; the inference is clear enough: he does not need to.

Thus the four men can be comparatively described, à propos their homosexuality, as follows:

*Director*: a man imaginative and passionate by nature who has had many lovers. But his belief in reason and his public position (and clear delight in it) make it difficult for him to accept homosexuality as a full and determinant part of his personality; he prefers merely to let it lead him to pleasant activities on the side. For that reason he has to 'invent' women – to whom in fact he denies inclinations, even a proper nature. However the play concerns itself with his hesitations, doubts and resolutions, and by its close – even though he dies – we feel, more strongly than with El Joven in *Así que pasen cinco años*, that he has attained knowledge of truth.

*Man 1*: he frankly and gladly views himself as homosexual. Not only does he instigate the 'screen test', it is he who is the greatest advocate of the true theatre which should acknowledge all desires and contradictory impulses within the human being. None of these shocks him; he is thus the opponent of the *weltanschauung* of certain important parts of the 'Oda a Walt Whitman'. Honesty and courage, however, don't necessarily mean happiness – at least of an exterior kind. Among his other 'avatars' during the course of this play are Romeo and a nameless, naked young youth dying in a hospital. Romeo died as a result of his love, and the nude 'red with a crown of blue thorns' plainly represents Christ who superbly had the ability to be himself. (This kinship with Christ is made explicit by quotations or half-quotations from the Passion chapters of the New Testament.) At the end of the play it would seem that Man 1 (Gonzalo) has died – attaining a sacramental form which will be noted later.

*Man 2*: equivocal and woman-imitating, effeminate, an approximation to the bitch of the dressing-table/boudoir of Lorca's imprecations in the 'Oda'. However here he is reprimanded more for the secrecy with which he enshrouds his desires than for these desires themselves.

*Man 3*: another equivocator and dissembler. His amorous activities are detailed to us by Helen, his approaches to whom tell us all-important things about his character and Lorca's attitude to him. His dishonesty leads to the sort of psychic distortions that manifest themselves in the perversity of sexual sadism (symbolised in the whip).

Thus the rewards in the play go to those who practise an absolute honesty – who want to establish the Theatre Beneath the Sand, one which is acknowledging and concerned with the roots of desire; existing, too, beneath what is made up of an infinity of particles, each beautiful and perfect in itself. We remember Blake (and this should not be the only time that we do so, for the resemblances between the two poets are considerable):

> To see a World in a Grain of Sand
> And see a Heaven in a Wild Flower,
> Hold Infinity in the palm of your hand
> And Eternity in an hour.[22]

Belief in the interpenetrative multiplicity of essence-informed exterior forms and of interior psychic elements (which have exterior counterparts) is axiomatic to the play. In the second scene, entitled 'Ruina romana' ('Roman ruin') and set where this would suggest, we have a long, mysterious conversation between a Figure of Little Bells (*Figura de cascabeles*) and a Figure of Vine Leaves (*Figura de pámpanos*), a conversation that seems a veritable *ne plus ultra* of Lorca's Platonist preoccupation with transmutation:

> FIGURE OF LITTLE BELLS. And if I turned myself into a cloud?
> FIGURE OF VINE LEAVES. I would turn myself into an eye.
> FIGURE OF LITTLE BELLS. And if I turned myself into dung?
> FIGURE OF VINE LEAVES. I would turn myself into a fly.
> FIGURE OF LITTLE BELLS. And if I turned myself into an apple?
> FIGURE OF VINE LEAVES. I would turn myself into a kiss.
> FIGURE OF LITTLE BELLS. And if I turned myself into a chest [human]?
> FIGURE OF VINE LEAVES. I would turn myself into a white sheet.
> FIGURE OF LITTLE BELLS. And if I turned myself into a moon-fish?
> FIGURE OF VINE LEAVES. I would turn myself into a knife.[23]

It will be observed that the metamorphoses the second figure proposes always offer strength and, together with this, either sustenance or destructive action (both related to assertion) towards those the first figure considers. The final two images are particularly important – for this cycle of changes is ongoing for the length of the play, and it is not long before we realise that these two strangely attired figures are, respectively, the Director and Man 1. The knife of the Vine-Leaves figure reminds us immediately of the Amargo, but an Amargo splendid in his dark sexuality and divested of his hostility (though not of his savage strength). The knife can dismember the moon-fish – with its connotations of sexual passivity and consummation through death. But eventually in the cycle it is the Figure of Vine Leaves/Man 1 (Gonzalo) who wants to become moon-fish. And just as in *Así que pasen cinco años* the dream-like image of the Dead Boy and his Cat attached itself from psychic life to exterior reality and we learned that such a pair had been known in the house where El Joven lived and had indeed died, so, in the sombre, strange last scene of *El público* Gonzalo's moon-fish identity becomes part of external life. His mother appears and agonisedly asks the Director:

> Where is my son? The fishermen brought me this morning an enormous moon-fish, pale, decomposed, and they cried out to me: Here you have your son.[24]

Meanwhile the Director is – like the Amargo himself – preparing to die.

These elaborate metamorphoses which follow a close internal logic and well repay study are demonstrations of a Heraclitan process of flux in constant and joyous operation in the world. And this itself makes all possibilities of sexual intercourse acceptable and valid. It is now time to examine the many faces – faces stripped of masks, masks simulating or hiding faces – that homosexuality wears in this extraordinary and immensely rich play.

And first we must turn our attention back to *Romeo and Juliet* which not merely haunts Lorca's own play but forces itself into it. The third scene – which takes us to the Theatre Beneath the Sand – opens out into Juliet's life in the tomb. She is desired by the Horses who manifest themselves again. Three of the Horses (who are white) declare they want to sleep with her:

> Because we are real horses, coach-horses, who have broken with our sex-organs the timber of the manger and the windows of the stable.[25]

They embody all the sexual emotion which animates most people into watching or reading work which deals with sexual subjects; for if

*Romeo and Juliet* did not, in some way, address itself to us sexually, it could hardly work as it should do. But polite audiences haven't been able to acknowledge this.

However the Fourth Horse (who is black – the colour endowed in dreams upon socially disapproved love-objects) has the most disconcerting utterance to deliver:

> Who passes through whom? Oh love, love that needs to pass your light through the dark warmths! Oh sea resting in the shadow and flower in the arse of the dead man![26]

This reference to anal sex, which after all can play a part in heterosexual love-making begins to take on homosexual significance when we remember that Shakespeare's theatre would have had Juliet played by a boy. Just as beneath the romantically rhetorical Romeo there was, Man 2 had insisted, a man who could piss, so beneath this luminous and beautiful girl (who inhabits a region of the dead similar to that in which dwells the Dead Boy and his Cat in *Así que pasen cinco años*) there is a boy, a boy who could be fucked in the arse. And indeed the Director's *Romeo and Juliet* appears to follow Shakespeare's practice.

We learn this in the most baffling scene (V, IV being non-extant), a scene in which a hospital where Man 1/Figure of Vine Leaves/Romeo lies dying, attended by a cryptic Male Nurse, coexists with a theatre in the process of being taken over by revolutionary students. These – pointers to a future world of different predominant values from those of Lorca's own day – believe in the true theatre, that beneath the sand and dealing with the most basic passions in their most urgent forms. Not all these students think exactly the same, but there is among them, it transpires, a sort of spiritual unanimity. They discuss Juliet and the fact that she was boy, not girl, and compare their own reactions to this to those (disturbed; incensed) of the conventional audience they seek to displace:

> STUDENT 4. Romeo was a man of thirty years and Juliet a boy of fifteen. The denunciation of the audience has been effective.

and later:

> The repetition of the act has been marvellous because undoubtedly they [Romeo and Juliet] loved each other with an incalculable love, although I might not justify it. When the nightingale sang I could not contain my tears.

He then asks his friend, Student 5:

Have you taken into account that Juliet who was in the tomb
was a boy in fancy dress, a trick of the Director of the scene, and
that the real Juliet was gagged beneath the stalls?

Whereupon Student 5 breaks into laughter:

Then I like it! It seemed to me very beautiful and if it was a boy
in fancy dress it doesn't matter to me at all.[27]

These revolutionaries are indeed heralds of a new age, one in which
Lorca's own preferred love-making – and that of the Director, the
three bearded Men and the avatars of Man 1, of the Black Horse, the
Male Nurse and the Emperor, of whom more presently – will be
happily accepted by all, and even practised in non-doctrinaire fashion
by many whose principal mode of sexual self-expression it isn't. And
that this means proper intercourse and all it entails – knowledge of the
dark depths of man – is made clear in the most curious exchange
between Man 1 and Man 2 in the Theatre Beneath the Sand of Scene
III: 'The arse is the downfall of man,' Man 1 says, 'it is his shame and
his death.'[28]

These sombre words – echoed by others later in the same scene –
may not amount to the indictment of anal sex they would first seem to
be; defecation and penetration (with its spillage of seed) can bring
embarrassment, humiliation, pain, and remind one constantly of the
vulnerability, the ultimate helplessness of man. The arse thus
constitutes a *momento mori*.

One reads this statement so because the man who speaks it is the
one, out of all the major characters, who most exults in his sexual
nature. Indeed as the dying Christ-like nude of Scene V he achieves a
near-literal apotheosis from which his homosexuality cannot be
extricated. In point of fact he had been accorded a gay transfiguration
long before the sad and haunted last pages, before even his words on
the arse. In the second scene, that set in the Roman Ruin, a Centurion
arrives, bringing to the two figures a message from an Emperor.
(Centurion and Emperor are, I have little doubt, engendered by the
ruins – symbols of the glorious but fallen classical world; only thus
could they coexist with a roughly present-day Director and actors,
however transmogrified!) The message is this:

The Emperor is looking for the One.[29]

It never occurs to either the Figure of Little Bells or the Figure of
Vine Leaves not to take these words on a sexual level – rightly, it turns
out – and each believes himself to be the One, that twin for whom the
man of Gemini, such as Lorca himself, is constantly searching. And it
is the Figure of Vine Leaves, Man 1, who has been most honest and

consistent about his sexuality, who is rewarded with the Emperor's embrace, much to the Director's distress. Rafael Martínez Nadal's supposition that the Emperor is Hadrian with his love for Antinous seems to me justified.[30]

That *El público* asserts the validity of all sexual communication is also borne out by the references to another Shakespeare play, *A Midsummer Night's Dream*. What Lorca admired in this play, what indeed he thought its central and pivotal feature, was Titania's infatuation with Bottom as ass. As in 'Thamar y Amnón', heterodoxy is seen to count for nothing besides the forces of genuine obsession and passion. (One must also add that *A Midsummer Night's Dream* with its watching duke and courtiers also makes significant use of an audience whose secret wishes are reflected in the play they witness.)

*El público*'s phantasmagoric round of homosexual desire and love abruptly broken by death is meant, as increasingly in Lorca's work, to be viewed ontologically. Homosexual relations differ from heterosexual ones in that while making love, and confronting each other's *otherness*, the lovers also see in the bodies they are embracing 'speaking images' of their own. However bizarre the transvestite disguises, whatever the role-difference accentuated in sadomasochistic ritual, this fact cannot but be evident. It highlights, I think, awareness of the mortality of the human being, and certainly *El público* presents all life, including the most outrageous sexual frolics, as enshadowed by Death. The windows of the first scene are made up of X-ray sheets, reminding us who have read Lorca's later poetry of the *'gráfico de huesos'* ('diagram of bones') of the sonnet 'Adán' ('Adam').[31] In the last act a great eye stares at us from the right of the stage, and a severed horse's head rears up from the floor. Sex is to be cherished, but it should help us – rather than divert us – from realisation of the might of death. Coming after the fifth scene, where the passion of Christ is half parodied, half re-enacted, and where the revolution seizes the theatre, these stage properties are peculiarly telling and pregnant with dark meaning.

This last scene – in which the Director will sink into coldness, quiet and death – is that in which Lorca makes us understand and acknowledge the superiority of the Theatre Beneath the Sand, that which deals with the deep forces within the psyche and eschews the persona. The Director has in truth come a long way from his proud boasts about his Theatre of Open Air, and his views can now be taken as those of his creator who, after his journey through his own multi-layered homosexual nature, wanted to make only art that was at once bold and deep:

> All true theatre has a profound stench of over-ripe moon. When the costumes speak, the living persons are already buttons of bone on the walls of Calvary. . .

If I spent three days struggling with the roots and the waterfalls it was in order to destroy the theatre. . .and to demonstrate that if Romeo and Juliet suffer and die in order to wake up smiling when the curtain falls, my characters, on the other hand, destroy the curtain and die in reality in the presence of the spectators. . .

I knew a man who swept the roof and cleaned the skylights and railings only out of gallantry towards the sky. . .

The true drama is a circle of arches where the wind and the creatures can go in and out without having a place to rest. Here you are treading upon a theatre where authentic dramas are given and where has been maintained a real combat which has cost the life of all the interpreters.[32]

This talk of truth, death, creative combat unites *El público* – and the conclusions reached in its final scene – with those theories of the *duende* on which Lorca was engaged at the time of much of its writing.

### 3

As in the pieces concerning El Amargo, Lorca in 'Juego y teoría del duende' takes an ancient Andalusian supernatural belief and interprets the object of this according to his own idiosyncratic temperament and creative needs, endowing it indeed with a new identity that enables it to have general Spanish and, beyond this, universal reference. There is a difference between the Amargo and the *duende*; the first manifests himself externally, forcing attention by means of his aggressive stare, etc; the second is an internal force. The *duende* enters the human being, wounding him or her in the process, establishes itself, and so a lifelong struggle ensues. In Lorca's view great art is born of this conflict, is manifest only with the assertion of the *duende* (for by implication art lacking in *duende* has, even at its best, an only partial application to the universal condition). Lorca's examples in the first pages of the lecture are from the *cantaores* and *tocaores* with which *El poema del cante jondo* made us familiar; indeed the names of Manuel Torres and Silverio Franconetti, whom Lorca had celebrated in earlier poems, are produced as illustrative of creation brought about by the struggle with the *duende*. How do we recognise it? Lorca suggests that in its presence – and it is usually manifested in the performing arts of song, dance, theatre and spoken poetry – one is in no doubt: the conflict, the ensuing passion *is*, and we are invaded as a result:

'All that has dark sounds has *duende*.' And there is no greater truth.

These 'dark sounds' are the mystery, the roots thrusting into the fertile loam known to all of us, ignored by all of us, but from which we get what is real in art. . .Thus the *duende* is a power and not a behaviour, it is a struggle and not a concept. I have heard an old guitarist master say: 'The *duende* is not in the throat; the *duende* surges up from the soles of the feet.' Which means that it is not a matter of ability, but of real live form; of blood; of ancient culture; of creative action.[33]

However it is not just simply a matter of waiting for what loosely might be termed inspiration, for *duende*-possession; one can be receptive to it, unstifling of it if one apprehends it imminent within. One can also try to ascertain that the culture of which one is part is itself sensible of *duende*. Anglo-Saxon America was not; Black Harlem was. But the great country of the *duende*, as Lorca views it, is Spain itself.

For all that the *duende* might seem to defy intellectualisation, Lorca proceeds to try to define further – often by example; indeed no work reveals the extent of Lorca's knowledge of cultural matters, Spanish or otherwise, more than this essay, which for all its seeming espousal of unsophisticated mores, of primitivism, should be compulsory reading for all those who insist on talking about Lorca as if he were a mere deliverer of some native woodnote wild.

First he contrasts the *duende* with two other art-engendering forces, the muse and the angel. 'The angel,' Lorca pronounces, remembering his own archangels of the *Romancero gitano*, 'guides and endows with gifts like San Rafael, or defends and wards off like San Miguel, or warns like San Gabriel. The angel may dazzle, but he merely hovers over the head of man; he bestows his graces, and man quite effortlessly achieves his work, his sympathy, or his dance.'[34] The muse, on the other hand, 'dictates and, occasionally, inspires'. I must confess that repeated readings over many years of this essay have failed to make satisfactorily clear to me exactly what – apart from being associated with an intellectual, over-formal kind of art – the muse's qualities are, why Apollinaire was destroyed by it and why Germany – with its great romantic tradition, land of Beethoven, Hölderlin, Nietzsche – should be seen as the chief land of the muse. But what becomes clear about both the muse and the angel, however we (or Lorca himself for that matter) interpret them, is that they fail, as guardians of the spirit and in their artistic manifestations, where death is concerned. Using startlingly Daliesque terminology Lorca tells us that the muse, the intellect, 'makes [the poet] oblivious of the fact that he may suddenly be devoured by ants, or a great arsenic lobster may fall on his head':

> The *duende*, on the other hand, does not appear if it sees no possibility of death, if it does not know that it will haunt death's house, if it is not certain that it can move those branches we all carry, which neither enjoy nor ever will enjoy any solace.

In idea, in sound, or in gesture, the *duende* likes a straight fight with the creator on the edge of the well. While angel and muse are content with violin and measured rhythm, the *duende* wounds, and in the healing of this wound which never closes is the prodigious, the original in the work of man.

The magical quality of a poem consists in its being always possessed by the *duende*, so that whoever beholds it is baptised with dark water. Because with *duende* it is easier to love and to understand, and also one is *certain* to be loved and to be understood; and this struggle for expression and for the communication of expression reaches at times, in poetry, the character of a fight to the death.[35]

The last paragraph here is particularly significant; apprehension of death, reverence for its power increases sense of life. *Así que pasen cinco años* and *El público* show this, are vessels for *duende*, though for that spirit's triumphal epiphany we shall have to wait for poetry wholly born of Spain and Spanish experience; the long elegy 'Llanto por Ignacio Sánchez Mejías' and the wonderful *gacelas* and *casidas* of the *Diván del Tamarit*. For in distinction to almost every other country:

Spain is always moved by *duende*, being a country of ancient music and dance, where the *duende* squeezes lemons of daybreak, as well as being a nation of death, a nation open to death.

In every country death has finality. It arrives and the blinds are drawn. Not in Spain. In Spain they are lifted. Many Spaniards live between walls until the day they die, when they are taken out to the sun. A dead person in Spain is more alive when dead than is the case anywhere else – his profile cuts like the edge of a barber's razor.[36]

It will be remembered that in an earlier *conferencia*, that on the lullabies, Lorca said that a dead man was more dead in Spain than elsewhere, Spain refusing the shadow-lands of most other popular mythologies. In fact these two statements, far from being contradictory, as at first sight they might seem, are mutually complementary. If death is unsparingly emphasised, its presence is the more inescapable, the more influence-exerting. The dead man emphasised in all his deadness thus becomes a living presence even while the process of decay, of drawing nearer to that '*gráfico de huesos*', has begun. Similarly the man who feels in himself his own mortality becomes the quicker, the more responsive to life in all its multiplicity.

All major Spanish art in Lorca's view exhibits *duende* in that a sense of death, a struggle with mortality, conditions and impregnates it:

The moon-frozen heads which Zurbarán painted, the butter-yellow and the lightning yellow El Greco, the prose of Fr

Sigüenza, the whole of Goya's work, the apse of the church at El Escorial, all our polychrome sculpture . . . all these are the cultured counterpart of the pilgrimages to San Andrés de Teixido, where the dead have a place in the procession. . .and of the innumerable Good Friday ceremonies which, together with the most civilised spectacle of bull-fighting, constitute the popular triumph of death in Spain. Of all the countries in the world, only Mexico can match Spain in this.[37]

Certainly the works that Lorca himself produced after his return to Spain, and by which he is best known – what I call, in the next chapter, his 'classical masterpieces' – show a wholly Spanish permeation with sense of death; *Bodas de sangre, Yerma, La casa de Bernarda Alba* exhibit the *duende* as fully as the more overtly death-concerned 'Llanto.'

That the theory of the *duende* owes its full being to Lorca's stay in America – which, by shutting the door to confrontation with mortality, had in fact created a society the poet found nigh unbearably cold and cruel – seems to me beyond doubt. The work that Lorca was to go on to produce on his return from Cuba shows a marked intensity on the author's part of a wish to be part of a great Spanish artistic tradition. After 1930 there is no conflict between the Spanish and the universal, or between the personal and the universal; a work like the 'Llanto' is all in one a conscious tribute to the Spanish literary tradition, a personal act of mourning on Lorca's part, and a work of wholly international reference, being concerned with emotions and intellectual problems that belong to everybody.

So that the period which had begun in such despair and confusion ended in a wholly creative discovery of his own nature and his own culture on the part of the poet. Before making some concluding remarks about this, however, I feel it only fair to comment briefly on the limitations of that vision at which Lorca had arrived – limitations inevitable in any *weltanschauung*, for – with the possible exception of Shakespeare in Dryden's famous phrase – no one human being can be all mankind's epitome. First, Lorca's rejection of America must be considered too complete; in life he may have appreciated its many-facetedness, in art not. America – it need hardly be said – is infinitely more than the sum of rapacity and jungle economics that *El poeta en Nueva York* makes it out to be. Of course *El poeta* does not pretend to be an objective, sociological document, quite the reverse, but all the same to find a sad absence in it of salutation to America's capacity for humanitarian activity seems to me not wholly lacking in pertinence. This feeling is compounded by the knowledge that after the Civil War, Lorca himself having been cruelly murdered, his family were glad to find in America a hospitable home.

Similarly there is a contraction of vision in the whole concept of *duende*. Indisputably Lorca is right when he chastises the creeds that have developed out of the Enlightenment for their dishonesty concerning death; but one can, I believe, counter by suggesting that too great an emphasis on what, after all, must at one level or another be obvious to all can have considerable dangers. These dangers, paradoxically, are not dissimilar to those very ones Lorca would seem to be in protest against. This comes out very strongly, I feel, in Lorca's eulogies about the bull-fight which indeed receive development from the passage quoted for the greater remaining part of the essay. Determined to view the *corrida* symbolically, to see it as a life-and-death rite, analogous to the Catholic mass, that gives the lie to comfortable humanist evasions of reality, Lorca pays no attention at all to the unjust, squalid, wanton and, above all – totally *real* pain of the bull. The bull exists in no state of awareness of the symbolic nature of what is going on and of what happens to him. Anyone who has witnessed the hideous rolling-over of the bull in his death-agonies, looking out with waning eyes at humankind in bewildered incomprehension at what has been dealt to him in pre-arranged and carefully practised ritual, knows that here is no telling spontaneous demonstration of the forces of existence, but merely a bloody and sensationalist spectacle – with atavistic roots, no doubt – indulged in for a whole host of reasons, all of them morally dubious to say the least: blood-lust, money, fetishistic addiction to age-old ceremony. One can only quarrel deeply and openly with a point of view that can find this commercialised brutality 'civilised'.

But one must surely also say that no one – not even a genius of Lorca's calibre – can escape from the society into which he is born. Lorca's love for Andalucía, for Spain altogether, led him into a reverence for all its most ancient arts which we can sympathise with, even if we do not take all of it on board. His theory of the *duende* – inspiring to Spaniards – is also of the greatest spiritual use to those of us from a very different tradition. Like those worshippers in the pilgrimage to San Andrés de Teixido – to whom Lorca referred – we need to make the dead, and with them the state in which they exist, part of what we do. Lorca's confrontations with the New World and with his own homosexuality, confrontations which resulted in three complex and highly individual masterpieces, enabled him to write poems and plays which in their artistic effect can truly be said – as he said of the *duende* – to 'burn the blood like powdered glass'. And we do Lorca the gravest disservice if we do not recognise continually that his apprehension of death was self-promoted in the knowledge that it would intensify his love of all living things and his perception of them as flawed but lovable versions of what knows perfection in the Platonist world of the Ideal. Let us close this concluding discussion of the first and principal section of the book with the last words of the lecture on the *duende*. Lorca has imagined three arches containing respectively the muse, the angel and the *duende*. In her arch the muse is quiet, the angel stirs diffidently –

> The *duende* – where is the *duende*? Through the empty arch
> comes air of the mind that blows insistently over the heads of the
> dead, in search of new landscapes and unsuspected accents; an air
> smelling of a child's saliva, of pounded grass, and medusal veil
> announcing the constant baptism of newly created things.[38]

It is this constant baptism of which the works of Lorca's classical
period, and of the period prior to his tragic death, make us so
gratefully aware.

★

Lorca returned to the Spain of the Republic, and to an atmosphere at
first more congenial and hopeful than any he had lived and worked in
before. His enthusiasm for those hopes for Spain propagated by
Zamora and Azaña can be seen by the eagerness with which he threw
himself into his theatre company, 'La Barraca' ('The Caravan'). This
visited the remotest parts of the Spanish provinces bringing to people
the glories of their own classical drama, as well as more recent works.
His faith in culture, his republicanism, were shared by all his friends
and by his family; it must be utterly repudiated that – as is sometimes
articulated by those of conservative opinion – Lorca was not fully and
committedly involved with what was happening in Spain in the
Thirties. (See Introduction and Chronology.) He followed the ailings
of the Republic with sorrow – the right-wing, punitive though
democratically valid victories of 1934 – and bitterly opposed the
savage reprisals against the Asturian miners that October. Similarly he
signed protest letters against the unjust imprisonment of Azaña. Later
he was delighted at the success of the Frente Popular though anxious
about its fortunes. Ian Gibson in his seminal essay '"L'apolitisme" de
Lorca' makes clear just how strong Lorca's democratic convictions
were, and his two exemplary studies *The Death of Lorca* and *The
Assassination of Federico García Lorca* have demonstrated how little dear
to the Right Lorca was, as well as convincingly demolishing the whole
paraphernalia of convenient theories invented after Lorca's murder in
August 1936 to explain it. It was not accident, nor was it – as rumour
once strongly had it – connected with some homosexual vendetta
somehow absorbed into Civil War activities. Lorca was murdered by
the violent Right because like his friends, he was not one of them and
never could be, and had behind him a career and a corpus of literary
works to demonstrate this. His murder acted – and very effectively –
as a *pour encourager les autres* for other Spaniards, an earnest of the
terrible things to come. Lorca's famous pronouncement that he was
for an all-inclusive Spain which also meant Monarchists and Catholics
would have only confirmed his haters in their opinion of him. The

Falangist Right, indeed the Right of any strong leadership, doesn't much care for plurality.

1930 to 1936 were, for all the external turmoil, years of a truly wonderful activity for Lorca; and the *Romancero gitano* excepted, all the work by which he has been best known came from that period – a period in which, in social and personal life, his old character had quite returned, ebullient, sensitive, friendly, full of plans and schemes, an amazing number of which he carried out (his visit to Argentina and Uruguay of 1933–34, for example), but with that awareness of his own *raíz amarga* which we have already noted.

The major part of my task has been done. I have shown how the crisis of 1928–29 forced from Lorca – especially when it took him to America with all its bewildering confusions – a recognition of the complexities of his own homosexual nature. I have tried to show that homosexuality had, in fact, animated his previous productions, being often responsible for what is most alive and disturbing in them, and that after his period in New York – during which he confronted it in a different way – he was able to use it to create works of major emotional and intellectual reference which have still not been accorded their full due. This balance I have attempted to put right.

On the other hand volumes already exist on the major achievements of the Thirties – achievements in which at first sight homosexuality plays little part. In the next section I look at these famous works but strictly from this point of view: that the homosexuality which we have seen so dominant in Lorca's imaginative, artistic life does *not* disappear from *Bodas de sangre* (1932), *Yerma* and the 'Llanto por Ignacio Sánchez Mejías' (1934), *Doña Rosita la soltera* (1935) and *La casa de Bernarda Alba* (1936). Rather it can be seen again as a figure in the carpet, and I hope that my revelation of this can be helpful and can make some contribution to further acknowledgement of just how richly worked and complex these achievements are. Even at the time they enjoyed great acclaim, and no wonder, because they speak to so many regions of the personality.

Contemporaneous with these so public achievements are the private ones which are the subject of the last section of my book: the poems of the *Diván del Tamarit* and, later, the *Sonetos del amor oscuro (Sonnets of the Dark Love)*. These last return to the subject of homosexual love, or rather visit the subject again and in an even bolder way, since they *are* written *in propria persona*. The two collections of poems amount, in my view, to Lorca's most advanced and visionary work. Once again I hope that my organisation of this discussion of Lorca's work, as imposed by my theme, can assist in a revaluation of the poet, and that these remarkable performances can begin to be given their full due, which in my opinion they have not yet quite received.

# PART TWO
# The Classical Masterpieces

## 1

Lorca had found the story of *Bodas de sangre* (*Blood Wedding*) some years before he wrote the play itself – in newspaper accounts of the elopement, on her wedding day, of a bride in Almería and her former lover.[1] The groom pursued the pair, and the two men proceeded to fight to the death. The play Lorca came to write ends with a choral account of this tragic conclusion to the story:

> Vecinas: con un cuchillo,
> con un cuchillito,
> en un día señalado, entre las dos y las tres,
> se mataron los dos hombres del amor.

> Neighbours: with a knife,
> with a little knife,
> on an appointed day, between two and three,
> the two men of love killed themselves.[2]

'*En un día señalado*': this phrase is crucial to the work. The events in Almería had composed themselves in Lorca's mind, not as a history of a crime and its repercussions, but as a terrible doomed sequence of irresistible compulsions. The Bride's lover exclaims at the play's climax:

> Que yo no tengo la culpa,
> que la culpa es de la tierra. . .

> Oh, it isn't my fault –
> The fault is the earth's. . .[3]

and, addressing the girl he loves:

> Clavos de luna nos funden
> mi cintura y tus cadenas.

Nails of moonlight have fused
my waist and your chains.[4]

Lorca's rejection of both socio-psychological and moralistic views of the incidents went hand in hand with a literary rejection of any naturalistic treatment of them. For the naturalistic is a collusion with beliefs in the supremacy of the rational and in the possibility of apportioning blame in, and finding solutions to, intricate human problems. *Bodas de sangre* is of Lorca's three great tragedies the most defiantly non-naturalistic. It is, as the lines just cited should make plain, the fruit of Lorca's absorption in Greek tragedy: it is also, this being no contradiction, a distinctly expressionist work. Such a fusion of classical and expressionist can be found also in the work of a dramatist ten years Lorca's senior, the American Eugene O'Neill. Stark and haunting achievements of his like *Desire Under the Elms* (1925), *Strange Interlude* (1928) and *Mourning Becomes Electra* (1936) provide interesting points of comparison with Lorca's major dramatic work, and embody the same cultural impulse: to clear the theatre of the clutter and *trompe l'oeil, trompe l'oreille* devices of the realistic drama, and to return to something purer, more atavistic and closer to drama's origins as a 'mystery' relating to the well-springs of human behaviour. Classical and expressionist features of *Bodas de sangre* are the rite-like *tableaux* that replace expected confrontations between characters, the discarding of prose for verse at high points of the play, the use of minor characters as a chorus, and the denial of names to all the characters except one, Leonardo, the Bride's old lover and present seducer.

It is the third act, however, which shows us most plainly the ritual and expressionist intentions of Lorca. Where the unsuspecting boulevard theatre-goer might anticipate a scene in which the wronged Bridegroom catches up with Leonardo and the Bride, we are presented with a masque of symbolic figures, none of whom has appeared before, speaking to us from a nocturnal forest as much a domain of the psyche as the actual place to which the guilty pair have fled. These figures are two Woodcutters, the Moon (in the guise of a Woodcutter) and an aged Beggarwoman – Death's acolyte and Death in person – both from Lorca's private but already much-projected mythology. Their exchanges and speeches show the people, their community, and the land in which it stands in the appropriate ontological context – one in which *un día señalado* is the most significant feature and everything is immanent with *duende*. These figures indicate to us that *Bodas de sangre* is, above all else, a rite-like progression towards acknowledgement of Death's supremacy.

This is also evidenced by Lorca's carefully thought-out, firmly insisted upon and wholly expressionist allotment of a colour to each scene, a paradigm of colours thus evolving. We move through yellow, rose, silver, and a general darkness to, first, an 'intense blue radiance' which the stage must take on for the advent of the Moon, and then the 'shining white' – with 'not a single grey nor any shadow, not even what is necessary for perspective' – of the final scene. It is therefore drenched in the frightening purity of an absolute and shadowless white that the Mother stands to deliver her last, gnomic lines:

> Y esto es un cuchillo,
> un cuchillito
> que apenas cabe en la mano;
> pez sin escamas ni río,
> para que un día señalado, entre las dos y las tres,
> con este cuchillo
> se queden dos hombres duros
> con los labios amarillos.
> Y apenas cabe en la mano,
> pero que penetra frío
> por las carnes asombradas
> y allí se para, en el sitio
> donde tiembla enmarañada
> la oscura raíz del grito.

> And this is a knife,
> a tiny knife
> that barely fits the hand;
> fish without scales, without river,
> so that on their appointed day, between two and three,
> with this knife,
> two men are left stiff,
> with their lips turning yellow.
> And it barely fits the hand
> but it slides in clean
> through the astonished flesh
> and stops there, at the place
> where trembles enmeshed
> the dark root of a scream.[5]

These lines about the power of the knife must remind us of the 'Diálogo del Amargo' in which the Amargo was offered by the Rider 'knives . . . that go in looking for the hottest spot'. In fact the kinship between the close of *Bodas de sangre* and the Amargo poems was first perceived and commented on by Lorca himself. In his lecture on the *Romancero gitano* Lorca would read the last couplet of the 'Canción de la madre del Amargo' (see above, p. 54) and add: 'at the end of my tragedy *Bodas de sangre*, they [women] weep again, I don't know why, over this enigmatic figure.'[6] So – *Bodas de sangre* is yet another emanation of the Amargo, another attempt to grapple with and contain him, and our conclusions from reading the Amargo poems must be highly pertinent to our consideration of this, Lorca's first dramatic masterpiece.

But who in the play stands for the Amargo? It is, after all, a *pair* of men that the women are weeping over in the final tableau, the Bridegroom and Leonardo.

It is tempting to see the latter as the Amargo's embodiment. He is both violent and a producer of violence; he, like the Amargo as we have already encountered him, is sullen, cussed, anti-social, yet burning with intense feeling. 'Why do you always have to make trouble with people?' his mother-in-law asks him, and his wife, bemusedly: 'What idea've you got boiling there inside your head?'[7] The Bride makes it clear to us that she believes herself to have chosen the rougher, the less virtuous of the two men. Like the Amargo in Lorca's childhood vision Leonardo offers the anti-domestic lot to her, beckons to her on behalf of the wild instinctual life beyond windows and walls. He is one with the horse that he rides so often and so ruthlessly during the course of the play, and on which he places the Bride for seduction:

> Pero montaba a caballo
> y el caballo iba a tu puerta.
> Con alfileres de plata
> mi sangre se puso negra,
> y el sueño me fue llenando
> las carnes de mala hierba.

> But I was riding a horse
> and the horse went straight to your door.
> And the silver pins of your wedding
> turned my red blood black.
> And in me our dream was choking
> my flesh with its poisoned weeds.[8]

His concept of love and of love-making is at variance with the vision of these implicit in the wedding service. Leonardo can lead us – as the Amargo would do – to an appreciation of the full, the double irony of the title Lorca gave his play:

> Vamos al rincón oscuro,
> donde yo siempre te quiera,
> que no me importa la gente,
> ni el veneno que nos echa.

Let's go to a hidden corner
where I may love you for ever,
for to me the people don't matter
nor the venom they throw on us.[9]

'*Que no me importa la gente*' – the line is rich in Lorquian ambiguity; he
is both critical of and sympathetic to such a notion, such a wish.

By contrast the Bridegroom would appear to embody the kindly
virtues of domesticity: he is a good son to his widowed Mother, he
works the vineyards well, he longs for nothing more than to live,
uninterruptedly, side by side with the girl who so stirs him physically
and who touches his heart. 'I'll hug you for forty years without
stopping,' he says to the Bride before they are married.[10] Yet when he
learns of her elopement he knows no tame hesitation or doubt. 'Let's
go after them!' he cries, 'Who has a horse?'[11]

The impassioned verse exchanges of Leonardo and the Bride in the
forest reveal that they are both prepared for a *liebestod* – ecstasy and
union in death. But in fact it is Leonardo and the Bridegroom who
achieve a kind of *liebestod*: carried away by their love they plunge
knives into each other. And it is *here*, in my view, that the Amargo can
be found. He is the *knife* – no matter which of the two men is its
owner – as it mortally enters the other's flesh. And the knife is the
penis which thrusts and enters where it lists. *This* is what the women
are weeping over, tragically bathed in the harsh whiteness – the
Amargo, the knife, the cock, responsible for dark rapture and spilled
blood alike.

Leonardo himself says:

To burn with desire and keep quiet about it is the greatest
punishment we can bring on ourselves.[12]

The penis, it must never be forgotten, can instruct the heart.
Together how can they not defy and annihilate reason's repressing
admonitions?

What good was pride to me – and not seeing you, and letting you
lie awake night after night? No good! It only served to bring the
fire down on me! You think that time heals and walls hide
things, but it isn't true, it isn't true! When things get that deep
inside you there isn't anybody can change them.[13]

His homosexual recognition of desire's might makes Lorca able to
empathise with women in the grip of anti-conventional desire. Listen
to the Bride's confession to the Bridegroom's mother:

I was a woman burning with desire, full of sores inside and out, and your son was a little bit of water from which I hoped for children, land, health; but the other one was a dark river, choked with brush, that brought near me the undertone of its rushes and its whispered song. And I went along with your son who was like a little boy of cold water – and the other sent against me hundreds of birds who got in my way and left white frost on my wounds, my wounds of a poor withered woman, of a girl caressed by fire. I didn't want to; remember that! I didn't want to. Your son was my destiny and I have not betrayed him, but the other one's arms dragged me along like the pull of the sea, like the head toss of a mule, and he would have dragged me always, always, always – even if I were an old woman and all your son's sons held me by the hair![14]

Mutatis mutandis this (like Leonardo's speech) could be the cry of a young man who, after courtship, engagement, a wedding, after all the business of orthodox sexuality and home-planning, surrenders to his deeper and stronger drives and realises (in both senses of that word) what he has been evading and denying for so long a time.

The classical (and expressionist) nature of *Bodas de sangre* does not prevent Lorca from giving in it an entirely convincing delineation of Spanish country life and its suffocating socio-sexual mores. Indeed, as in *La·zapatera prodigiosa* with its villagers, a veritable Devil's Bible could be built up from the precepts on the comparative behaviour of the two sexes delivered throughout the play, particularly by the Mother:

MOTHER [*to her son, the Bridegroom*]. I'd like it if you were a woman. Then you wouldn't be going out to the arroyo now and we'd both of us embroider flounces and little woolly dogs.[15]

MOTHER [*somewhat proudly*]. It's twenty years since I've been up to the top of the street.[16]

FATHER [*about his daughter, the Bride*]. No need to tell you about my daughter. At three, when the morning star shines, she prepares the bread. She never talks: soft as wool, she embroiders all kinds of fancy work and she can cut a strong cord with her teeth.[17]

MOTHER [*to her future daughter-in-law*]. Do you know what it is to be married, child?
BRIDE, *seriously*. I do.
MOTHER. A man, some children and a wall two yards thick for everything else.

BRIDEGROOM. Is anything else needed?
MOTHER. No. Just that you all live – that's it![18]

The young Woodcutter who is the Moon (where, we recall, sits the Amargo after death) provides us – literally – with the appropriate light in which to view these dicta of the prison-house. His lines make it quite clear that his rays are also knives and cocks which not only crave but joyfully force entries everywhere, entries illuminated and illuminating:

> No quiero sombras. Mis rayos
> han de entrar en todas partes,
> y haya en los troncos oscuros
> un rumor de claridades. . .

> I want no shadows. My rays
> must get in everywhere,
> even among the dark trunks I want
> the whisper of gleaming lights. . .[19]

However animated by the unconscious, the phallic imagery here is, it hardly need be said, completely intentional and conscious. The light of the Moon – which shows us Life-and-Death as Siamese twin reality – shines into vagina and anus alike, and makes nonsense of the kind of conventions that the Mother and all her fellow-upholders of the law are pleased so continually to remind us of.

## 2

*Yerma* takes us into the same world as *Bodas de sangre*, a Spanish rural community coffin-narrow with prescription. Its story contains no scenes of escape, no moon-irradiated forest; and it culminates in a horrific act that only increases the sense of claustrophobia engendered by both setting and characters. For this reason the play eschews many of the expressionist devices that made *Bodas de sangre* so rich a work; Lorca wishes form to be mimetic of the subject-matter – frustration in a restricted society. *Yerma* is a relentlessly concentrated study, intent on its two central characters with a fixity of purpose proper to the classical drama (of France and Spain as well as of Greece and Rome). Paradoxically it is of far wider emotional reference than *Bodas de sangre* and, shot through with ambiguity, offers us complexities that are difficult indeed. To an even greater extent than was the case with its predecessor we find that *Yerma*'s power is inextricably linked to its creator's sexuality. Even an account of its situations and action can make that evident.

Yerma – her name is the feminine of the adjective *yermo*, waste, deserted, barren – cannot, through no deficiency or fault of her own, conceive a child. When we first meet her she has been married to her young smallholder husband, Juan, for two years. Juan, speaking about their life together, says 'smiling': 'Our work goes well, we've no children to worry about,'[20] but Yerma does not see their position in the same happy light. Already she minds bitterly about being childless, and reminds her husband of how willingly she entered the marriage-bed:

> I know girls who trembled and cried before getting into bed with their husbands. Did I cry the first time I went to bed with you? Didn't I sing as I turned back the fine bedclothes? And didn't I tell you, 'These bedclothes smell of apples!'[21]

The apple has, as we have seen, been much used by Lorca as a symbol of sexual love and fecundity. Juan tells his wife to hush. 'I have a hard enough job hearing all the time that I'm . . .'[22]

But what is this word, this phrase that he does not, cannot speak? As we become more intimate with Yerma and Juan – and we are made privy to their lives over a period of several years – our knowledge about their sexual relations, about the reasons for Yerma's failure to become pregnant, grows progressively less certain. It becomes plain that Juan finds sex with his wife an onerous duty rather than a pleasure and an expression of love. This is partly the result of exhaustion; his acceptance of the conventional rural role for the male means that he works so hard in the fields and in the orchards that he comes home too tired to do anything, let alone make love:

> I had a hard day yesterday [he complains to his sister]. I was pruning the apple trees, and when evening fell I started to wonder why I should put so much into my work if I can't even lift an apple to my mouth.[23]

But perhaps it is not as sad for Juan as it should be that he cannot please his wife amorously. And certainly the fact of his not having begotten children does not upset him. Indeed in the final scene he tells Yerma: 'Without children life is sweeter. I am happy not having them.'[24]

This statement, of course, in no way clarifies *why* he does not have them. We know that he is tepid in his love-making but then tepid love-makers can also beget children. It is, I think, implied in the play that Juan fails to achieve erection, but the last lines – spoken by Yerma after she has killed him – would seem to contradict this: 'Now I'll sleep without startling myself awake, anxious to see if I feel in my blood another new blood.'[25] If Juan, on the other hand, is incapable of fertilising emissions, then no beratement of him is justifiable. Were we in life presented with the case of Yerma and Juan we might cast doubts on the procreative powers of them as a couple – or even have Yerma undergo an examination! But it is axiomatic to Lorca's work that Yerma *is* capable of having children.

Yerma, for her part, has ceased to respond to Juan with sexual excitement. He has changed from the swimming, climbing, healthy youth she married into a pale-complexioned man with weary movements. We know that she is physically attracted by another, Victor, who indeed, before she met Juan, had given her her most memorable experience of physical joy. But in spite of all the rumours and suspicions to the contrary, Yerma desires a child only from her husband. Maybe in emphasising this point Lorca is engaging in criticism of the sexual mores of the kind of community with which he is concerned; honour, we learn from Yerma in the latter part of the play, demands that Juan – and Juan only – must be the father of her child. But I do not in fact think that Lorca here is indulging in tacit rebuke of rural morality; Yerma, whose nature is a constant one, has given herself to Juan completely, and certainly in the early days of their life together she yearned for him with her body as much as with her spirit. What she is subjected to therefore is a double denial – of proper attention from the man of her choice, and of a child from him.

Her plight leads her, first, to obsessive questioning of the happier people about her, then to consultation with the sorceress Dolores, and finally to her one deed of triumphant passion, her murder of Juan with her bare hands – which is also, of course, the murder of any child that she could honourably have had. The ironic significance of this is not lost on her:

> My body dry for ever! . . . Don't come near me, because I've killed my son. I myself have killed my son![26]

To come to terms with the sterility of his position, with the inexorable fact that his love-making can never lead to a child, is perhaps the hardest, the most anguishing problem for the homosexual, and many probably never achieve true acceptance of the situation. For Lorca who, as we have seen, loved children and was from all accounts very good with them, who had written on childhood and childish things with a tenderness unsurpassed by any writer this century, the problem must have been acute indeed. It is, I am convinced, his grief and rage at not being able to father a child that make *Yerma* the powerful work it is, that raise it from case history of frustration to great tragedy. Paradoxically it is also this personal investment in the play which is responsible for those uncertainties, those inconsistencies of thought that I have already noted. Lorca's vacillations about what is really the matter with Juan in relation to

Yerma derive from his having identified with *him* as much as with the eponymous Yerma. Indeed in an important way the identification with Juan is the more complete, for Juan's inability or refusal to do his sexual duty by a woman is far nearer Lorca's homosexual condition than is Yerma's denied motherhood. Which is not to say that Lorca does not present Yerma with empathic feeling; the success of his portrayal of her is surely shown by the fact that so many critics of the play have concentrated on Yerma at the expense of Juan.

The pain of the predicaments of both Yerma and Juan is compounded by the observations of the chorus of villagers with their cruelly role-enforcing rebukes and maxims. (The kinship here of *Yerma* to *Bodas de sangre* will be obvious.) Juan is made to feel shame that he has not sired a child, Yerma that she has not borne one. Maybe in a kinder, looser-structured society they would not feel their respective impotency and barrenness so intensely (just as the homosexual is happier in more amorphous and therefore tolerant societies). But I would not want it thought that *Yerma* is primarily a play of social criticism. Once again we can get help towards a proper understanding of the play from a consideration of its literary nature. Lorca describes it as a 'tragic poem'. Though the dialogue is eminently convincing – Yerma, Juan and Victor are not archetypes like those who make up the cast of *Bodas de sangre* – the play is not the naturalistic affair that would be suitable if the poet's intentions were sociological. *Yerma* is expressionist in the sense that it presents its characters bathed in the light of one predominant mood – in this case, frustration over childlessness. Like a poem, every line is shaped to contribute to the intensification of this mood, until the terrible and yet inevitable end is reached.

Moreover Lorca has not altogether forsaken those other features of the expressionist stage in which he rejoiced in *Bodas de sangre*. Here are Lorca's opening stage instructions:

> When the curtain rises YERMA is asleep with an embroidery frame at her feet. The stage is in the strange light of a dream. A SHEPHERD enters on tiptoe looking fixedly at YERMA. He leads by the hand a CHILD dressed in white. The clock sounds. When the SHEPHERD leaves, the light changes into the happy brightness of a spring morning. YERMA awakes.[27]

So, before we confront the characters in their wounded and workaday aspects, we have been taken into the collective unconscious – into a world of tenderness and fecundity. Excursions into the same realms are made in the beautiful lullaby that Yerma and her friends sing:

¿De dónde vienes, amor, mi niño?
'De la cresta del duro frío.'
¿Qué necesitas, amor, mi niño?

From where do you come, my love, my baby?
'From the mountains of icy cold.'
What do you lack, sweet love, my baby?[28]

– in the sudden ventures into verse, most notably Yerma's dreamily delivered description of her landscape of pain:

¡Ay, qué prado de pena!

Oh, what a field of sorrow![29]

– and, above all, in the near-pagan fertility pilgrimage, which forms the background to the dark events of Act Three. Lorca wants us, therefore, to view the play both in the wider context of human dreams and desires and *sub specie aeternitatis*.

And seeing it thus increases rather than diminishes our sense of Yerma and Juan's tragic lot. I referred just now to Lorca's grief and rage; what I did not say then is that they are directed at Nature herself, and at whatever has permitted her intransigent laws. It is intolerable that good, naturally maternal Yerma cannot have the children she so longs for; it is intolerable that good, naturally paternal homosexuals also cannot. Juan's transformation from healthy young man into wan-faced misanthrope, Yerma's from loving, high-hoping girl into murderess (one remembers Hardy's Tess) are totally unjust, and to greet them with Promethean anger is, perhaps, but the strongest and sincerest form of full acknowledgement of life.

That the power of *Yerma* derives from the strong personal significance of its theme for Lorca is confirmed by the presence of this last in that remarkable ultimate *suite* 'En el bosque de las toronjas de luna' ('In the Wood of the Moon's Grapefruit'), written eleven years earlier. The culmination of this series of poems is surely 'Encuentro' ('Encounter'). Here the poet ('*Yo*') and a mysterious female figure ('*Ella*') discuss unborn children they will never have. They can be heard in the girl's throat and seen shimmering before her eyes, but the serpent (some deep innate predilection?) disturbs the young man's breast and renders their birth impossible. 'Flor del sol/flor del río' ('Flower of the sun/flower of the river') say the identical opening and closing couplets, and fire (sun) dries water (river) and water extinguishes fire. A quietly Promethean expression of rage indeed![30]

*3*

*Yerma* and Lorca's most famous and ambitious poem, 'Llanto por Ignacio Sánchez Mejías' are intimately related in two ways. Though written in September 1934, less than a month after Sánchez Mejías' death in Madrid, the 'Llanto' (Lament') was first read publicly – by the poet himself – at a performance of *Yerma* (its hundredth) in April 1935. This, as Lorca himself must presumably have felt, is wholly appropriate, for the 'Llanto' continues *Yerma*'s Promethean rage at the cruelty of Nature's laws, a rage all the more violent because of the poet's deep love for the dead man who is at the poem's centre. The 'Llanto's' occasional nature should not be forgotten or underplayed. As much as *Bodas de sangre* with its Amargo-informed closing speeches or *Yerma* with its charged interchanges between heroine and husband, the 'Llanto' moves us by its rhetorical devices – its sense, if you like, of theatre. We must not be swayed when considering it by an Anglo-Saxon prejudice against poetry for which audience is important, against the studiedly monumental; the fact that it is consciously declamatory in no way mitigates its sincerity, the real personal suffering behind it. *Yerma* was subtitled by Lorca 'a tragic poem', the 'Llanto' could with equal aptness be described as a 'drama for the speaking poet'.

Something should be said here about Ignacio Sánchez Mejías himself. When Lorca first got to know him in 1927, during the celebrations of Góngora's tercentenary, he had retired – so he thought – from the arena in which he had earned a considerable reputation for himself. Later accounts have made him out to be a fairly indifferent *torero*, and certainly in no way comparable with a folk-hero like Belmonte. He was very interested in the arts, gathering poets and playwrights about him in his estate at Pino Montano, and he even wrote a play himself, *Sinrazón (Abuse)*.† He became the lover of Lorca's great friend, the dancer La Argentinita (real name: Encarnación López Julvez). Lorca saw much of the pair during his period in New York, where they went to stay in 1929, and was again very frequently in Ignacio's company after his return to Spain. Rafael Martínez Nadal has said that it seemed as if Lorca could never talk or be with the man enough, though there is no suggestion of any sexual relation between them.[31]

In May 1934 Ignacio decided to go back into the arena, a tragically mistaken decision as it turned out. He received the fatal wound –

---

†Lorca's admiration for all his talents was boundless. In a New York presentation to Ignacio – in which he extolled the bull-fight as the only serious thing in the modern world, uniting us all with antiquity – he described his friend as the embodiment of faith, heroism, and said his 'theatre' would make that of others seem vulgar, bourgeois.

exactly as the poem tells us – '*a las cinco de la tarde*' ('at five o'clock in the afternoon') in the arena at Manzanares, on 11 August 1934. He was rushed to Madrid and died there two days later at 1 p.m. Though the poem might seem to intimate otherwise, Lorca was not present when the *torero* received his fatal wound, and though on learning of it he made hourly inquiries about Ignacio's worsening condition, he did not visit him. When Ignacio died, he reacted – so he told his friend and distinguished French biographer, Marcelle Auclair – as if he had heard of his *own* death.[32] This reaction, this sentiment, are borne out by the whole tone of the elegy, the subject of which, over and above the mourned Ignacio, is Death itself – that of every member of the human race, and indeed Lorca's own.

The poem's dramatic elements work on us even in our silent readings: the famous octosyllabic line '*a las cinco de la tarde*' sounds bell-like and obsessively throughout the poem's first part, of which indeed it constitutes the constant alternate line to the sequence of dodeca- and hendeca-syllabic utterances (themselves rhetorically significant, since they hark back in prosody to the Renaissance and earlier, and are thus deliberate departures from the conventional romantic and post-romantic elegiac mode). In the second part the verb is in the first person singular for the first time; '*Que no quiero verla!*' ('Oh, I do not want to see it)'[33] it begins, and the pronoun object is the spilled blood of Ignacio. Five times Lorca repeats this cry, and then, to conclude the section, he subtly changes it, to intensify the personal feeling dictating it: '*Yo no quiero verla.*' The second part is distinguished also by two most dramatically effective bursts of lyrical apostrophes. The first of these proceeds by means of imaginative antitheses:

> ¡Qué gran torero en la plaza!
> ¡Qué buen serrano en la sierra!
> ¡Qué blando con las espigas!
> ¡Qué duro con las espuelas!
> ¡Qué tierno con el rocío!
> ¡Qué deslumbrante en la feria!
> ¡Qué tremendo con las últimas
> banderillas de tiniebla!

> What a great bullfighter in the ring!
> What a good countryman in the sierra!
> How gentle with the ears of corn!
> How hard with the spurs!
> How tender with the dew!
> How dazzling at the fair!
> How tremendous with the final
> *banderillas* of darkness![34]

The second places Ignacio in a wider context; a Spanish art had brought about his death, and Lorca can cry out:

> ¡Oh blanco muro de España!

> Oh white wall of Spain![35]

Interspersed with further personal exclamations of refusal to see his friend's blood, these lines develop an awareness of a cruelty, a mercilessness in Nature herself – who brings violent death but not the physical solace that should accompany it in a more kindly ordained providence.

The third section of the poem, 'Cuerpo presente' ('The Laid-Out Body') consists of quatrains in measured alexandrines: the mood is meditative, but still agonised. No peace of mind has come to the man mourning his friend, and this is indicated rhythmically by sudden lines broken into short sentences – ejaculations, questions – generally following much longer sentences that have been musically moving towards a deeply registered acknowledgement of stark reality.

> Ya está sobre la piedra Ignacio el bien nacido.
> Ya se acabó; ¿qué pasa? Contemplad su figura. . .

> Already Ignacio the well-born is on the stone.
> It's all over; what's happening? Look at his figure . . .[36]

The fourth section, 'Alma ausente' ('The Absent Soul') is also made up of quatrains in hendecasyllables (save for its fifth stanza of five lines), but once more rhetorical devices are used with great deliberation and effect: the repetition of the phrase '*no te conoce*' ('does not know you') to emphasise the total passing out of existence of Ignacio, so that everything about him is incomprehensible – and of the line (one surely very important in considering Lorca's religious point of view):

> porque te has muerto para siempre.

> because you have died for ever.[37]

The poem now builds up to its grand and formal perorative pronouncements on Ignacio. First the oxymoronic:

> Tu apetencia de muerte y el gusto de su boca.
> La tristeza que tuvo tu valiente alegría.

> Your appetite for death and the taste of its mouth.
> The sadness that your valiant gaiety possessed.[38]

Certainly Lorca is raising Ignacio to a Spanish pantheon; it is hard to imagine a non-Spaniard being praised in such terms. Perhaps even a non-Andalusian, and this aspect is stressed in the solemn final stanza, solemn yet not without that sad gaiety of which Lorca has just spoken:

> Tandará mucho tiempo en nacer, si es que nace,
> un andaluz tan claro, tan rico de aventura.
> Yo canto su elegancia con palabras que gimen
> y recuerdo una brisa triste por los olivos.

> A long time will pass before there is born, if ever,
> an Andalusian so noble, so rich in adventure.
> I sing his elegance with words that moan
> and I remember a sad breeze among the olive-trees.[39]

One notes that intimacy of memory is quite out of place here; Ignacio the socialite and cultural dilettante does not make an appearance. Ignacio is stripped of idiosyncratic identity in two respects – his life is presented in its quintessence, as crystalised by the art he served, and in death he passes into the world of mystery of which Lorca is a celebrant here. I use the words 'mystery' and 'celebrant' advisedly, since the 'Llanto' corresponds to another public event – the mass. The first part, 'La cogida y la muerte' ('The Tossing and Death') is a kind of introit, the words '*a las cinco de la tarde*' the communion bell bidding worshippers draw near. Just as in the story of the Passion, we have to believe in its divine preparation for it to have the appropriate significance, so here Lorca – conjuring up the *plaza de toros* for us – lays great stress on the preordination of the sudden and shocking moment at which Ignacio died. All the clocks say five in the afternoon, but in fact '*la muerte puso huevos en la herida*' ('death laid eggs in the wound')[40] and so the moment of time becomes at once both of the greatest significance and of no importance at all. The same idea is indeed repeated in the powerful second part of the poem:

> Por las gradas sube Ignacio
> con toda su muerte a cuestas.
> Buscaba el amanecer,
> y el amanecer no era.

> Up the tiers Ignacio climbs
> with all his death on his back.
> He was looking for the dawn,
> but the dawn did not exist.[41]

This second part, 'La sangre derramada' ('The Spilled Blood') is, of course, analogous to the wine, the blood of Christ in the mass; in the Roman Catholic Church until recently only the priests took this part of the sacrament, and this may be reflected in the wish of Lorca, Catholic-educated, not to see or have to do with the blood of his friend. (Though there are obvious personal reasons for this.) Nevertheless the blood is given the redemptive quality the Christian story gives to that of the Saviour of mankind; Lorca – in the lecture on the *duende* – had already stressed to the point of obsessiveness the kinship between the mass and the *corrida*. In writing the lines about the mystic property of the so recently spilled blood Lorca is too, I think, remembering 'El rey de Harlem' in which blood was extolled as a violent force driving, it was to be hoped, all to deeds of overthrow. Blood in this poem by contrast reminds one of the transcendent sweetness beyond pain:

> Y su sangre ya viene cantando:
> cantando por marismas y praderas,
> resbalando por cuernos ateridos,
> vacilando sin alma por la niebla,
> tropezando con miles de pezuñas
> como una larga, oscura, triste lengua,
> para formar un charco de agonía
> junto al Guadalquivir de las estrellas.

> And his blood now comes singing:
> singing through marshes and meadows,
> sliding down horns stiff with cold,
> hesitating without soul in the mist,
> stumbling with thousands of hooves,
> like a long, dark, sad tongue
> to form a pool of agony
> next to the starry Guadalquivir.[42]

Part Three is 'Cuerpo presente', in which the wounded and dead Ignacio lies on the stone ready for his final resting-place. Here Lorca confronts the body which is and is not his friend, and permits that Promethean protest of which we have recently been speaking to break through. He wishes there were other ways of dying and other ways of being dead than those meted out to us (and here death in the bull-ring is only a symbol of the way mortality gores and then seizes us all). The processes of decay (even more, the feeble attempts to arrest decay by those tending the body) are seen as a humiliation of the man whose form had housed so brave a spirit. Lorca even doubts for a few minutes (holy awe in the presence of the emptied human temple) his own ability artistically to surmount the tragedy:

Yo quiero que me enseñen un llanto como un río
que tenga dulces nieblas y profundas orillas,
para llevar el cuerpo de Ignacio . . .

I want them to teach me a lament like a river
that might have sweet mists and deep banks,
to bear the body of Ignacio . . .[43]

We remember how to be a river symbolised in the 'Oda a Walt Whitman' the wish, the need to identify oneself with all that is calming in Nature and contrary to the fret of human life. The river is also a symbol of flux. And the last stanza of the third part finds a grim consolation in the idea of this last; what has happened to Ignacio, his disintegration and absorption into timelessness happens to everybody, everything:

Vete, Ignacio: No sientas el caliente bramido.
Duerme, vuela, reposa: ¡También se muere el mar!

Go, Ignacio: Don't feel the warm bellowing.
Sleep, soar, rest. Even the sea dies.[44]

Christ ascended into heaven, and the mass – while reminding us of the reality of His death and ours – is also an earnest of eternal life. Ignacio, on the other hand, knows only extinction. It is not possible to read the last section without acknowledging this to be Lorca's belief. He may dwell on the separation of the dead man from all earthly life – never will he know autumn again nor autumn him – but above this he insists that the soul is absent not just in the sense of not being in the body any longer, but absent altogether:

Porque te has muerto para siempre,
como todos los muertos de la Tierra. . .

Because you have died for ever,
like all the dead of the Earth. . .[45]

Thus the sacrament that Lorca finally celebrates in the 'Llanto' is a humanist one – a reverence for a life that existed and then, terribly, ceased to exist, the mysteries of personality and the mysteries of that state we all have to accept when that personality ends. In the *gacelas* and *casidas* – with which the last part of this book will be concerned – we shall find a more mystic attitude to death: even Nothing can be viewed creatively so that its shadow ceases to frighten, indeed the reverse, intensifies our sense of life. The 'Llanto' is perhaps Lorca's bleakest work, but one of the most tremendous and exemplary courage. And it took his love of a man – even if this love was not of an overtly sexual kind – to bring out this courage to its full – and so beautifully articulated – extent.

## 4

The homosexual writer, with singular qualification, can view women as autonomous beings; freed from the endowments of desire or acquisition they can stand before him in all their complexity and their tragedy. Tragedy – because he, more than his heterosexual fellows perhaps, can understand just what cost to their psychic life their enforced surrender to convention so frequently entails. Just as the gay man has had to put up with expectations from those around him that he has neither inclination nor ability to fulfil, so women, especially in traditional societies, have had to acquiesce to criteria of judgement – founded on others' convenience – which may find them wanting and which, in their inmost beings, they resent and despise. Lorca's last two plays, *Doña Rosita la soltera* and *La casa de Bernarda Alba* make use of his experience as a homosexual to apprehend the lives of women trapped and suffocated by custom.

*Doña Rosita la soltera* (*Doña Rosita, the Spinster*) is described by the author as 'a poem of 1900 Granada, divided into various gardens, with scenes of song and dance'. Together with the poems of the *Diván del Tamarit* it constitutes Lorca's fullest tribute to his own city, with its arcane, sequestered gardens, its courteous, centuries-evolved social life, its ability to impart both a sense of time and timelessness. A strange tribute – and an ironically apt one, considering the cruelty the city was to deal out to its most distinguished son so soon after this play's completion. Life in the city is revealed as one of stultifying stupidity and enslavement to formality. Even the character who most amply loves the flowers and gardens of Granada (Doña Rosita's Uncle who has brought her up) is treated unsympathetically; he is a fool and a bore, and finally incompetent in dealing with the money which has sustained the restrictive life all the women around him have been forced to lead. The quotidian round in the city turns most of the women into empty shadows of themselves, the more depressing if they haven't succeeded in getting married. Lorca gives us wholly convincing and wholly appalling examples of the gossip, the frippery and the stratagems to conceal deepest frustration which make up the social intercourse of most of the female characters.

'A poem of 1900 Granada' needs qualification. In many ways *Doña Rosita la soltera* is most closely related to *Así que pasen cinco años* among Lorca's former works: it is a play in which Time is one of the *dramatis personae* and a cruel one. The first act takes place in 1885; Rosita, a lovely and gentle-natured girl, loves and is loved by her cousin, but it is not thought a good idea for them to marry. He must go off to Argentina, and she must wait until such time as he feels he has succeeded in his business undertakings and so can make her his wife. Inwardly – and in the bursts of poetry which appear in this play like operatic arias – Rosita protests against the arrangement, for she is very deeply committed to the young man. But what else can she do? Act Two takes us to the 1900 of the 'poem'; in the fifteen years that have elapsed Rosita and her cousin have not been united, though she hears from him. As in *Así que pasen* – of which this can be seen as a feminine counterpart – time stands still in the lover's head. Rosita sees her cousin as he was when he departed for Tucumán; she even follows a puppeteer in the town because of his resemblance to her love. A message comes from him towards the end of the act – he wants the two of them to be married by proxy, an obviously deceiving plan which, however, Rosita agrees to. Act Three takes us ten years on into the century. Of course Rosita was the victim of a trick of her cousin's; he married a rich Argentinian woman, and she has perforce joined the huge unemployed army of upper-class Granadine women, headed by her aunt who is threatened with poverty after her husband's recent death. As in a play by Chekhov the set of the last act is charged with a heart-touching air of departure, of reduction of life and retreat into an analogue of death. Against this Doña Rosita is moved to speak lines which bring home to us the burning agony she must carry through her quiet life. She has been referring to her deception by her cousin:

> . . . every one knew it, and I found myself pointed out with a finger that made my engaged girl's modesty ridiculous, and gave a grotesque air to my maidenly fan. Every year that passed was like an intimate garment torn from my body. And today one friend gets married, and another and another, and tomorrow, she has a son and he grows up and comes to show me his examination marks . . . and I stay the same, with the same trembling, the same . . . [A child says:] 'There's the old maid,' and another [. . .]: 'No one would cast an eye at her any more.' And I hear it, and I can't even cry out, but go on, with a mouth full of poison and an overpowering desire to flee, to take off my shoes, to rest, and never, never move out of my corner again.[46]

And later:

> There are things that cannot be told because there are no words to tell them; and even if there were, no one would understand their meaning. You understand me if I ask for bread or water, or even for a kiss, but you would never be able to understand, nor remove, this dark hand that freezes or burns my heart – I don't know which – every time I'm left alone.[47]

The play was conceived long before it was written (1935), in the mid-Twenties after Lorca's friend José Morena Villa, librarian of the Royal Palace in Madrid, had read to him an 18th-century account of the *rosa mutabile*, a rose that changes colour as it ages. This is the central image of Lorca's drama, and the *rosa mutabile* is of course, on an important level, Doña Rosita herself and such as she. The poetry recounting the rose is of an almost painful tenderness:

Cuando se abre en la mañana,
roja como sangre está;
el rocío no la toca
porque se teme quemar.
Abierta en la mediodía
es dura como el coral.
El sol se asoma a los vidrios
para verla relumbrar.
Cuando en las ramas empiezan
los pájaros a cantar
y se desmaya la tarde
en las violetas del mar,
se pone blanca, con blanco
de una mejilla de sal.
Y cuando toca la noche
blando cuerno de metal
y las estrellas avanzan
mientras los aires se van,
en la raya de lo oscuro
se comienza a deshojar.

When it opens in the morning,
it is red as blood;
the dew does not touch it
because it is afraid of burning.
Open at mid-day
it is hard as coral.
The sun looks in through the windows
to see it glow.
When in the branches
the birds begin to sing
and the afternoon faints
on the violets of the sea,
it becomes white, with the white
of a cheek of salt.
And when night plays
a smooth metal horn
and the stars draw near

while the winds disperse,
on the edge of darkness
it begins to lose its petals.[48]

But there is a difference between the rose and the woman named after it; the rose's position is natural to it, and each weather, each fluctuation of season, however sad, is borne by the flower with expressions and changes wholly acceptable, indeed organic, to it. Doña Rosita, though, wishes her movement through life to be informed with love for and from others – more specifically, for and from men. But fate and convention between them have seen that it isn't, and change is the only experience that comes deeply her way. Thus while she follows the ways of the rose, she cannot do so as if she were one. Or rather, she is denied secret properties the rose must have if sensate as to its earthly career.

There is one moment of transitory redemption. One of the sons of an old friend of Rosita's comes to call on her house; his half grown-up ways are a further proof of time's passing. But he wishes her well, and tells her how greatly he has enjoyed dressing-up, as a joke, in old dresses that fashion-conscious women wore in Rosita's heyday. He is the last of the kindly, life-enhancing boys of double sexual identity that Lorca was to create, and when we meet him we remember the sweetness of the boy in *La zapatera prodigiosa* and of the Dead Boy and the Second Friend in *Así que pasen cinco años*.

★

The wonderful *La casa de Bernarda Alba* (*The House of Bernarda Alba*) was Lorca's last play, and not performed in his lifetime; indeed two months after its completion he was dead. It has a power that is very nearly unbearable, and is unquestionably one of the supreme dramatic achievements of this century. It fills one with a grief and, almost harder to endure, a terrible anger which, for me, beggars parallel. *La casa de Bernarda Alba* is tauter than Lorca's other work – his now increased knowledge of Greek and European classical tragedy is perhaps an important factor here – and is certainly the one with the most surface realism. Indeed the evocation of Bernarda Alba's household, and the tight village community without, would have satisfied a naturalist of an earlier generation from Lorca's. All the same it is not a naturalistic work, and shouldn't be discussed as such; it has, rather, the emotional intensity of early expressionist works, such as those of Strindberg (*Miss Julie*) or Wedekind (*Spring Awakening; Pandora's Box*), which in painterly fashion drench all characters and incidents in one colour, one mood. One can use the word 'colour' with great aptness where *Bernarda Alba* is concerned, since, as in other plays of Lorca's, one colour has an important role: white, the colour of the imprisoning walls of Bernarda Alba's house, the colour of the stallion who, restless, embodies what that house is shutting out, the colour of the purity to which Bernarda cruelly sacrifices her family, the colour of the Nothing to which she has wilfully reduced their life. The use of colours, symbols (walls, stables, windows, horse and rider), and verbal phrases that echo and distort each other is as controlled and imaginative as in any poem of Lorca's; indeed were it not so superbly of the theatre, one would say that this – in the usual meaning of the word – most 'unpoetic' of Lorca's plays is, in point of fact, that which best deserves the description 'tragic poem'.

The play opens shortly after the death of Bernarda's second husband; a wake for him has recently been held. A loveless, hypocritical marriage has come to an end; Bernarda's husband was never happier than when lifting up the skirts of the servantwoman, but for Bernarda her lack of feeling for the deceased does not prevent her from announcing the beginning of an eight-year period of mourning. All her family, over whom she rules despotically, must partake in this – all except her eldest daughter by a previous and richer husband, the pallid, lifeless heiress, Angustias (thirty-nine years old). Her destiny will be to accept the proffered hand of the beau of the village, Pepe el Romano. No one imagines that Pepe, twenty-five and of considerable sexual experience, is in love with Angustias – not even, in her honester moments, herself. The girl he was in love with, and may indeed still love (we never know), is the youngest and most attractive of her half-sisters, Adela. For her part she loves him, and even in the climate of imposed mourning and arranged marriage contrives to have clandestine meetings with him.

The situation which develops out of this has a terrible inevitability; the play continually stresses the restriction, the airlessness of life in Bernarda's house. Among the many poignant illustrations of the poisonous atmosphere prevailing in it is the behaviour of another daughter, the sickly, unattractive Martirio who, jealous of both her sisters and herself infatuated with the attractive Pepe, steals his photograph from Angustias and hides it under her pillow. The life built up in this small landholding family – closed yet ever mindful of what is thought in the village world – cannot admit of spontaneity, openness, steady and organic growth; everything twists upon itself, becomes tainted just as, apparently, the water of the well has turned polluted. Bernarda's mother – living out the long tedious years of her widowhood – babbles at the age of eighty of finding a handsome young lover by the seashore, and of having a child (or it may be a lamb! – lambs and children are kin) – and who can say whether or not her dotty fantasies are preferable to the gloomy half-life thrust upon her. Martirio's masturbatory habits are the only release possible for a plain and untalented girl whom her mother is determined to martyr (the choice of Christian name is an apt one). As for Adela – passionate and aware of her beauty – she is forced into a secrecy distateful to her and contrary to her real nature. She is the one character perhaps in whom love is stronger than sense of shame. When Bernarda, having discovered Pepe el Romano's visits to the house, shoots at him – not hurting him; symbolically he gallops away unscathed – Adela hangs herself: a twenty-year-old girl has to be cut down as if she were a bundle of goods hooked to a beam. Her mother is moved to burst out:

> Pepe, you're running now, alive, in the darkness, under the trees, but another day you'll fall. Cut her down! My daughter died a virgin. Take her to another room and dress her as though she were a virgin. No one will say anything about this! She died a virgin. Tell them, so that at dawn, the bells will ring twice.[49]

Proprieties, even if based on falsehood, must be observed! Otherwise the whole psychological edifice of Bernarda's inner house would collapse!

And all determining these horrors, moral and actual, a refusal to accept Nature, to obey its dictates and to go out in reverence and joy towards others as one does so. Talking of the stallion, Adela says: 'The stallion was in the middle of the corral. White. Twice as large. Filling all the darkness,' which is what sexual love does. But her sister replies: 'It was frightening. Like a ghost.'[50]

In his rage at the malformation of life to which the women of his drama – maybe even the terrible Bernarda herself – are subjected, Lorca must have been thinking of the denial of natural impulses and feelings to homosexuals in the conservative Spanish countryside. How many a boy, loving – or even merely desiring – another, was imprisoned in secrecy for fear of scandal, or else – like Angustias and Martirio – festered inwardly until both the inner mind and the outer man were diseased because unfulfilled. Another animus in the play that must, I think, emanate from Lorca's having been made to suffer for his sexuality in the convention-bound countryside, is that against the rollicking young men of the village epitomised by Pepe el Romano. A macho buck, good-looking and of reasonable family, can, as is observed in the play, get away with anything – seducing girls, even knowing the social consequences of this, trifling with their feelings, deceiving them, sacrificing them to self-advancement or pure pleasure. And yet the result of so much amorality is not necessarily, by any means, the censure one would expect of a society obsessively concerned with right-doing; unlike the gay man or the girl who give in to their sexual promptings and do no one any harm, he is admired for his dashing and will reap no consequences of his recklessness over others.

What conserves this unjust system is, of course, property – the preservation of property among the landed classes. It is interesting that in this, his last play, Lorca shows himself intransigently against those who build up treasures on this earth at the expense of their fellows: *La casa de Bernarda Alba* is in its own way as anti-capitalist as the 'Oda a Walt Whitman': here it is the capitalism of the Old World, of the hierarchical society centring on ownership of land. The poor of the village – whom the young Federico had known about from the stories of his family servants – do not live in the dread and distortion of sex that their social superiors do. Repeatedly throughout the play we learn about their greater sexual freedom and happiness. But their lot is, despite this, an unhappy one, and the maintenance of the have and have-not situation only furthers this, increasing the guilt-determined cruelty of the first, the passivity of the second.

'The poor are like animals,' says Bernarda haughtily, 'they seem to be made of different stuff.'

The peasant woman, to whom she is speaking, objects: 'The poor feel their sorrows too.'

And Bernarda is pleased to reply: 'But they forget them in front of a plateful of peas.'[51]

Faced with the evidence of this play of Lorca's last months, charged with that compassion which burned so creatively in him during his New York years, we need ask ourselves no questions about how the poet would have reacted to the regime of Franco – a regime his appalling death happily prevented him from seeing. And once again the sensibility that informs the last play he wrote and makes it so powerful a cry against all injustices must have ultimately been nurtured by his membership of a class which knew what rejection and denial meant, the homosexual.

★

This view of Lorca, and of *La casa de Bernarda Alba*, is vindicated by our present knowledge that its composition was flanked in time by resumed work on what have become all but mythological, the *Sonetos del amor oscuro* (*Sonnets of the Dark Love*), in which, with a heartfelt honesty and a total lack of self-pity, the poet voices, in a form as spare, classical and concentrated as that of his last dramatic masterpiece, the ebbs and flows of his emotional/psychic life during his love-affair with a man. Lorca had been writing sonnets in the Twenties, often in the strictest Gongorine form; it has been claimed that Lorca's projected volume of sonnets *Jardín de los sonetos* (*Garden of the Sonnets*) – half of which was to contain these earlier productions, half (roughly 17) new sonnets of his *amor oscuro* – originated in his New York years, though maybe only as a remote literary *desideratum*.[52] What we now know for sure is that in May 1935 Lorca, recovering from the creation of *Doña Rosita*, began to turn his mind back to a sonnet-sequence, on which he proceeded to work all that summer, and later, during November of the same year. In an interview of 7 April 1936 he was pleased to tell a journalist that he had finished a volume of sonnets; this seems to be a case of articulating a wish rather than a deed. In the terrible last month of his life, when in the now hate-charged city of his boyhood Lorca took shelter with his old friend, the poet and rightist Luis Rosales,[53] he returned to the sonnets. It is a thought at once tragically moving and strangely uplifting that amid bloody chaos – which was to culminate in his own ghastly murder – Lorca was devoting his imaginative energies to crystalline presentation of his intimate life, of the anguish and joy to which his homosexual direction had brought him.

The *Sonetos* were for a long time thought to have disappeared altogether; only recently have they been rescued from the Lorca family archives to confirm the awed memories of those who heard the poet read them (for instance shortly before his doomed departure for Granada in July 1936), men such as Rafael Martínez Nadal and Vicente Aleixandre who exclaimed:

Federico, what a heart! How much you must have loved, how much you must have suffered![54]

The present recovery of the sonnets and their placing, when taken together to form a whole, as the last achievement of Lorca's barbarously terminated life, causes us to revise our conventional image of the poet's progress. But, I submit, even without this so significant literary restoration, a reassessment along the lines it has, so to speak, redefined or strengthened was necessary. For, with the exception of the 'Llanto por Ignacio Sánchez Mejías', the poetry of Lorca's post-American years has suffered at the expense of his (justly) popular and admired plays. There was until very recently – and indeed perhaps still is, in the mind of the general public – a view that, apart from the 'Llanto', Lorca devoted himself after the surrealist explosion of *El poeta en Nueva York* to the theatre, and that it is as a dramatist that we must think of him in his maturity. And this despite the continuous appeal of a handful of late poems. In point of fact the *gacelas* and *casidas* that go to form the posthumously published *Diván del Tamarit* seem to me creations of the most astonishing genius, eclipsing even the dramatic *chefs d'oeuvre*. These poems also – though to a lesser extent than the *Sonetos* – have had a confused and confusing bibliographical history, and this may be a factor in their having been lost sight of in the dazzling forward-moving highway that Lorca's oeuvre should present. Some words of clarification are therefore now required.

The earliest of the poems included in the *Diván del Tamarit*, the 'Casida del sueño al aire libre' ('Casida of a Dream in the Open Air') dates from August 1931. A number of poems in comparable idiom were written during the next three years; then in the summer of 1934 Lorca, during a dinner, told the celebrated Arabist Emilio García Gomez, author of the anthology *Poemas arabigoandaluces* (*Arabo-*

*Andalusian Poems*, 1930) that he himself had completed a collection of Arabic-style poems, of *gacelas* and *casidas*, to honour the Moorish culture of his own Granada. Once again wish seems to have been anterior to achievement, and a number of the poems that go to make what we know as the *Diván del Tamarit* date from 1935. The poet would appear to have himself prepared the book for publication; a case therefore could be made for ending an account of Lorca's career with it.

Of these two last sequences the poems of the *Diván del Tamarit* are perhaps the richer and more imaginatively challenging, the *Sonetos* the bolder, the more surprising, the more painful. But in many respects their worlds are one, and of the most extraordinary beauty. The last part of this study tries to take readers into that world, the landscape of which is often strange and hard to traverse. First I will lead them into the arcane orchard that is the *Tamarit*, then into the secret garden of the last sonnets.

# PART THREE
# Dark Love, Gay Power

A year after Lorca's death, Freud's last major theoretical paper on psychoanalysis appeared: 'Analysis Terminable and Interminable'. In this he wrote:

> It is not a question of an antithesis between an optimistic and a pessimistic theory of life. Only by the concurrent or mutually opposing action of the two primal instincts – Eros and the death-instinct –, never by one or the other alone, can we explain the rich multiplicity of the phenomena of life.[1]

This continuous duet between Eros and Thanatos in the human soul – manifest in all Lorca's work – receives, I believe, its most sublime expression not in the more widely accepted plays but in the poems of his last years: the 'Llanto por Ignacio Sánchez Mejías', the *gacelas* and *casidas* of the *Diván del Tamarit*, and the pared and personal *Sonetos*.

The fact that the *gacelas* and *casidas* have not been saluted as the profound achievements that they are is partly due to the reasons cited in the last chapter, partly because they are even more difficult of access than Lorca's other poetry. Difficulty, it might be said, is a familiar enough problem for the reader of Lorca – parts of *El poeta en Nueva York* and *El público* being difficult to the point of virtual opacity. However the difficulties in these two works and others kin to them are wholly different in kind from those we have to face in the poems of the *Diván*. In the earlier work the associative process – influenced by the poet's reception of Dalí and Freud – led to a profligacy of images, one suggesting another. Logic comes through making the journey through the poem with the poet himself, though often – especially in the New York poems – the journey is a rough and wild one, suggesting the turbulence in the poet's mind. (This is not to deny what I stressed in Part One, that an overall unity is imposed upon the material, unity of thought and art.)

In the *gacelas* and *casidas*, however, the obscurities are quite other: the movement from image to image, the long and hard journey through a psychic landscape, these have already been accomplished by the poet *before*, as it were, he decided to commit the poem to paper. Each *gacela*, each *casida* constitutes a *place* in itself – ordered according to a logic fully comprehensible to the poet but not to others until after many readings. The comparative formal simplicity and verbal restraint of the poems of the *Diván del Tamarit* have also, I think, contributed to their relative critical undervaluation, as has the fact that they are contemporaneous with Lorca's most accessible and emotionally direct work, the classical masterpieces which were the subject of the previous chapter. Though forged from that Lorquian grammar of images with which we should have grown familiar, the later poems are, it must be conceded, remote, elusive.

However, for all this, they can, in one important respect, be related back to the interests and ambitions of his young manhood; like *El poema del cante jondo* they show the author's concern with the recovery of the ancient cultures of his native Andalusia, in this instance the Moorish/Arab. The confusions of the New World have been truly put behind him now. The title of the volume needs explanation. The *Tamarit* was the principal administrative office of the Moorish authorities, the *Diván* the assembly of men who met there. But – of more personal import – Tamarit was also the name of an orchard in possession of the Lorca family, where indeed many of the poems were written (it is indeed specifically referred to during the sequence). And *diván* is also the traditional Arabic name for a collection of poems (c.f. Goethe's famous *West-Östlicher Divan* of 1819).

In the 1922 lecture on the *cante jondo* Lorca had already spoken of the kinship of the Andalusian art-form that was his subject to the poetry of the Islamic world:

> When our songs reach the very extremes of pain and love they become the expressive sisters of the magnificent verses of Arabian and Persian poets.
> The truth is that in the air of Córdoba and Granada one still finds gestures and lines of remote Arabia, and remembrances of lost cities still arise from the murky palimpsest of the Albaicín . . .
> But where the resemblance is most striking of all is in the sublime amorous *ghazals* of Hafiz, the national poet of Persia, who sang the wine, beautiful women, mysterious stones, and infinite blue night of Shiraz.[2]

The *ghazal* becomes the *gacela* – a short lyrical poem, minimum four lines, maximum fifteen, and by preference on an erotic theme. The *casida* – Arab not Persian – is a lyrical poem of medium length with a strong internal structure: the majority of Lorca's *casidas* are arranged in quatrains of longish, slow-rhythmed lines. The poems themselves remind us from time to time of their origins, both ultimate and more immediate (i.e. Granada). For example, in the very first *gacela* of the sequence of twelve we read:

> Mil caballitos persas se dormían
> en la plaza con luna de tu frente. . .

> A thousand little Persian horses were sleeping
> in the moonlit square of your forehead. . .[3]

– a lovely tribute to the inner and erotic imaginative world of a sleeping loved one. And in 'Casida de los ramos' ('Casida of the Branches') the *'arboledas del Tamarit'* ('the groves of the Tamarit') are richly evoked – where long ago councillors conferred and where Lorca is now writing. But –

> El Tamarit tiene un manzano
> con una manzana de sollozos.

> The Tamarit has an apple-tree
> with an apple of sobs.[4]

So once again we are brought back to the postlapsarian world, to the Eden supposedly situated in Arab lands. Once again we apprehend *all* sensate nature as suffering, not just men alone. Among the loves that inform the *Diván* eminent is Lorca's for that disseminating centre of Islamic poetry, Granada herself. (As I have said, the volume must be taken together with *Doña Rosita la soltera* as Lorca's supreme act of homage to his city.) In the 'Gacela del amor que no deja ver' ('Gacela of Love that Doesn't Allow Itself to See'), Lorca pays tribute to the great bell of Granada's cathedral, La Vela, and tells us:

> *Granada era una luna*
> *ahogada entre las yedras.*

> *Granada was a moon*
> *drowned among the ivies.*[5]

But we remember the death-associations of 'moon', and are moved to think of the sufferings as well as joys that Granada brought to Lorca and was yet to bring him. 'Gacela del niño muerto' ('Gacela of the Dead Boy') reminds us:

> Todas las tardes en Granada,
> todas las tardes se muere un niño.

> All the afternoons in Granada,
> all the afternoons a small boy dies.[6]

Just such a small boy as Lorca himself was and – immersing himself in
Granadine matters – had remembered himself as being. The two
sequences contain many references to *niños*, emphasising the back-
ward journey the poet was often imaginatively making, as well as
linking us with the various *niños* of the *Libro de poemas* and the
*Canciones* and with the Dead Boy and his Cat of *Así que pasen cinco
años*.

Also among the loves must be that dark and gay one which Lorca
was perhaps beginning to treat in sonnets contemporaneous with the
later *gacelas* and *casidas*. If sexuality as a whole seems freed from gender
in the *Diván*, this means that the poet embraces in his art all possible
manifestations of it. And yet Lorca, on his own confession, was
drawn to Arabic poetry because of its homoerotic quality, which his
Arabist friend Emilio García Gomez had already stressed.[7] The *Diván*
contains clear references to the poet's own kind of loving. Of 'Gacela
de la terrible presencia' ('Gacela of the Terrible Presence') both these
last two observations are true, particularly in its last four couplets:

> Puedo ver el duelo de la noche herida
> luchando enroscada con el mediodía.
>
> Resisto un ocaso de verde veneno
> y los arcos rotos donde sufre el tiempo.
>
> Pero no ilumines tu limpio desnudo
> como un negro cactus abierto en los juncos.
>
> Déjame en su ansia de oscuros planetas
> pero no me enseñes tu cintura fresca.
>
> I can see the duel of the wounded night
> struggling entwined with midday.
>
> I resist a sunset of green poison
> and the broken arches where time suffers.
>
> But you may not shine your pure nakedness
> like a black cactus open among the reeds.
>
> Leave me in a dread of dark planets
> but do not show me your cheeky waist.[8]

The image of night's battle with day has, as we have seen, been
recurrent in Lorca's poetry – c.f. 'Romance Sonámulo', 'Thamar y
Amnón', 'Aurora' (in *El poeta en Nueva York*), and in the *Sonetos* the
'Noche del amor insomne' ('Night of Sleepless Love') employs it with

particularly resonant effect, the sun bringing about the full union of the lovers and therefore the temporary appeasement of the poet with his *corazón amartajado* ('shrouded heart'). The image of the perpetual duel appeals because it symbolises other perpetual duels necessary to, indeed indissolubly part of, life: the duel between the unconscious and the conscious; between sexuality and the heart; between the heart and the mind; between Eros and Thanatos. In the 'Sonetos' Lorca is to emphasise the duelling element to be found in any love-affair, satisfactory or unsatisfactory.

In this *gacela*, however, Lorca appears positively to want to *preserve* this struggle, realising that it gives hue (Freud's 'multiplicity') and meaning to life; he opposes or resists the sunset, which has the greenness associated with sexuality and now said to be poisonous. The first line of the second couplet quoted is a (deliberately ambivalently couched) refusal to surrender either to abstinence from loving (for sunset closes the struggle between day and night) or to any 'change' to conventional amorous behaviour (the green poison being *imposed* heterosexuality). The ruins in the line that follows bring us once again to *El público*; the classical civilisation which accepted homosexuality is now only a series of ruins.

In the penultimate couplet the black cactus – whose light Lorca seems fearful of – has obvious phallic significance, as have the reeds surrounding it, another favourite Lorquian symbol (c.f. the *remansos* in the *Canciones*). Lorca appears spiritually ready to accept unhappiness, that '*ansia de oscuros planetas*' – and it is hard *now*, especially with our present knowledge, to dissociate the word *oscuro* from homosexuality. But the waist – clearly an extremely important erogenous zone for Lorca – is called *fresca* – 'calm', 'serene', or, in familiar usage, 'cheeky'. So even at the close of the poem the duel hasn't ended for Lorca. His resigned state of mind might be seriously disturbed by a glimpse of his beloved's provocative waist.

The night/day, *yo/tu* conflict appears again in 'Gacela del amor desesperado' ('Gacela of the Desperate Love'). It is carried forward by a balancing of *ir* (to go) and *venir* (to come). Difficulties are involved in both processes and for both parties.[9] The 'I' prepares to go through the daylight and experiences '*un sol de alacranes*' ('a sun of scorpions') devouring his temple, an image which takes us back to the cruelly rapacious scorpion of *El maleficio*. The 'you' has to make a journey through '*las turbias cloacas de oscuridad*' ('the muddy sewers of darkness'). This phrase – particularly if once more according homosexual connotations to the last word – reminds us that for the gay man, to an even greater extent than for the straight, love has, to use Yeats' words, 'pitched its mansion in/The place of excrement'. (And here then is another ongoing antithesis; cleanliness and shit, soiling consummation and pure abstinence.) The poem concludes:

> Ni la noche ni el día quieren venir
> para que por ti muera
> y tú mueras por mí.

> Neither the night nor the day want to come
> in order that I may die for you
> and you may die for me.[10]

In so far as it is imaginable, fusion of night and day would mean mutual cancellation. And yet people feel when in love that they could die for each other. Maybe mutual cancellation can also be *liebestod* and apotheosis.

An important result of admitting one's love – above all one's sexual love – into every region of the psyche is that death becomes on the profoundest level acceptable, appears a natural culmination of life. As the late Mario Mieli wrote in *Homosexuality and Liberation*:

> Even the charm of death can be rediscovered and enjoyed, once
> life has been refound, and human beings live in harmony with
> their community, with the world, and with the other who is part
> of our own existence.[11]

The *gacelas* and *casidas* are able to achieve a marriage of Eros and Thanatos, of life-force and *duende*, that does amount to endowing death with life's charms, life with death's infinity.

In 'Gacela del recuerdo del amor' ('Gacela of the Memory of Love') Lorca says:

> Un muro de malos sueños
> me separa de los muertos.

> A wall of bad dreams
> separates me from the dead.[12]

We bring to the contemplation of our inevitable end all the bad faith that living separated from Nature entails. Lorca's most complete exploration of death – even more complete than the 'Llanto' where the thought of the individual dead intervenes – comes in 'Gacela de la muerte oscura' ('Gacela of the Dark Death'):

> Quiero dormir el sueño de las manzanas,
> alejarme del tumulto de los cementerios.
> Quiero dormir el sueño de aquel niño
> que quería cortarse el corazón en alta mar.

No quiero que me repitan que los muertos no pierden la
        sangre;
que la boca podrida sigue pidiendo agua.
No quiero enterarme de los martirios que da la hierba,
ni de la luna con boca de serpiente
que trabaja antes del amenecer.

Quiero dormir un rato,
un rato, un minuto, un siglo;
pero que todos sepan que no he muerto;
que hay un establo de oro en mis labios;
que soy el pequeño amigo del viento Oeste;
que soy la sombra inmensa de mis lágrimas.

Cúbreme por la aurora con un velo,
porque me arrojará puñados de hormigas,
y moja con agua dura mis zapatos
para que resbale la pinza de su alacrán.

Porque quiero dormir el sueño de las manzanas
para aprender un llanto que me limpie de tierra;
porque quiero vivir con aquel niño oscuro
que quería cortarse el corazón en alta mar.

I want to sleep the sleep of the apples,
to distance myself from the tumult of the cemeteries.
I want to sleep the sleep of that child
who wanted to cut his heart on the high sea.

I don't want them to tell me that the dead don't lose their
        blood;
that the putrid mouth goes on asking for water.
I don't want to learn about the tortures that the grass gives,
nor about the moon with a mouth of a snake
that labours before daybreak.

I want to sleep a while,
a while, a minute, a century;
but all should know that I haven't died;
that I've got a stable of gold in my lips;
that I am the little friend of the West wind;
that I am the immense shadow of my tears.

Cover me at dawn with a veil,
because it will throw at me fistfuls of ants,
and moisten with hard water my shoes
in order that the pincers of its scorpion may slide.

Because I want to sleep the sleep of apples
in order to learn a lament that'll cleanse me of earth;
because I want to live with that dark child
who wanted to cut his heart on the high sea.[13]

No more need be said about the apple's symbolic richness for Lorca. Both the first and the last stanzas of the poem make use of the apple to assert Lorca's desire to fuse the timeless-seeming moment of sexual communication and the entry into the timeless that is death. Lorca is fearful of the divorce of Eros and Thanatos, and the confusion that would result he dramatises as '*el tumulto de los cementerios*'. The sleep of the boy who wanted to cut his heart on the high sea I take to be another analogue for that openness to death which we heard Lorca praise in his lecture on the *duende*. The sea has always stood, throughout Lorca's art, for infinity (which equals death), and to be wounded by it in this life is to be prepared for one's eventual destiny and to be able to accept it more peacefully.

The second stanza is perhaps the bravest piece of writing that Lorca accomplished. For all his mystical apprehensions Lorca was in fact a rationalist with no belief whatever in immortality (c.f. 'Llanto por Ignacio Sánchez Mejías'). In these lines he may, I think, have been ruminating the work of Unamuno, whom we know him to have much admired. Man according to Unamuno needs immortality, though he also fears it; his desire and his terror are what animate him through life's course. They render life both infinitely meaningful and ultimately meaningless. Lorca is surely saying here though, that – to use Jorge Luís Borges' words – he wishes to die completely. And in saying that he has the courage to face up to what is (*pace* Poe) perhaps the most terrifying notion of all: that as our bodies rot away, we are aware of this – in some trapped, flickering consciousness. In fact, of course, the strange character of the Dead Boy in *Así que pasen cinco años* has already adumbrated this predicament for us, but at a remove from the poet himself. But while it is a possibility that must be imaginatively faced, Lorca does not believe it, and begs people not to render the fear any more vivid with details about the tortures the grass can give, etc. (This image too can be found, slightly differently worded, in *Así que pasen*.)

Returning to a sort of agnostic orthodoxy Lorca presents us with a vision of himself entering timelessness from time – '*Quiero dormir un rato/Un rato, un minuto, un siglo*'. The last two lines of this stanza are, I think, intentionally ambivalent: '*que no he muerto*' could be read as words coming from a dead Lorca surveying his condition or from a living Lorca who acknowledges that – as Bruno Bettelheim put it: 'as long as there is life in us we can keep Eros victorious over Thanatos'.[14] Either way Lorca finds – in terms remarkably similar to Yeats' 'Sailing to Byzantium' – that '*hay un establo de oro en mis labios*': this somehow invalidates the terrors inherent in any image of death that seeks to divorce it from the whole flux of human life, which art enhances, as it seems always to have done. In Yeats' words:

> Consume my heart away; sick with desire
> And fastened to a dying animal
> It knows not what it is; and gather me
> Into the artifice of eternity.
>
> Once out of nature I shall never take
> My bodily form from any natural thing,
> But such a form as Grecian goldsmiths make
> Of hammered gold and gold enamelling
> To keep a drowsy Emperor awake;
> Or set upon a golden bough to sing
> To lords and ladies of Byzantium
> Of what is past, or passing, or to come.[15]

Lorca's trust that the stable of gold in his lips may lead – as in Yeats – to a personal transcendence of death is not accompanied by quite the rejection of the physical world that mars (as thought, not art) 'Sailing to Byzantium'. He sees himself as the friend of the kindly West wind, and, even in the somewhat Daliesque fourth stanza, accepts the fistfuls of ants and the (possibly metaphoric) scorpion, even though as he dies, he may wish to be protected from these.

The last line suggests more overtly what has been implicit throughout Lorca's art, especially in the 'Llanto por Ignacio Sánchez Mejías': that the very act of lamentation constitutes a triumph over mortality, over death, can be an act of Eros to make us equal to Thanatos. Lorca wants to learn the lament that can cleanse him of earth. Interestingly an earlier version of the poem has '*que limpie la tierra*' – simply, 'which may clean the earth'. Thus, paradoxically, the very making of this *gacela* – by facing up to what is frightening in earthly life – is also a delivery of earth from distress, hence the significant change in the repetitions of the fifth stanza, lines 3–4: Lorca wants now to live (*vivir*) with (*con*) the boy who cut his heart on the high sea, not merely be at rest with him. Life is the victor after all.

★

The nine *duende*-possessed *casidas* also assert this; bathed in the light of confronted and transfiguring death, the inspirited transmutatory Lorquian landscape stands before us. A nightingale collects the sighs of living creatures, and the pheasants scatter them in the dust of the ground ('Casida de los ramos') ('Casida of the Branches').[16] The jasmine wages against the beheaded bull a battle which is resolved in the dreams of a young girl; the jasmine turns into water, the girl becomes a nocturnal branch, and her skeleton establishes itself in the bull ('Casida del sueño al aire libre') ('Casida of the Dream of the Open Air').[17]

'Casida de la muchacha dorada' ('Casida of the Gilded Girl') gives us an even more complex and joyous cycle. A gilded girl ('*la muchacha dorada*') enters the water and makes it gold (c.f. the lemon that Antoñito el Camborio threw into the river in the *Romancero gitano*). Her bathe leaves the girl white; the water turns into flame; the nightingale cries at the girl's plight; she decides to immerse herself in the flames which singe the nightingale's wings. As a result she becomes a heron – or like a heron – and the water, restored to itself again, gilds her back to her former beautiful self.

What we are given here almost certainly owes something to Heraclitus, to Plato and to the neo-Platonists, whom Lorca would have been familiar which from his late adolescent readings of Machado onwards. Certainly to read such poems as 'Casida del sueño al aire' or 'Casida de la muchacha dorada' is to remember accounts of Heraclitus such as that H.D.F. Kitto gives us:

> The essence of the universe is Change; everything is in a state of flux. You cannot step into the same river twice, for the second time it is not the same river – a statement which a successor wittily emended to read: 'You cannot step into the same river once,' since it is changing while you step. Can you say then that a thing *is*, when it is always becoming something different? . . . This Heraclitan philosophy had a profound influence on Plato, for the distinction between the changing, imperfect and ultimately unknowable world of sense, and the unchanging, perfect and knowable world of Reality is of course fundamental to Platonism.[18]

Repeatedly, from *El maleficio* onwards, we have invoked Plato because Lorca finds everywhere in the created world indwelling essences which seem to have proceeded from the world of perfect forms. In the *gacelas* and *casidas* this vision – attained with such strength of will after so much suffering – achieves ecstatic status comparable, in my view, to that of Beethoven's Op. 131 or 132. (Did Lorca, one wonders, admire the late quartets of Beethoven, then receiving belated critical due?) This ecstasy produces an extraordinary telluric tenderness, with cosmological application.

As in the *Romancero gitano* and *El poeta in Nueva York*, Lorca would appear to have thought the sequence in which he arranged the poems, irrespective of when they were written, significant in itself. The first *casida* is the strange 'Casida del herido por el agua' ('Casida of One Wounded by Water'). Placed as it is in Granada, Lorca in presenting us with a *niño herido* is leading us back to the *niños* of the *Canciones* and the

Dead Boy of *Así que pasen cinco años*. Those boys stood representative of Lorca's wounded self now healed through self-knowledge. Is Lorca revisiting himself in these lines?

> El niño estaba solo
> con la ciudad dormida en la garganta.

> The boy was alone
> with the city asleep on his throat.

The poem ends with a quatrain which is an adumbration of both Lorca's past tensions concerning death and his present sense of union with it:

> Quiero bajar al pozo,
> quiero morir mi muerte a bocanadas,
> quiero llenar mi corazón de musgo,
> para ver al herido por el agua.

> I want to descend the well,
> I want to die my death in mouthfuls,
> I want to fill my heart with moss,
> in order to see one wounded by the water.[19]

By '*morir mi muerte a bocanadas*' Lorca doesn't mean, of course, that terrible awareness of the ebbing of one's life of which he spoke in the 'Gacela de la muerte oscura'; he means rather that death should never take him by surprise, that he wishes his living and dying to interpenetrate each other, as they do in his art. And the object of this appears to be to see the little boy wounded by water (i.e. life); in other words all his energies will be exercised on compassionate empathy with living beings who are suffering and who thus remind him of his own earlier years. The anathemas of *El poeta en Nueva York* are vindicated here; here is the philosophy of New York's denunciator pared to its quintessence.

The *Diván del Tamarit* ends with the 'Casida de las palomas oscuras' ('Casida of the Dark Doves'). In fact this final poem of Lorca's last complete book was written some time before the others, possibly several years earlier; this shows the continuity of Lorca's imaginative art, and that at important points he anticipated himself. Certainly here are gathered together a truly comprehensive and psychically reverberative selection of images from Lorca's unique grammar. Here is Franciscan innocence and Heraclitan/Platonist complexity, here is recognition of the infinite lovability and value of all matter, and of the eternal coexistence with it of Nothing:

Por las ramas del laurel
vi dos palomas oscuras.
La una era el sol,
la otra la luna.
'Vecinitas', les dije,
'¿dónde está mi sepultura?'
'En mi cola', dijo el sol.
'En mi garganta', dijo la luna.
Y yo que estaba caminando
con la tierra por la cintura
vi dos águilas de nieve
y una muchacha desnuda.
La una era la otra
y la muchacha era ninguna.
'Aguilitas', les dije,
'¿dónde está mi sepultura?'
'En mi cola', dijo el sol.
'En mi garganta', dijo la luna.
Por las ramas del laurel
vi dos palomas desnudas.
La una era la otra
y las dos eran ninguna.

In the branches of the bay-tree
I saw two dark doves.
One was the sun,
the other the moon.
'Neighbours,' I said to them,
'Where is my grave?'
'In my tail,' said the sun.
'In my throat,' said the moon.
And I who was walking
with the earth round my waist
saw two eagles of snow
and a naked girl.
The one was the other
and the girl was neither.
'Little eagles,' I said to them,
'Where is my grave?'
'In my tail,' said the sun.
'In my throat,' said the moon.
In the branches of the bay-tree
I saw two naked doves.
The one was the other
and both were neither.[20]

The poet has walked with love and sympathy through the entirety of Creation, and the lines are tantamount to a mystic abolition of gender.

The homosexual man is bound to have special attitudes towards both sex and death. Because sex is not associated for him with procreation, he can see it in all its unadulterated splendour, terror and beauty; because when he is dying he cannot think of his continuation through descendants, death appears as an indefatigable finality to be faced nakedly. In truth sex has, of course, other significance than the procreative for heterosexuals; and for them, too, death exists as a reality quite separate from their having begotten or produced children. In these respects, I believe, heterosexuals may have reason to be grateful to the homosexual artist for his ability absolutely to confront these major realities of existence, to explore them and to transcend them through his art. That Lorca can assist readers in these matters whatever their sexual orientation, has, I hope, been demonstrated in this study.

But to make our quotidian life significant we also have to love – or perhaps better put, learn to love – our fellow-creatures. Again I will have written to no purpose if Lorca does not stand before the reader as one whose heart went out to all. His art was a kind one from the very earliest, intimately associated with peace; New York's social barbarities enraged him, and from the early New York poems onwards his kindness has a fierceness that did not desert him and which perhaps illustrates the paradox that pacifist, non-resistant Christ said he had come both to offer universal love and to bring a sword. Here too Lorca's homosexuality played an inestimable part in the development of his art; his charity had been learned through not belonging to a secure majority and through knowing what it felt like to be insulted and injured.

In his last year Lorca said that he was going to write the poetry of those who hate war; he would have been perfectly equipped for the task, but in point of fact his extant works can – by extension – be so described. Those of us who love and pursue peace find in them repeated, inexhaustible inspiration. Repeatedly too Lorca spoke of his feelings for the poor, for those who have nothing ('even the tranquility of nothingness is denied to them . . .'). He said: 'If I were to be presented with a pair of scales, my own suffering on one side, and on the other Justice for all, I would come down with all my strength for the latter.'[21]

★

But what Lorca did create in the last year of his life (whenever conceived and begun) was the poetry of those who stand before the world loving their own sex, loving another because there is no alternative to do so; homosexual love is the love that *is*, and therefore must be. No social imperatives dictate or sustain it. The *Sonetos*† with which Lorca unknowingly said farewell to the world are, as has been said, his fullest excursions into the *propria persona* – indeed in an important sense the only true excursion. Even in *El poeta en Nueva York* Lorca was not concerned with baring himself in the way that he does in the last sonnets. Unwittingly(?) he stands for us before his forced entry into death in all his nakedness as sexually-driven man, as a homosexual man desirous of speaking out about all that he has felt during a relationship which took him – to use conventional words for what are supposed to lie beyond this life – to both hell and heaven.

If the *gacelas* and *casidas* have reminded us of string quartets, the *Sonetos* recall the austere, supremely intimate art of the sonata, perhaps for the unaccompanied instrument, like Bartok's superb, tortured yet life-enhancing Violin Sonata. Even taking into consideration the 'Llanto' and *La casa de Bernarda Alba*, the *Sonetos* – perhaps paradoxically considering the passion that both informs and dictates them, though Lorca must have thought of how the severe sonnet had served Michelangelo and Shakespeare to bare ardent (and homosexual) love – are works of the most rigorous literary discipline. They positively rejoice in their condition, Gongorine sonnets that in all cases except one adhere to the following tight rhyming scheme – ABBA/ABBA/CDC/DCD. (That one exception among the eleven poems, 'El poeta habla por teléfono con el amor' ('The Poet Speaks on the Telephone to his Love') has the related pattern ABBA/ABBA/CDC/CDC.) The language of the *Sonetos* (the grammar of images employed) is as spare as the form is rigid. This gives them a directness of utterance which connects them – for all the obvious differences of genre and theme – more to the classically taut and naturalistically spare *Casa de Bernada Alba* than to any of Lorca's other works. It cannot be insignificant that they date from the same time, belong to the same mental climate.

Certainly it is not hard to see why Aleixandre responded as we have heard that he did to these sonnets, for they contain the most unabashed self-exposure Lorca had ever made, a self-exposure surprising perhaps in the context of his art. Whether or not the sequence really is made up of vignettes from a relationship of Lorca's own, it purports to be this, demands to be *taken* as such, to be read as authentic revelations of the soul from one who has hitherto eschewed the confessional mode. The first line of the first sonnet, 'Soneto de la guirnalda de rosas' ('Sonnet of the Garland of Roses') imparts the agitation that never leaves the sequence. '¡Esa guirnalda! ¡Pronto! ¡Que me muero!' ('This garland! Quick! Oh, I'm dying!').[22] There will follow a number of other occasions when Lorca disturbs the surface symmetry of the sonnet by breaking up a line and using ejaculations. The imperative voice (Lorca addressing his love) is used extensively

†We have eleven, forming an apparently whole sequence. More, possibly as many as eight more, were projected or maybe written.

throughout. The sonnet 'El poeta pregunta a su amor por la ciudad encantada de Cuenca' ('The Poet Questions his Love in the Enchanted Town of Cuenca') is made up entirely of nervous, charged inquiries of the loved one. The untitled ninth sonnet repeats again and again that traditional agonised cry of the *cantaor* – *¡Ay!* – and ends with an urgent exhortation of two lines both doubled by being broken up into paired excited phrases:

> ¡Apiádate de mí, rompe mi duelo,
> que soy amor, que soy naturaleza!
>
> Have compassion on me, break my sorrow,
> for I am love, I am naturalness.[23]

This concluding couplet can legitimately be taken as a summary of the basic plight that animates the sonnets – the last word of all is particularly significant, especially if balanced against *amor*. When reading the poems I am often reminded of sensible words written by the critic Stephen Adams in *The Homosexual as Hero in Contemporary Fiction* à propos the American novelist James Purdy:

> Purdy neither proselytises for homosexuality nor depicts it as an 'affliction'. He simply accords it the same power to damn or to save as any other kind of love.[24]

In the *Sonetos* Lorca neither examines the philosophical/cultural aspects of his homosexuality as in the 'Oda a Walt Whitman' nor invites the reader to share his homoerotic experiences. (In this respect a more oblique poem like 'San Gabriel (Córdoba)' in the *Romancero gitano* is far more triumphantly gay than any of the *Sonetos*, and certainly they lack that fecundity of sexual suggestion which we find in the *Diván del Tamarit*.) What is important about them, in fact, is the complete opposite – to an equal extent – of either of these approaches. The poems' intention is to present, in formal terms, the spiritual pain consequent on intense love – especially an unequal one, for the sonnets would certainly suggest that Lorca loved more than was loved. Lorca was homosexual so the loved one is male, but a man anguishedly loving a woman, or a woman anguishedly loving a man, would be able not only to recognise the emotions in the poems but to salute them as accurate. By his consistent use of the first person singular, by his unashamed saying of '*yo*', so much more pointed and emphatic in Spanish than in English, Lorca is standing before readers not only as a man who has suffered emotionally, but as a man who has suffered *and* is also homosexual. Lorca has indeed reached another milestone on his remarkable artistic/spiritual journey, one which, however, does not diminish that of the *gacelas* and *casidas* where he was able so memorably to encompass *all* sexuality.

But the matter cannot be left at this. What, it must be asked, constitutes the homosexuality of the *Sonetos*? How clear is it that this *amor oscuro* is homosexual?

That the sequence takes us through various stages of *one* affair – sometimes blissful but for the most part unhappy – seems to me virtually certain; the very titling of them would suggest this. Thus just as the '*yo*' is constant, so is the '*tú*'. Certainly in the presentation of the '*tú*' there seems to me satisfactory consistency: the loved one is changeable, less committed to the idea of a relationship than the poet, but nonetheless capable of ardour, passion. In the penultimate and very moving sonnet 'El amor duerme en el pecho del poeta' ('The Loved One Sleeps on the Breast of the Poet')[25] the adjective describing the '*tú*' is incontestibly masculine: '*estás dormido*' ('you are asleep'). And indeed if one reads the sequence with a male '*tú*' in mind, other and specifically homosexual features of the relationship under scrutiny become clearer. The '*yo*', Lorca himself, is the yielding, more passive one of the pair.

In the 'Soneto del dulce llanto' ('Sonnet of the Sweet Lament') Lorca tries to establish certain acceptances of conditions on his own part that should be met by his love's fidelity. He protests:

> Si tú eres el tesoro oculto mío,
> si eres mi cruz y mi dolor mojado,
> si soy el perro de tu señorío . . .

> If you are my dark treasure,
> if you are my cross and my moistened pain,
> if I am the dog of your lordship . . .[26]

The haunting 'Noche del amor insomne' ('Night of Sleepless Love') puts the situation in more direct sexual language. Indeed the poem can be read as an account of Lorca's erotic conduct with his loved one:

> Noche arriba los dos con luna llena,
> yo me puse a llorar y tú reías.
> Tu desdén era un dios, las quejas mías
> momentos y palomas en cadena.

> Noche abajo los dos. Cristal de pena,
> llorabas tú por hondas lejanías.
> Mi dolor era un grupo de agonías
> sobre tu débil corazón de arena.

> La aurora nos unió sobre la cama,
> las bocas puestas sobre el chorro helado
> de una sangre sin fin que se derrama.

Y el sol entró por el balcón cerrado
y el coral de la vida abrió su rama
sobre mi corazón amortajado.

Night above the two of us with full moon,
and I began to cry and you were laughing.
Your scorn was a god, my lamentations
moments and doves in chains.

Night below the two of us. Crystal of grief,
you were crying for deep distances.
My pain was a cluster of agonies
about your weak heart of sand.

Dawn united us upon the bed,
our mouths placed on the frozen jet
of a blood without end which is overflowing.

And the sun entered through the closed balcony
and the coral of life opened its branch
over my shrouded heart.[27]

The first quatrain makes clear the respective roles of the two men;
when the poet cries, the loved one laughs. There is something
impressive and alluring to the 'I'-figure about this disdain, and Lorca
sees himself in his distress as a chained prisoner. (The image of a
fettered dove and the image of a prison occur elsewhere in the
sequence, e.g. in the 'Soneto góngorino en que el poeta manda a su
amor una paloma' ('Gongorine Sonnet in Which the Poet Shows his
Love a Dove').[28]) Night now settles in more thickly. The *'hondas
lejanías'* for which the loved one is crying can be read, it seems to me,
for what lies beyond the arsehole. He is – in a usage of synecdoche
wholly appropriate – called *'cristal de pena'*, a crystal of grief/pain, a
hurting tool which can however attain the distant region, i.e. the
penis. This reading is enhanced by the fact that in Spanish there is a
near-pun: *pena* = grief, pain; *pene* = penis. We can infer then that
Lorca's loved one wants sexual satisfaction from him rather than love;
he is prepared however to avail himself of the latter to obtain the
former, hence the bitterness of the last two lines of the second quatrain
– which confirm with two strong words *dolor* and *agonías* the physical
pain of the *'yo'*, and show in the phrase *'débil corazón de arena'* the
emotional tepidity of the *'tú'*.

Dawn brings the two men together in lines of peculiar beauty – and
boldness. For surely *'las bocas puestas sobre el chorro helado/de una sangre
sin fin que se derrama'* refer to fellatio – and in the 69 position at that!
Both mouths (the plural is significant) are placed upon a jet described

as *helado*, which in Spanish is used as the noun for icecream which male issue rather resembles. As for the blood of the second of these two lines, it was widely believed until well into this century that semen was blood that had been changed in the testicles.

After dawn the sun! Light comes through the balcony. As in the *canción* 'Suicidio' I think the balcony can be taken as connotative of the arsehole, thus of Lorca's finally allowing the 'sun' to enter him, i.e. his loved one to fuck him. Happiness ensues, solace for his heart which has been so badly wounded that it can be described as *amortajado*.

Other lines which strengthen one's picture of Lorca's relationship include these from 'El poeta pide a su amor que le escribe' ('The Poet Asks his Love to Write to Him'):

> Pero yo te sufrí. Rasgué mis venas,
> tigre y paloma, sobre tu cintura,
> en duelo de mordiscos y azucenas.

> But I put up with you. I thrummed my veins,
> tiger and dove, upon your waist,
> in a duel of bites and lilies.[29]

Tiger, dove, the waist, the duel, lilies – we recognise these from the grammar of images and by receiving the resonances of each can travel beyond the individual situation of the sonnet in question. Often, it must be admitted, knowledge of the Lorquian *oeuvre* is invaluable (something true of the *Diván* poems too) but even without it there would be richness of suggestion. Let us look at the last two tercets of 'Llagas de amor' ('Sores of Love'):

> Son guirnalda de amor, cama de herido,
> donde sin sueño, sueño tu presencia
> entre las ruinas de mi pecho hundido,

> y aunque busco la cumbre de prudencia
> me da tu corazón valle tendido
> con cicuta y pasión de amarga ciencia.

> They are a garland of love, a bed of a wounded man,
> where without sleep, I dream your presence
> among the ruins of my buried breast,

> and although I search for the acme of wisdom
> your heart gives me a stretched-out valley
> with hemlock and passion of a bitter science.[30]

'*Las ruinas de mi pecho hundido*' has more force if we remember the Roman ruins and the burying sands of *El público*; the hemlock that grows in the metaphoric valley given the poet by his loved one's heart reminds us of those hemlocks of the 'Diálogo del Amargo' that bristled on the mountainsides after the Amargo accepted the Rider's lift. The recollection is endorsed by the word *amarga* existing in the same line as *cicuta*, referring here to *ciencia* (perhaps in contrast to Nietzsche's 'gay science'). Knowledge of loss and selfhood brings death-associated bitterness with it. The hemlock must also bring to mind Socrates; it brought oblivion to a good and unjustly vilified homosexual. Thus the particular complaint of Lorca's concerning his lover takes us both to a landscape of the psyche and to places in real history that have acquired psychic significance.

Above all the *sonetos* are expressions of that *pena* that Lorca saw as the central character of the *Romancero gitano*. Unrequited – or only partially requited – love brings about the most intense awareness of the otherness of someone else – who evades or cannot meet what he-she has, just by being him-herself engendered. This in turn produces a sense, sometimes desperate, of one's *own* irremediable uniqueness. The *sonetos* move between need for dialogue (dualogue), for reciprocity at *some* level, and a desolate solitude comparable to that articulated in the poems of solitude in New England (*El poeta en Nueva York*):

> Entre lo que me quieres y te quiero,
> aire de estrellas y temblor de planta . . .

> Between your loving me and my loving you,
> a breeze of stars and a trembling of plants . . .[31]

says the first sonnet of the sequence, and the last:

> Que no se acabe nunca la madeja
> del te quiero me quieres siempre ardida
> con día, grito, sal y luna vieja,

> que lo que me des y no te pida
> será para la muerte que no deja
> ni sombra por la carne estremecida.

> How it never is finished the skein
> of I love you, you love me always bold
> with day, scream, salt and old moon,

> how what you may give me and I may not ask you
> will be for death which doesn't leave
> any shadow for the shaken flesh.[32]

For Lorca death came – with terror and pain – on the morning of 19 August 1936. Of all his works, the *Sonetos del amor oscuro* are the hardest to imagine being heard, let alone read or published, in the benighted Spain that succeeded the Civil War. It is perhaps not the least tribute to the intensity and courage of his gay art that under an unspeakable regime his last creations are unthinkable.

The sufferings that Lorca must have experienced, during the concluding days of his life, and above all on that August morning itself, are almost too terrible to contemplate. But justice has come down – after his murder, after a savage war, after the darkness that his murderers' ultimate leader forced upon his vital and splendid country, after the belated lifting of that darkness – firmly on Lorca's side.

Stephen Spender, in one of his best poems of the Thirties, 'Exiles from their Land, History their Domicile' wrote:

> History has tongues
> Has angels has guns – has saved has praised –
> Today proclaims
> Achievements of her exiles long returned
> Now no more rootless, for whom her printed page
> Glazes their bruised waste years in one
> Balancing present sky.[33]

History is here viewed in terms Lorca would have found sympathetic: as the Platonists' good, beyond temporal events. To adapt words from this poem, Federico García Lorca is one of history's angels who, with all his rich achievements, has returned to us; and we, in our own dark times, have perhaps more need than ever of the courage and compassion of his art. An art which, as this book may have helped to show, is truly a triumph of the gay imagination.

# Chronology

1898  5 June: Federico García Lorca born in Fuente Vaqueros, son of Federico García Rodriguez and Vicenta Lorca Romero.

1906  The Lorca family move to a nearby village, Asquerosa, later called Valderrubio.

1908  Lorca begins to study piano and composition with Antonio Segura, a disciple of Verdi. Musical studies will dominate the boy's life for the next nine years.

1909  The family move to Granada and Lorca enters the Colegio del Sagrado Corazón, the director of which was his uncle. From now on the family spend only the summer in the country.

1914  Matriculates in the faculty of letters and law at the university of Granada. Frequents *tertulia* called El Rinconcillo. First poems written.

1916  Travels with Martín Domínguez Berrueta around Spain in June and in October–November. During the first of these meets Antonio Machado in Baeza.

1917  Writes articles based on travels. His friendship with Manuel de Falla begins, and he comes under the friendly notice of the university's professor of law, the socialist Fernando de los Ríos, an important influence upon his life. Decides to devote himself to literature rather than to music.

1918  Publication in Granada of his first book (prose) *Impresiones y paisajes*. First published poems written. First stay in Madrid, where he is introduced to the cultural circle of the *Ateneo*.

1919  Under the advice of Fernando de los Ríos goes to live in Madrid, in the Residencia de Estudiantes where he retains a room until 1928. It is here that he meets Luis Buñuel and José Moreno Villa, and will meet many another of the brilliant poets of his generation: Alberti, Guillén (both in 1924) etc. Writes more poems and passes through a kind of crisis of religious faith.

1920  Gets to know the world of the theatre in Madrid. Gregorio Martínez Sierra commissions from him and produces *El maleficio de la mariposa*. This is performed – one night only – at the Teatro Eslava on 22 March.
      In September Falla settles in Granada and the friendship strengthens.

1921    Falla and Lorca go to Sevilla for Holy Week, which inspires the 'Poema de la saeta' sequence of the *Poema del cante jondo*; this book was probably conceived then, and was written (in two weeks) in November.

15 June: *Libro de poemas* published.

Towards the end of the year the friendship with Salvador Dalí begins.

1922    19 February: Gives lecture on the *cante jondo* at the Centro artístico de Granada.

13–14 June: Organises a festival of *cante jondo* with Falla in the Alhambra at Granada.

5 August: A version of *Tragicomedia de don Cristóbal y la seña Rosita* finished.

1923    6 January: Epiphany festival in Lorca's own house in Granada – again organised with Falla. An evening of puppet-plays and chamber-music, including Lorca's (now lost) *La niña que riega la albahaca y el príncipe preguntón* and Falla's arrangement of Stravinsky's *L'histoire du soldat*.

July: *Suites* finished. First act of *La zapatera prodigiosa* written. Also works on *canciones* and *romances gitanos*.

13 September: The dictatorship of Primo de Rivera results in the exile of Miguel de Unamuno and the dismissal of Fernando de los Ríos. Lorca begins work on *Mariana Pineda* as indirect protest.

1924    Spring and summer: Further *canciones* and poems that will become part of the *Romancero gitano*.

July: Juan Ramón Jiménez and his wife pass ten days in Granada and meet the Lorca family.

Moreno Villa tells Lorca about the *rosa mutabile* which gives him the idea for his later (1935) play *Doña Rosita la soltera*. Writes libretto for Falla, *Lola la comediante*.

December: Begins three-year correspondence with Jiménez.

1925    8 January: Completes third and final version of *Mariana Pineda*. Spring: First stay in Cadaqués with the Dalí family.

July: *Cinco diálogos* including the 'Diálogo del Amargo'.

September: Writes last section of the *Canciones*, 'Eros con batón'.

1926    13 February: Gives lecture in the *Ateneo* of Granada on the poetic image in Luis de Góngora.

March: 'Oda a Salvador Dalí'.

Works throughout summer on *Romancero gitano*, all but complete by November. Reworks first act of *La zapatera prodigiosa*. A feeling persists throughout the year that his career has not progressed as he would have wished.

1927    Tercentenary of the death of Luis de Góngora.

17 May: *Canciones* published to acclaim.

Spends much of May and June with Dalí, working with him on sets and costumes for *Mariana Pineda* and on *El sacrificio de Ifigenia* which in September he claims to have finished.

24 June: Première in Barcelona of *Mariana Pineda* and the start of his theatrical collaboration with the actress Margarita Xirgu.

25 June–2 July: Exhibition of 24 of Lorca's drawings in Barcelona arranged by Dalí and others.

12 October: *Mariana Pineda* in Madrid. Rafael Alberti introduces Lorca to the poet Vicente Aleixandre.

16–22 December: Tercentennial celebrations of death of Góngora. Lorca invited with a number of his brilliant friends to Sevilla where he is entertained in the nearby house of the literary bullfighter, Ignacio Sánchez Mejías, later one of his most loved companions. The *Generación del '27* born. Begins friendship with Luis Cernuda.

1928    8 March: The review *El gallo* launched with great banquet in Granada to awaken the city from its cultural complacency. First issue appears next day. The second and last issue comes out in April.

End of July: *Romancero gitano* published as *Primer romancero gitano* to enormous success.

25 July: *ABC* – Spanish newspaper – publishes story of a *crime passionel* which gives Lorca the idea for *Bodas de sangre*.

August: 'Oda al santísimo sacramento del altar' written and dedicated to Manuel de Falla who does not greatly care for it, finding it doctrinally heterodox.

October: Receives sharply critical letter from Dalí about the *Romancero gitano* and this inaugurates the poet's own reaction against the book, as well as his own depression. Dalí leaves with Buñuel for Paris and it is not until 1935 that the two friends meet again.

December: Completes *Amor de don Perlimplín con Belisa en su jardín* and *Tragicomedia de don Cristóbal y Rosita*.

1929    Lorca experiences great anguish of spirit.

January: The censor of Primo de Rivera's government puts a stop to rehearsals of *Amor de don Perlimplín*.

March: Friendship with Chilean diplomat Carlos Morla Lynch.

April: Signs manifestation against Primo de Rivera.

11 June: Leaves Spain in company of Fernando de los Ríos. Visits Paris, London and Oxford and embarks the *Olympic* at Southampton for New York where he arrives 28 June.

July: Enrolls at Columbia and establishes himself in John Jay Hall. Writes first poems of his impressions of America.

August–September: In Vermont and the Catskill mountains, then back to New York for the autumn term. Experiences much internal agony, but also plunges himself into the exciting

Black world of Harlem.

1930    30 January: End of Primo de Rivera's dictatorship. Under the direction of General Berenguer Spain prepares for re-establishment of democracy and Unamuno makes a widely saluted return to his country. In New York Lorca continues to work on poems. Associates with fellow-Spaniards Dámaso Alonso and Andrés Segovia, and arranges songs for La Argentinita.

7 March: In response to invitation from the Institución Hispano-Cubana de Cultura arrives in Havana, Cuba where, with delight, he finds himself back in the Spanish world. Gives famous lecture on the *duende* ('Teoría y juego del duende'), one of his most seminal pieces. Begins work on *El público*.

12 June: Embarks for Spain, where he arrives 22 June.

July–August: Finishes first version of *El público*, which he reads to Carlos Morla Lynch and his wife who are shocked by it.

24 December: In Madrid first performance of *La zapatera prodigiosa*.

1931    January: Four poems to be part of *El poeta en Nueva York* appear in *Revista de occidente*.

14 April: Second Republic proclaimed in Spain, and Lorca participates with joy in public celebrations in Madrid. Manuel Azaña becomes *jefe* in May.

23 May: Publication – after ten years – of *Poema del cante jondo*.

June: Lorca reads to Carlos Morla Lynch and his wife, the dedicatees of *El poeta en Nueva York*, extensive extracts from it.

Summer: Writes *Así que pasen cinco años*, conceived in New York.

November: Conceives the project of a travelling theatre bringing to the Spanish people their own classical masterpieces, to be called La Barraca ('the caravan').

1932    First poems later to be included in the *Diván del Tamarit* published in reviews.

March–June: Embarks on a series of lectures all over Spain, pre-eminently *Un poeta en Nueva York*.

10 July: La Barraca – approved officially by the Minister of Education, Fernando de los Ríos, and attached to the socialist union of students – recruits members of the troupe from the student sector. Lorca flings himself into its performances and itineraries with a whole-hearted enthusiasm. He does not mind if he has to abandon literary work temporarily. Nevertheless during that summer writes *Bodas de sangre* which he reads to Carlos Morla Lynch on 17 September.

10 August: Lorca and La Barraca give performances in front of the President of the Republic and important members of the Cortés.

1933    8 March: First performance of *Bodas de sangre* in Teatro Infanta
Beatriz, Madrid; a great success.
5 April: First performance – by an amateur company – of *Amor
de don Perlimplín*.
Begins work on *Yerma* and on what he describes as the third of
the trilogy *La destrucción de Sodoma*.
1 May: Along with many other Spanish intellectuals signs
protest against Hitler: 'We protest against the fascist barbarism
which imprisons German writers.'
June: Collaborates with Falla on the production of his *El amor
brujo*.
September: Collapse of Azaña cabinet. Replaced by right-wing
coalition.
29 September: Lorca embarks for Montevideo, Uruguay
having accepted an invitation to visit Argentina following the
great success in Buenos Aires of *Bodas de sangre*. Spends the
next six months in Argentina (with a fortnight in Uruguay) –
until 27 March 1934. The day of his arrival in Buenos Aires, he
meets Pablo Neruda, then Chilean consul there, and together,
later, they give a public homage to the great Nicaraguan poet,
Rubén Darío, at the P.E.N. club – in the manner of
bullfighters' *al alimón*.

1934    A year of great political tension in Spain following the victory
of the Right; the *bienio negro* (dark two years). Gil Robles enters
the government.
January: Lorca announces that *Yerma* is ready.
April: Great celebrations in Madrid to welcome Lorca back
from Argentina, with special performance by La Barraca.
5 May: Pablo Neruda becomes Chilean consul in Barcelona,
but spends much of his time in Madrid associating with artists
there.
June: Actually completes *Yerma*.
11 August: Ignacio Sánchez Mejías wounded in the arena at
Manzanares and taken to Madrid hospital.
13 August: Ignacio Sánchez Mejías dies.
By the end of the summer Lorca says he has finished a volume
of poems and has decided to call it *Diván del Tamarit*,
honouring Arab poetic tradition. Some of the poems in this
volume as we now know it were, however, written later.
5 September: Receives invitation from Luigi Pirandello to visit
Italy with La Barraca.
4 October: Reads Carlos Morla Lynch his 'Llanto por Ignacio
Sánchez Mejías'. That very day news comes of the uprising of
the miners in Asturias. This is to be put down with the greatest
brutality by General Franco; almost 4,000 killed, 7,000
wounded and 30,000 taken prisoner. Lorca cancels perform-

ances of La Barraca in response; Barcelona declares Estat Catalá.

1 November: Lorca signs letter protesting against the imprisonment of Azaña.

15 December: Declares, the actress Margarita Xirgu at his side, that 'I am always on the side of the poor'.

29 December: Triumphantly successful first night of *Yerma* which however a rightist group tries to disrupt on account of its 'immorality'.

1935   January: Claims to have finished *La destrucción de Sodoma*.

1 February: Special lecture on the educational role of the theatre. A few days later announces that he is engaged on a work against war and the inevitable miseries it brings.

12 March: At the hundredth performance of *Yerma* reads aloud the 'Llanto por Ignacio Sánchez Mejías'.

May: Asks the sculptor Angel Ferrant to make marionettes for performances of his puppet-plays which accompany the book fair in the Paseo de Recoletos, Madrid.

June: Finishes *Doña Rosita la soltera*.

September–December: In Barcelona, to much acclaim, giving conferences and lectures and attending performances of his works.

24 October: Presides over gala in honour of Margarita Xirgu, the proceeds of which go to the prisoners of right-wing repression. Participates in Pablo Neruda's review, *Caballo verde para la poesía*.

6 November: Takes part in big anti-fascist demonstration. Later in the month on a visit to Valencia works on a number of the *Sonetos del amor oscuro*.

1936   21 January: *Bodas de sangre* published.

28 January: *Primeras canciones* (*1922*) published.

February: Elections put the *frente popular* in power. Lorca signs a manifestation in favour of peace in *El sol*. Granada falls into a state of great unrest, and Lorca abides by his principles and lets *El defensor de Granada* publish his views.

9 February: Lorca reads an anti-fascist declaration at a banquet held to celebrate Rafael Alberti's return from Russia.

8 March: Tells fellow-poet Gabriel Celaya that he wishes to devote himself to a disciplined form of poem, the sonnet – the *Sonetos del amor oscuro*.

22 May: Takes part in a reception given to three distinguished literary members of the French *front populaire*, Malraux, Cassou, Lenormand.

June: Finishes *La casa de Bernarda Alba*.

5 July: Lorca's parents return to Granada to stay with their daughter Concha and her husband Manuel Fernández Montesi-

nos (to become, for a few days only, the socialist mayor of Granada). Lorca promises to be with them for 18 July, his name-day.

13 July: Calvo Sotelo, head of the opposition, assassinated. Lorca entrusts manuscript of *El poeta en Nueva York* to José Bergamín, and of *El público, Así que pasen cinco años* and many poems to Rafael Martínez Nadal, who accompanies him to the station.

15 or 16 July: Arrives in Granada.

20 July: Centre of Granada falls to the Right, the Albaicín resisting until 23 July.

Lorca stays in family country house, 'La Huerta de San Vicente', ill and threatened. Appeals to his friend, Luis Rosales, honourable Falangist who gives him sanctuary in his own house.

16 August: Brother-in-law Manuel Fernández Montesinos shot. Lorca arrested at midday by Ramón Ruiz Alonso. Luis Rosales and Manuel de Falla, at great personal risk, try to intercede with the governor of Granada, Valdes, but in vain.

19 August: Executed in the village of Viznar, in an olive-grove, along with countless others.

(For full elucidation of the complex events of these last terrible days the reader is referred to Ian Gibson's *The Death of Lorca* and *The Assassination of Federico García Lorca*.)

# Bibliography

A) Editions of Federico García Lorca quoted and consulted in Spanish:
*Obras completas* vol. I, edited by Arturo del Hoyo, Aguilar, Madrid, 1973.
Alianza ediciones, Madrid; each volume edited by Mario Hernández, the series editor, unless otherwise stated:
  1. *Primer romancero gitano*, 1981.
  2. *Yerma*, 1981.
  3. *Diván del Tamarit; Llanto por Ignacio Sánchez Mejías; Sonetos*, 1981.
  4. *La casa de Bernardo Alba*, 1981.
  5. *Primeras canciones; Seis poemas galegos; Poemas sueltos; Canciones populares antiguas*, 1981.
  6. *Canciones 1921–1924*, 1982.
  7. *La zapatera prodigiosa*, 1982.
  8. *Poema del cante jondo*, 1982.
  9. *Epistolario I* (ed. Christopher Maurer), 1983.
  10. *Epistolario II* (ed. Christopher Maurer), 1983.
  11. *Conferencias I* (ed. Christopher Maurer), 1984.
  12. *Conferencias II* (ed. Christopher Maurer, 1984.
  13. *Bodas de sangre*, 1984.
Ariel ediciones, Madrid:
  *Libro de poemas* (ed. Ian Gibson), 1982.
  *Suites* (ed. André Belamich), 1983.
  *El poeta en Nueva York; Tierra y luna* (ed. Eutimio Martín), 1982.
*Autógrafos* (Dolphin Book Company, Oxford), edited by Rafael Martínez Nadal:
  I. *Poemas*, 1975.
  II. *El público*, 1976.
  III. *Así que pasen cinco años*, 1979.
Cátedra ediciones, Madrid:
  *Poema del cante jondo/Romancero gitano* (eds Allen Josephs and Juan Caballero), 1982.
Novelas y Cuentos ediciones, Madrid, edited by Ricardo Domenech and José Luís Sastre:
  *Amor de don Perlimplín; Así que pasen cinco años; El maleficio de la mariposa*, 1975.
  *Mariana Pineda; La zapatera prodigiosa, Bodas de sangre*, 1968.
  *Yerma; La casa de Bernarda Alba; Doña Rosita la soltera*, 1974.
  *Sonetos del amor oscuro*, privately printed by friends of the poet in a limited edition of 250 copies, Granada, 1983.

B) Editions quoted and consulted in French:
   *Oeuvres complètes*, vol. I; Bibliothèque de la Pléiade, Gallimard, Paris, 1981. Edited by André Belamich, with translations by André Belamich, Jacques Comincioli, Claude Couffon, Robert Marrast, Bernard Sesé and Jules Supervieille.

C) Editions quoted and consulted in English:
   *Selected Poems*, introduced and edited by J.L. Gili; Penguin, Harmondsworth, 1960.
   *Three Tragedies* (*Blood Wedding; Yerma; The House of Bernarda Alba*), translated by James Graham-Luján and Richard L. O'Connell, with an introduction by Francisco García Lorca; Secker and Warburg, London, 1965; Penguin, Harmondsworth, 1983.
   *Five Plays: Comedies and Tragi-Comedies* (*The Billy-Club Puppets; The Shoemaker's Prodigious Wife; The Love of Don Perlimplín and Belisa in the Garden; Doña Rosita, the Spinster; The Butterfly's Evil Spell*), translated by James Graham-Luján and Richard L. O'Connell, with an introduction by Francisco García Lorca; Secker and Warburg, London, 1965; Penguin, Harmondsworth, 1970.
   *Selected Letters*, edited and translated by David Gershator; Marion Boyars, London, 1983.
   *Deep Song and Other Prose*, edited and translated by Christopher Maurer; Marion Boyars, London, 1980.

In the case of Lorca's poetry, all translations are by the author and have been made to follow the Spanish as closely as possible, even at the risk of a distortion of conventional word order. Where prose is concerned, I have – unless otherwise stated in the Notes – quoted from those English translations currently available and easy of access, as cited above. For the two major dramas *El público* and *Así que pasen cinco años*, I have translated myself directly from the *Autógrafos* editions of the Dolphin Book Company.

# Notes

## Notes to Chapter One

1. *Epistolario*, vol. II, p. 128.
2. 'Un poeta en Nueva York', *Obras completas*, vol. I, p. 1094.
3. ibid.
4. *Selected Letters*, p. xii.
5. 'A Poet in New York', *Deep Song and Other Prose*, p. 87.
6. ibid, p. 96.
7. ibid, pp. 96–7.
8. Walt Whitman, *The Complete Poems* (Penguin, 1975), pp. 485–6.
9. *Oeuvres complètes*, vol. I, pp. 1461–76.
10. *Selected Letters*, p. 151.
11. ibid, p. 152.
12. ibid, pp. 154–5.
13. 'A Poet in New York', *Deep Song and Other Prose*, p. 101.
14. *Obras completas* [= tomo I (vol. I) throughout], p. 447. The manuscript of this poem is in fact dated 'Bushnell-ville (E.S.U.)' (sic), 6 September 1929, Bushnellville being in the Catskills. Thus some other poems in the cycle predate this in writing, if not in inception. See *Oeuvres complètes* for satisfactory dating of all individual poems.
15. T. S. Eliot, *The Waste Land* (Faber, 1971), p. 135.
16. *Obras completas*, p. 448.
17. The computation of editors Allen Josephs and Juan Caballero in the Cátedra edition of *Poema del cante jondo/Romancero gitano*, p. 224.
18. *Obras completas*, p. 452. Guillén's line is taken from his 'Los jardines' in *Cántico* (1928).
19. ibid.
20. ibid, p. 450.
21. ibid, p. 451.
22. *Oeuvres complètes*, vol. I, p. 1510.

## Notes to Chapter Two

1. *Obras completas*, p. 399.
2. 'On Lullabies', *Deep Song and Other Prose*, p. 9.
3. ibid, pp. 14–15.
4. *Obras completas*, p. 1058.
5. 'On the *Gypsy Ballads*', *Deep Song and Other Prose*, pp. 117–8.

6. 'From the Life of García Lorca, Poet', ibid, p. 133.
7. *Obras completas*, p. 47.
8. ibid, p. 104.
9. ibid, pp. 24–6.
10. ibid, p. 9.
11. *Five Plays: Comedies and Tragi-Comedies*, p. 196.
12. ibid, pp. 222–3.
13. ibid, p. 207.
14. Introduction by Francisco García Lorca to *Three Tragedies*, p. 9.
15. ibid, p. 10.
16. *Oeuvres complètes*, vol. I, p. xxxiv.
17. 'Holy Week in Granada', *Deep Song and Other Prose*, pp. 54–5.
18. 'Casida del herido por el agua' ('Casida of One Wounded by Water'), *Obras completas*, p. 589.
19. ibid, p. 375.
20. *Selected Letters*, p. 14.
21. ibid, p. 18.
22. ibid, p. 23.
23. ibid, p. 33.
24. V.S. Pritchett, *The Spanish Temper* (Chatto, 1973), p. 164.
25. Ronald Crichton, *Falla* (BBC Publications, 1982), p. 53. In Buenos Aires, in a conversation with Pablo Suero (*Noticias Gráficas*, 15 October 1933), Lorca called Falla 'a saint, a mystic. I don't revere anyone as I do Falla.'
26. *Obras completas*, pp. 809–925.
27. Also translated in Valentine Cunningham (ed.), *The Penguin Book of Spanish Civil War Verse* (Penguin, 1980), p. 205.
28. Introduction by Francisco García Lorca to *Five Plays: Comedies and Tragi-Comedies*, p. 19.
29. 'Deep Song', *Deep Song and Other Prose*, p. 25.
30. ibid, p. 40.
31. Manuel de Falla, *On Music and Musicians* (Marion Boyars, 1979), pp. 104–5.
32. 'Deep Song', op. cit., p. 25.
33. ibid, pp. 30–1.
34. ibid, p. 30.
35. ibid, p. 32.
36. ibid, p. 34.
37. ibid.
38. ibid, pp. 34–5.
39. *Obras completas*, pp. 395–7.
40. ibid, pp. 400–3.
41. 'Deep Song', op. cit., p. 32.
42. ibid, p. 33.
43. ibid, p. 36.
44. *Obras completas*, p. 407.
45. 'On the *Gypsy Ballads*', *Deep Song and Other Prose*, p. 105.
46. 'Saeta' from *Poema del cante jondo*, *Obras completas*, p. 184.
47. In conversation with the author.
48. 'On the *Gypsy Ballads*', op. cit, p. 105 – the words *retablo* and *pena* preserved in Spanish.

49. *Obras completas*, p. 234.
50. 'On the *Gypsy Ballads*', op. cit., p. 119.
51. ibid, p. 120.
52. ibid.
53. ibid, p. 120–1.
54. *Obras completas*, p. 241.
55. 'On the *Gypsy Ballads*', op. cit., p. 121.
56. *Obras completas*, p. 423.
57. ibid.
58. ibid, p. 424.
59. ibid.
60. Catedra edition of *Poema del cante jondo*, p. 276.
61. *Obras completas*, p. 414.
62. W.B. Yeats, *Selected Poems* (Macmillan, 1962), p. 42.
63. *Obras completas*, pp. 408–9.
64. ibid, pp. 417–8.
65. ibid, p. 419.
66. 'On the *Gypsy Ballads*', op. cit., p. 117.
67. Arturo Barea, *Lorca: The Poet and His People* (Faber, 1944), pp. 18–19.
68. *Obras completas*, p. 426.
69. ibid, p. 429.
70. Arturo Barea, op. cit., p. 17.
71. *Selected Letters*, p. 73.
72. Arturo Barea, op. cit., p. 17.
73. 'On the *Gypsy Ballads*', op. cit., p. 105.
74. ibid, p. 106.
75. *Obras completas*, p. 400.
76. 'On the *Gypsy Ballads*', op. cit., p. 111.
77. *Obras completas*, p. 401.
78. ibid.
79. ibid, p. 425.
80. ibid, p. 313.
81. ibid, pp. 402–3.

## Notes to Chapter Three

1. 'A Poet in New York', *Deep Song and Other Prose*, p. 87.
2. *Obras completas*, p. 480.
3. ibid, p. 481.
4. 'Asesinato (Dos voces de madrugada en Riverside Drive)' ('Murder (Two Voices at Daybreak on Riverside Drive)'), ibid, p. 477.
5. ibid, p. 485.
6. ibid, p. 460.
7. 'El Rey de Harlem' ('The King of Harlem'), ibid, p. 459.
8. 'Paisaje de la multitud que vomita' ('Landscape of the Vomiting Crowd'), ibid, p. 473.
9. 'Navidad en el Hudson' ('Christmas on the Hudson'), ibid, p. 478.
10. 'Panorama ciego de Nueva York' ('Blind Panorama of New York'), ibid, p. 482.

11. *Obras completas*, pp. 505–6.
12. ibid, p. 92.
13. 'A Poet in New York', op. cit., p. 98.
14. *Obras completas*, p. 512.
15. ibid, p. 498.
16. ibid, p. 503.
17. ibid, p. 506.
18. ibid, p. 96.
19. Stephen Spender, *Love-Hate Relations: A Study of Anglo-American Sensibilities* (Hamish Hamilton, 1974), p. 12.
20. Dawn Ades, *Salvador Dalí* (Thames and Hudson, 1982), p. 74.
21. *Obras completas*, p. 517.
22. ibid. These vivid lines are thought to have been inspired by the abattoirs and many butchers' shops in the vicinity of Columbia University.
23. ibid, p. 518.
24. 'A Poet in New York', op. cit., p. 99.
25. *Selected Letters*, p. 135.
26. 'Suicidio en Alejandria', *Obras completas*, pp. 960–2.
27. 'Nadadora sumergida', ibid, pp. 963–4.
28. *Selected Letters*, p. 139.
29. Dawn Ades, *Salvador Dalí*, p. 38.
30. *Obras completas*, p. 755.
31. *Selected Letters*, p. 118.
32. ibid, p. 133.
33. Alianza edition of *Romancero gitano, p 190*.
34. *Selected Letters*, p. 136.
35. ibid, pp. 139–40. (To Jorge Zalamea.)
36. ibid, p. 146. (To Carlos Morla Lynch.)
37. Rafael Martínez Nadal, Introduction to vol. I of *Autógrafos*, p. xxx.
38. Ian Gibson, *The Death of Lorca* (W. H. Allen, 1973), p. 10, and in conversation with the author.

## Notes to Chapter Four

1. *Selected Letters*, pp. 2–3.
2. *Obras completas*, pp. 321–2.
3. Manuel de Falla, *On Music and Musicians*, pp. 8, 22, 23.
4. *Selected Letters*, p. 3.
5. *Five Plays: Comedies and Tragi-Comedies*, p. 207.
6. ibid, p. 195.
7. ibid.
8. *El maleficio de la mariposa* in *Amor de don Perlimplín* . . ., p. 199. Translation the author.
9. ibid, p. 165. Translation the author.
10. ibid, p. 208. Translation the author.
11. Francisco García Lorca, *Federico García Lorca y su mundo* (Alianza Tres, Madrid, 1980), p. 263.
12. André Gide, *Corydon* (GMP, 1985), pp. 69–70.
13. J.H. Fabre, *Social Life in the Insect World* (Penguin, 1937), pp. 162–7.

14. 'The Parable of the Old Man and the Young', *The Poems of Wilfred Owen* (Hogarth, 1985), p. 151.
15. Manuel de Falla, *On Music and Musicians*, p. 9.
16. ibid.
17. ibid, p. 11.
18. Ronald Crichton, *Falla*, p. 10.
19. Francisco García Lorca in Introduction to *Five Plays: Comedies and Tragi-Comedies*, pp. 10–13.
20. ibid, p. 12.
21. *Selected Letters*, p. 71.
22. *Five Plays . . .*, p. 23.
23. ibid.
24. ibid, p. 63.
25. *Selected Letters*, p. 19.
26. *Five Plays . . .*, p. 117.
27. ibid, p. 130.
28. ibid, p. 131.
29. ibid, p. 17.
30. *Obras completas*, pp. 19–20.
31. ibid, pp. 27–28.
32. ibid, pp. 32–33.
33. ibid, p. 36.
34. ibid, p. 37.
35. ibid, p. 51.
36. ibid, p. 90.
37. ibid, pp. 60, 130, 132.
38. ibid, p. 71.
39. *Selected Letters*, p. 5.
40. *Obras completas*, pp. 96–8.
41. ibid, p. 361.
42. ibid, p. 362.
43. ibid, p. 365.
44. ibid, p. 374.
45. 'On the *Gypsy Ballads*', *Deep Song and Other Prose*, p. 105.
46. 'The Poetic Image of Don Luis de Góngora', ibid, p. 66.
47. 'On the *Gypsy Ballads*', ibid, p. 114.
48. *Obras completas*, pp. 315–6.
49. ibid, pp. 412–3.
50. ibid, pp. 410–1.
51. Cátedra edition of *Poema de cante jondo/Romancero gitano*, p. 252.
52. *Obras completas*, pp. 404–5.
53. ibid, p. 440.
54. ibid, pp. 765–73. We should note that in the section 'Carne' ('Flesh') Lorca anticipates the New York poems, in imagery of apples and savage beasts and in referring to '*la verde sangre de Sodoma*' ('the green blood of Sodom') which makes shine '*un yerto corazón de aluminio*' ('a lifeless heart of aluminium').

## Notes to Chapter Five

1. 'A Poet in New York', *Deep Song and Other Prose*, p. 93.
2. 'Norma y paraíso de los negros' ('Norm and Paradise of the Blacks'), *Obras completas*, p. 457.
3. 'A Poet in New York', op. cit., p. 96.
4. ibid, p. 95.
5. 'On the *Gypsy Ballads*', ibid, pp. 105 and 117.
6. *Obras completas*, p. 460.
7. ibid, p. 459.
8. Rafael Martínez Nadal, *Lorca's The Public* (Calder & Boyars, 1974), p. 98.
9. *Obras completas*, p. 461.
10. ibid, p. 460.
11. Alianza edition of *Romancero gitano*, pp. 154–7.
12. *Obras completas*, p. 462.
13. ibid, p. 525.
14. ibid, p. 526.
15. ibid.
16. ibid, p. 527.
17. Madison Jones in conversation with the author. Paul Binding, *Separate Country*, (Paddington, 1979), p. 60.
18. Walt Whitman, *The Complete Poems*, p. 504.
19. 'Starting from Paumanok', ibid, pp. 50–1.
20. ibid, p. 53.
21. 'For You O Democracy', ibid, p. 150.
22. 'We Two Boys together Clinging', ibid, p. 162.
23. 'Starting from Paumanok', ibid, p. 63.
24. *Obras completas*, p. 528.
25. ibid.
26. ibid, p. 529.
27. ibid.
28. ibid.
29. ibid.
30. Walt Whitman, *The Complete Poems*, p. 153.
31. ibid.
32. *Obras completas*, p. 531.
33. ibid.
34. ibid, p. 530.
35 Matthew Arnold, *Poems* (Penguin, 1985), p. 181.
36. *Obras completas*, p. 532.
37. See introduction by Rafael Martínez Nadal to *Autógrafos*, vol. II.
38. *Obras completas*, pp. 1067–79. Translated by J.L. Gili in *Selected Poems*, pp. 127–39.

## Notes to Chapter Six

1. *Autógrafos*, vol. III, p. 15.
2. Gwynne Edward, *Lorca: The Theatre Beneath the Sand* (Marion Boyars, 1980), pp. 93 ff.

3. Reed Anderson, *Federico García Lorca* (Macmillan, 1984), pp. 134 ff.
4. T.S. Eliot, 'Burnt Norton', *Four Quartets* (Faber, 1959), p. 13.
5. *Autógrafos*, vol. III, p. 85.
6. ibid.
7. ibid.
8. Stephen Spender, *The Generous Days* (Faber, 1971), p. 1.
9. *Autógrafos*, vol. III, p. 99.
10. ibid.
11. ibid, p. 129.
12. ibid, p. 123.
13. ibid, p. 189.
14. ibid, p. 67.
15. ibid, p. 69.
16. *Obras completas*, p. 531.
17. ibid.
18. *Autógrafos*, vol. II, p. xv.
19. ibid, p. xvi.
20. ibid, p. xv.
21. ibid.
22. William Blake, 'Auguries of Innocence'.
23. *Autógrafos*, vol. II, p. xxl.
24. ibid, p. lv.
25. ibid, p. xxxiv.
26. ibid.
27. ibid, pp. xlvii–xlviii.
28. ibid, p. xxvi.
29. ibid, p. xxlv.
30. Rafael Martínez Nadal, *Lorca's The Public*, p. 61.
31. *Obras completas*, p. 264.
32. *Autógrafos*, vol. II, pp. liii–lv.
33. 'Theory and Function of the Duende', *Selected Poems*, p. 127.
34. ibid, p. 128.
35. ibid, p. 136.
36. ibid, p. 133.
37. ibid, p. 135.
38. ibid, p. 139.

## Notes to Part Two

1. In *A.B.C.*, 25–28 July 1928. See *Bodas de sangre* (Alianza edn), 'Apéndice 1', p. 175.
2. *Bodas de sangre*, p. 171. c.f. *Three Tragedies*, p. 95.
3. *Bodas de sangre*, p. 156. c.f. *Three Tragedies*, p. 83.
4. *Bodas de sangre*, p. 158. c.f. *Three Tragedies*, p. 85.
5. *Bodas de sangre*, p. 171. c.f. *Three Tragedies*, p. 96. In versions anterior to that established by Lorca in Buenos Aires, this concluding speech is divided between the Bride and the Mother.
6. 'On the *Gypsy Ballads*', *Deep Song and Other Prose*, p. 121.
7. *Three Tragedies*, p. 45.

8. *Bodas de sangre*, p. 156. c.f. *Three Tragedies*, p. 83.
9. *Bodas de sangre*, p. 157. c.f. *Three Tragedies*, p. 84.
10. *Three Tragedies*, p. 62.
11. ibid, p. 74.
12. ibid, p. 57.
13. ibid.
14. ibid, p. 93.
15. ibid, p. 34.
16. ibid, p. 37.
17. ibid, p. 49.
18. ibid, p. 50.
19. *Bodas de sangre*, p. 148. c.f. *Three Tragedies*, p. 78.
20. *Three Tragedies*, p. 100.
21. ibid.
22. ibid.
23. ibid, p. 123.
24. ibid, p. 146.
25. ibid, p. 147.
26. ibid.
27. ibid, p. 99.
28. *Yerma* (Novelas y Cuentos edn), 1974, p. 26. c.f. *Three Tragedies*, p. 100.
29. *Yerma*, p. 62. c.f. *Three Tragedies*, p. 126.
30. *Suites*, ed. André Belamich, pp. 204.
31. In conversation with the author.
32. *Oeuvres complètes*, vol. I, p. 1575.
33. *Obras completas*, p. 553.
34. ibid, p. 555.
35. ibid.
36. ibid, p. 556.
37. ibid, p. 558.
38. ibid.
39. ibid.
40. ibid, p. 552.
41. ibid, p. 554.
42. ibid, p. 555.
43. ibid, p. 557.
44. ibid.
45. ibid, p. 558.
46. *Five Plays: Comedies and Tragi-Comedies*, p. 185.
47. ibid, p. 186.
48. *Doña Rosita la soltera* (Novelos y Cuentos edn), p. 203. c.f. *Five Plays . . .*, p. 138.
49. *Three Tragedies*, p. 201.
50. ibid, p. 191.
51. ibid, p. 155.
52. *Oeuvres complètes*, vol. I, pp. 1599–1602.
53. Ian Gibson, *The Assassination of Federico García Lorca* (Penguin, 1983), pp. 119 ff.
54. Cited by J.L. Gili in *Selected Poems*, p. xxii.

## Notes to Part Three

1. Sigmund Freud, *Standard Edition* (Hogarth, 1964), vol. XXIII, p. 243.
2. 'Deep Song', *Deep Song and Other Prose*, pp. 36–7.
3. *Obras completas*, p. 573.
4. ibid, p. 591.
5. ibid, p. 576.
6. ibid, p. 577.
7. *Oeuvres complètes*, vol. I, pp. 1583–9.
8. *Obras completas*, p. 574.
9. ibid, p. 575.
10. ibid.
11. Mario Mieli, *Homosexuality and Liberation* (Gay Men's Press, 1980), p. 169.
12. *Obras completas*, p. 579.
13. ibid, p. 581.
14. Bruno Bettelheim, *Freud and Man's Soul* (Chatto, 1983), p. 111.
15. W. B. Yeats, *Selected Poems*, pp. 104–5.
16. *Obras completas*, p. 591.
17. ibid, p. 593.
18. H. D. F. Kitto, *The Greeks* (Penguin, 1957), p. 182.
19. *Obras completas*, p. 589.
20. ibid, p. 598.
21. Cited in *Federico García Lorca* issue of *Europe* (*revue litteraire mensuelle*), August–September 1980. ('Chronologie' by Charles Martilly and 'L'apolitisme de Lorca' by Ian Gibson.)
22. *Sonetos*, p. 9.
23. ibid, p. 15.
24. Stephen Adams, *The Homosexual as Hero in Contemporary Fiction* (Vision, 1980), p. 65.
25. *Sonetos*, p. 18.
26. ibid, p. 12.
27. ibid, p. 10.
28. ibid, p. 16.
29. ibid, p. 13.
30. ibid, p. 11.
31. ibid, p. 9.
32. ibid, p. 19.
33. Stephen Spender, *Collected Poems* (Faber, 1955), p. 77.

# Index

GMP publish a wide range of books, including Fiction, Art, Literature, Photography, Politics, Poetry, and the Heretic and Gay Modern Classics series. Send for our catalogue to GMP Publishers Ltd, P O Box 247, London N15 6RW.